ICTS 163

Special Education General Curriculum

Teacher Certification Exam

By: Sharon Wynne, M.S.
Southern Connecticut State University

"And, while there's no reason yet to panic, I think it's only prudent that we make preparations to panic."

XAMonline, INC.

Boston

XAMonline, Inc.
21 Orient Ave.
Melrose, MA 02176
Toll Free 1-800-509-4128
Email: info@xamonline.com
Web www.xamonline.com
Fax: 1-781-662-9268

Library of Congress Cataloging-in-Publication Data

Wynne, Sharon A.
    Special Education General Curriculum: Teacher Certification / Sharon A. Wynne. -2nd ed.
    ISBN 978-1-58197-576-5
        1. Special Ed. General Curriculum.   2. Study Guides.   3. ICTS
        4. Teachers' Certification & Licensure. 5. Careers

Disclaimer:
The opinions expressed in this publication are the sole works of XAMonline and were created independently from the National Education Association, Educational Testing Service, or any State Department of Education, National Evaluation Systems or other testing affiliates.

Between the time of publication and printing, state specific standards as well as testing formats and website information may change that is not included in part or in whole within this product. Sample test questions are developed by XAMonline and reflect similar content as on real tests; however, they are not former tests. XAMonline assembles content that aligns with state standards but makes no claims nor guarantees teacher candidates a passing score. Numerical scores are determined by testing companies such as NES or ETS and then are compared with individual state standards. A passing score varies from state to state.

Printed in the United States of America   œ-1

ICTS: Special Education General Curriculum
ISBN: 978-1-58197-576-5

Table of Contents

SUBAREA III.   NATURAL SCIENCES

Great Study and Testing Tips!

What to study in order to prepare for the subject assessments is the focus of this study guide but equally important is *how* you study.

You can increase your chances of truly mastering the information by taking some simple, but effective steps.

Study Tips:

1. Some foods aid the learning process. Foods such as milk, nuts, seeds, rice, and oats help your study efforts by releasing natural memory enhancers called CCKs (*cholecystokinin*) composed of *tryptopha*n, *choline*, and *phenylalanine*. All of these chemicals enhance the neurotransmitters associated with memory. Before studying, try a light, protein-rich meal of eggs, turkey, and fish. All of these foods release the memory enhancing chemicals. The better the connections, the more you comprehend.

Likewise, before you take a test, stick to a light snack of energy boosting and relaxing foods. A glass of milk, a piece of fruit, or some peanuts all release various memory-boosting chemicals and help you to relax and focus on the subject at hand.

2. Learn to take great notes. A by-product of our modern culture is that we have grown accustomed to getting our information in short doses (i.e., TV news sound bites or USA Today style newspaper articles.)

Consequently, we've subconsciously trained ourselves to assimilate information better in neat little packages. If your notes are scrawled all over the paper, it fragments the flow of the information. Strive for clarity. Newspapers use a standard format to achieve clarity. Your notes can be much clearer through use of proper formatting. A very effective format is called the *"Cornell Method."*

Take a sheet of loose-leaf lined notebook paper and draw a line all the way down the paper about 1-2" from the left-hand edge.

Draw another line across the width of the paper about 1-2" up from the bottom. Repeat this process on the reverse side of the page.

Look at the highly effective result. You have ample room for notes, a left hand margin for special emphasis items or inserting supplementary data from the textbook, a large area at the bottom for a brief summary, and a little rectangular space for just about anything you want.

3. <u>**Get the concept then the details**</u>. Too often we focus on the details and don't gather an understanding of the concept. However, if you simply memorize only dates, places, or names, you may well miss the whole point of the subject. A key way to understand things is to put them in your own words. If you are working from a textbook, automatically summarize each paragraph in your mind. If you are outlining text, don't simply copy the author's words.

Rephrase them in your own words. You remember your own thoughts and words much better than someone else's, and subconsciously tend to associate the important details to the core concepts.

4. <u>**Ask Why**</u>? Pull apart written material paragraph by paragraph and don't forget the captions under the illustrations.

Example: If the heading is "Stream Erosion," flip it around to read "Why do streams erode?" Then answer the questions.

If you train your mind to think in a series of questions and answers, not only will you learn more, but it also helps to lessen the test anxiety because you are used to answering questions.

5. <u>**Read for reinforcement and future needs**</u>. Even if you only have 10 minutes, put your notes or a book in your hand. Your mind is similar to a computer; you have to input data in order to have it processed. *By reading, you are creating the neural connections for future retrieval.* The more times you read something, the more you reinforce the learning of ideas.

Even if you don't fully understand something on the first pass, *your mind stores much of the material for later recall.*

6. <u>**Relax to learn so go into exile**</u>. Our bodies respond to an inner clock called biorhythms. Burning the midnight oil works well for some people, but not everyone.

If possible, set aside a particular place to study that is free of distractions. Shut off the television, cell phone and pager and exile your friends and family during your study period.

If you really are bothered by silence, try background music. Light classical music at a low volume has been shown to aid in concentration over other types.

Music that evokes pleasant emotions without lyrics are highly suggested. Try just about anything by Mozart. It relaxes you.

7. <u>**Use arrows not highlighters**</u>. At best, it's difficult to read a page full of yellow, pink, blue and green streaks. A quick note, a brief dash of color, an underline, and an arrow pointing to a particular passage is much clearer than a horde of highlighted words.

8. <u>**Budget your study time**</u>. Although you shouldn't ignore any of the material, *allocate your available study time in the same ratio that topics may appear on the test.*

Testing Tips:

1. <u>Get smart, play dumb</u>. **Don't read anything into the question**. Don't make an assumption that the test writer is looking for something else than what is asked. Stick to the question as written and don't read extra things into it.

2. <u>Read the question and all the choices *twice* before answering the</u> <u>question</u>. You may miss something by not carefully reading and then re-reading both the question and the answers.

If you really don't have a clue as to the right answer, leave it blank on the first time through. Go on to the other questions, as they may provide a clue as to how to answer the skipped questions.

If later on, you still can't answer the skipped ones *Guess.*

The only penalty for guessing is that you *might* get it wrong. Only one thing is certain; if you don't put anything down, you will get it wrong!

3. <u>Turn the question into a statement</u>. Look at the way the questions are worded. The syntax of the question usually provides a clue. Does it seem more familiar as a statement rather than as a question? Does it sound strange?

By turning a question into a statement, you may be able to spot if an answer sounds right, and it may also trigger memories of material you have read.

4. <u>Look for hidden clues</u>. It's actually very difficult to compose multiple-foil (choice) questions without giving away part of the answer in the options presented.

In most multiple-choice questions you can often readily eliminate one or two of the potential answers. This leaves you with only two real possibilities and automatically your odds go to Fifty-Fifty for very little work.

5. <u>Trust your instincts</u>. For every fact that you have read, you subconsciously retain something of that knowledge. On questions that you aren't really certain about, go with your basic instincts. **Your first impression on how to answer a question is usually correct.**

6. <u>Mark your answers directly on the test booklet</u>. Don't bother trying to fill in the optical scan sheet on the first pass through the test.

Just be very careful not to miss-mark your answers when you eventually transcribe them to the scan sheet.

7. <u>Watch the clock</u>! You have a set amount of time to answer the questions. Don't get bogged down trying to answer a single question at the expense of 10 questions you can more readily answer.

INTRODUCTION

This one-volume study guide was designed for professionals preparing to take a teacher competency test in special education or in any field in which the principles of special education are a part of the test content. Objectives specific to the field of special education were obtained from state departments of education and federal territories and dependencies across the nation. Educators preparing to take tests in the various areas of special education should find the manual helpful, for the objectives and the scope of the discussions concerning each objective cover a wide range of the field.

The study guide offers many benefits to the person faced with the necessity of making a qualifying score on a competency test in special education. A large number of source materials must be covered in order to study the conceptual knowledge reflected by the objectives listed in each state study guide. These objectives encompass the major content of the special education field. The term "objective" may be called "competency" in some states. These terms are synonymous and refer to an item of professional knowledge for mastery.

Many prominent textbooks used by preservice teacher training programs nationwide were researched for the content of this book. Other important resources (e.g., books, journal articles and media) were included in the discussions about the objectives. The compilation of this research alleviates the hardship imposed on a teacher who attempts to accumulate, as one individual preparing for an examination, the vast body of professional material. This one-volume study guide highlights the current knowledge and accepted concepts of the field of special education, thus reducing the massive amount of material, which would need to be assembled if one did not have it between a single set of covers.

The book is organized by major topical sections. These topics often correspond with course titles and textbooks in pre-service teacher training programs. The objectives and discussions about them comprise the main content within each section. The discussions feature important information from textbooks in the field of special education, reported in the books in a synthesized and summarized form. Specific references have been given for charts and quoted materials, which were included to enhance understanding of conceptual discussions. Complete reference citations can be located in the reference listings. A glossary of terms is located at the end of each topical section. The definitions are stated in the contextual usage of special education.

Finally, questions specific to the discussion of each objective have been written to help determine if the reader understands that material. Correctness of responses to questions can be checked for immediate accuracy in the Answer Key section. Test questions are written as teaching mechanisms and appear in the style and format to cover those used on tests by any state.

Though this manual is comprehensive, it in no way purports to contain all the research and applied techniques in every area of exceptionality. Research generates new applications and continuing in-service education is a requirement for all special education professionals. This manual gives the reader a one-volume summary of the fundamentals known and practiced at the time of writing.

COMPETENCY 1.0   UNDERSTAND THE NATURE OF THE READING PROCESS AND LITERACY DEVELOPMENT

Skill 1.1   Demonstrate knowledge of theoretical models of reading and philosophies of reading education and their relevance to instruction

Beginning Reading Approaches

Methods of teaching beginning reading skills may be divided into two major approaches—code emphasis and meaning emphasis. Both approaches have their supporters and their critics. Advocates of code emphasis instruction point out that reading fluency depends on accurate and automatic decoding skills, while advocates of meaning emphasis favor this approach for reading comprehension. Teachers may decide to blend aspects of both approaches to meet the individual needs of their students.

Bottom-up or Code-Emphasis Approach

1   Letter-sound regularity is stressed.

2   Reading instruction begins with words that consist of letter or letter combinations that have the same sound in different words. Component letter-sound relationships are taught and mastered before introducing new words.

3   Examples—phonics, linguistic, modified alphabet and programmed reading series, such as the Merrill Linguistic Reading Program and DISTAR Reading.

Top-down or Meaning-Emphasis Model

1   Reading for meaning is emphasized from the first stages of instruction.

2   Programs begin with words that appear frequently, which are assumed to be familiar and easy to learn. Words are identified by examining meaning and position in context and are decoded by techniques such as context, pictures, initial letters and word configurations. Thus, a letter may not necessarily have the same sound in different words throughout the passage.

3   Examples: whole language, language experience and individualized reading programs.

Other approaches that follow beginning reading instruction are available to help teachers design reading programs. Choice of approach will depend on the student's strengths and weaknesses. No matter what approach or combination of approaches is used, the teacher should encourage independent reading and build activities into the reading program that stimulate students to practice their skills through independent reading.

Developmental Reading Approaches

Developmental reading programs emphasize daily, sequential instruction. Instructional materials usually feature a series of books, often basal readers, as the core of the program.

Basal Reading

Basal reader series form the core of many widely-used reading programs from preprimers to eighth grade. Depending on the series, basal readers may be meaning emphasis or code emphasis. Teacher manuals provide a highly-structured and comprehensive scope and sequence, lesson plans, and objectives. Vocabulary is controlled from level to level and reading skills cover word recognition, word attack and comprehension.

Advantages of basal readers are the structured, sequential manner in which reading is taught. The teacher manuals have teaching strategies, controlled vocabulary, assessment materials and objectives. Reading instruction is in a systematic, sequential and comprehension-oriented manner.

Many basal reading programs recommend the <u>directed reading activity procedure</u> for lesson presentation. Students proceed through the steps of motivation preparation for the new concepts and vocabulary, guided reading and answering questions that give a purpose or goal for the reading, development of strengths through drills or workbook, application of skills and evaluation.

A variation of the directed reading method is <u>direct reading-thinking</u>, where the student must generate the purposes for reading the selection, form questions, and read the selection. After reading, the teacher asks questions designed to get the group to think of answers and to justify their answers.

Disadvantages of basal readers are the emphasis on teaching to a group rather than the individual. Critics of basal readers claim that the structure may limit creativity and not provide enough instruction on organizational skills and reading for secondary content levels. Basal readers, however, offer the advantage of a prepared comprehensive program and may be supplemented with other materials to meet individual needs.

Phonics Approach

Word recognition is taught through grapheme-phoneme associations, with the goal of teaching the student to independently apply these skills to new words. Phonics instruction may be synthetic or analytic. In the synthetic method, letter sounds are learned before the student goes on to blend the sounds to form words. The analytic method teaches letter sounds as integral parts of words. The sounds are usually taught in the sequence: vowels, consonants, consonant blends at the beginning of words (e.g., bl and dr) and consonant blends at the end of words (e.g., ld and mp), consonant and vowel digraphs (e.g., ch and sh), and diphthongs (e.g., au and oy).

Critics of the phonics approach point out that the emphasis on pronunciation may lead to the student focusing more on decoding than comprehension. Some students may have trouble blending sounds to form words and others may become confused with words that do not conform to the phonetic "rules." However, advocates of phonics say that the programs are useful with remedial reading and developmental reading. Examples of phonics series are *Science Research Associates, Merrill Phonics* and DML's *Cove School Reading Program.*

Linguistics Approach

In many programs, the whole-word approach is used. This means that words are taught in families as a whole (e.g., cat, hat, pat and rat). The focus is on words instead of isolated sounds. Words are chosen on the basis of similar spelling patterns and irregular spelling words are taught as sight words. Examples of programs using this approach are *SRA Basic Reading Series* and *Miami Linguistic Readers* by D.C. Heath.

Some advantages of this approach are that the student learns that reading is talk written down and develops a sense of sentence structure. The consistent visual patterns of the lessons guide students from familiar words to less familiar words to irregular words. Reading is taught by associating with the student's natural knowledge of his own language. Disadvantages are extremely controlled vocabulary, in which word-by-word reading is encouraged. Others criticize the programs for the emphasis on auditory memory skills and the use of nonsense words in the practice exercises.

Whole language Approach

In the whole language approach, reading is taught as a holistic, meaning-oriented activity and is not broken down into a collection of skills. This approach relies heavily on literature or printed matter selected for a particular purpose. Reading is taught as part of a total language arts program, and the curriculum seeks to develop instruction in real problems and ideas. Two examples of whole language programs are *Learning through Literature* (Dodds and Goodfellow) and *Victory!* (Brigance). Phonics is not taught in a structured, systematic way. Students are assumed to develop their phonetic awareness through exposure to print. Writing is taught as a complement to reading. Writing centers are often part of this program, as students learn to write their own stories and read them back or follow along with an audiotape of a book while reading along with it.

While the integration of reading with writing is an advantage of the whole language approach, the approach has been criticized for the lack of direct instruction in specific skill strategies. When working with students with learning problems, instruction that is more direct may be needed to learn the word-recognition skills necessary for achieving comprehension of the text.

Language Experience Approach

The language experience approach is similar to whole language in that reading is considered as a personal act, literature is emphasized and students are encouraged to write about their own life experiences. The major difference is that written language is considered a secondary system to oral language, while whole language treats the two as parts of the same structure. The language experience approach is used primarily with beginner readers but can also be used with older elementary and with other older students for corrective instruction. Reading skills are developed along with listening, speaking and writing skills. The materials consist, for the most part, of the student's skills. The philosophy of language experience includes:

1 What students think about, they can talk about?

2 What students say, they can write or have someone write.

3 What students write or have someone write for them, they can read.

Students dictate a story to a teacher as a group activity. Ideas for stories can originate from student artwork, news items or personal experiences, or they may be creative. Topic lists, word cards or idea lists can also be used to generate topics or ideas for a class story. The teacher writes down the stories in a first draft and the students read them back. The language patterns come from the students and they read their own written thoughts. The teacher provides guidance on word choice, sentence structure and the sounds of the letters and words. The students edit and revise the story on an experience chart. The teacher provides specific instruction in grammar, sentence structure and spelling, if the need arises, rather than using a specified schedule. As the students progress, they create their individual storybooks, adding illustrations if they wish. The storybooks are placed in folders to share with others. Progress is evaluated in terms of the changes in the oral and written expression, as well as in mechanics. There is no set method of evaluating student progress. That is one disadvantage of the language experience approach. However, the emphasis on student experience and creativity stimulates interest and motivates the students.

Individualized Reading Approach

Students select their own reading materials from a variety, according to interest and ability, and they are more able to progress at their own individual rates. Word recognition and comprehension are taught as the students need them. The teacher's role is to diagnose errors and prescribe materials although the final choice is made by the students. Individual work may be supplemented by group activities, with basal readers and workbooks for specific reading skills. The lack of systematic check and developmental skills and emphasis on self-learning may be a disadvantage for students with learning problems.

Skill 1.2   Demonstrate knowledge of the factors that affect the development of reading proficiency

In 2000, the National Reading Panel released its now well-known report on teaching children to read. In a way, this report slightly put to rest the debate between phonics and whole-language. It argued, essentially, that word-letter recognition was important, as was understanding what the text means. The report's "big 5" critical areas of reading instruction are as follows:

- Comprehension
- Fluency
- Phonemic Awareness
- Phonics
- Vocabulary

Methods used to teach these skills are often featured in a "balanced literacy" curriculum that focuses on the use of skills in various instructional contexts. For example, with independent reading, students independently choose books that are at their reading levels; with guided reading, teachers work with small groups of students to help them with their particular reading problems; with whole group reading, the entire class will read the same text and the teacher will incorporate activities to help students learn phonics, comprehension, fluency and vocabulary. In addition to these components of balanced literacy, teachers incorporate writing so that students can learn the structures of communicating through text.

Phonics
As opposed to phonemic awareness, the study of phonics must be done with the eyes open. It's the connection between the sounds and letters on a page. In other words, students learning phonics might see the word "bad" and sound each letter out slowly until they recognize that they just said the word.

Phonological awareness means the ability of the reader to recognize the sounds of spoken language. This recognition includes how these sounds can be blended together, segmented (divided up), and manipulated (switched around). This awareness then leads to phonics, a method for teaching children to read. It helps them "sound out" words.

Development of phonological skills may begin during the preschool years. Indeed, by the age of 5, a child who has been exposed to rhyme can recognize a rhyme. Such a child can demonstrate phonological awareness by filling in the missing rhyming word in a familiar rhyme or rhymed picture book.

You teach children phonological awareness when you teach them the sounds made by the letters and the sounds made by various combinations of letters, along with how to recognize individual sounds in words.

Phonological awareness skills include:

1. Rhyming and syllabification.
2. Blending sounds into words—such as pic-tur-bo-k.
3. Identifying the beginning or starting sounds of words and the ending or closing sounds of words.
4. Breaking words down into sounds—also called "segmenting" words.
5. Recognizing other smaller words in the big word by removing starting sounds—such as "hear" to ear.

The typical variation in literacy backgrounds that children bring to reading can make teaching more difficult. Often, a teacher has to choose between focusing on the learning needs of a few students at the expense of the group and focusing on the group at the risk of leaving some students behind academically. This situation is particularly critical for children with gaps in their literacy knowledge who may be at risk in subsequent grades for becoming "diverse learners".

Areas of Emerging Evidence

1. **Experiences with print (through reading and writing) help preschool children develop an understanding of the conventions, purpose and functions of print.** Children learn about print from a variety of sources, and in the process, come to realize that print carries the story. They also learn how text is structured visually (i.e., text begins at the top of the page, moves from left to right and carries over to the next page when it is turned). While knowledge about the conventions of print enables children to understand the physical structure of language, the conceptual knowledge that printed words convey a message also helps Children Bridge the gap between oral and written language.

2. **Phonological awareness and letter recognition** contribute to initial reading acquisition by helping children develop efficient word recognition strategies (e.g., detecting pronunciations and storing associations in memory). Phonological awareness and knowledge of print-speech relations play an important role in facilitating reading acquisition. Therefore, phonological awareness instruction should be an integral component of early reading programs. Within the emergent literacy research, viewpoints diverge on whether acquisition of phonological awareness and letter recognition are preconditions of literacy acquisition or whether they develop interdependently with literacy activities such as story reading and writing.

3. **Storybook reading affects children's knowledge about, strategies for, and attitudes towards reading.** Of all the strategies intended to promote growth in literacy acquisition, none is as commonly practiced, nor as strongly supported across the emergent literacy literature, as storybook reading. Children in different social and cultural groups have differing degrees of access to storybook reading. For example, it is not unusual for a teacher to have students who have experienced thousands of hours of story reading time, along with other students who have had little or no such exposure.

Design Principles in Emergent Literacy

Conspicuous Strategies

As an instructional priority, conspicuous strategies are a sequence of teaching events and teacher actions used to help students learn new literacy information and relate it to their existing knowledge. Conspicuous strategies can be incorporated in beginning reading instruction to ensure that all learners have basic literacy concepts. For example, during storybook reading, teachers can show students how to recognize the fronts and backs of books, locate titles or look at pictures and predict the story rather than assume children will learn this through incidental exposure. Similarly, teachers can teach students a strategy for holding a pencil appropriately or checking the form of their letters against an alphabet sheet on their desks or the classroom wall.

Mediated Scaffolding

Mediated scaffolding can be accomplished in a number of ways to meet the needs of students with diverse literacy experiences. To link oral and written language, for example, teachers may use texts that simulate speech by incorporating oral language patterns or children's writing. Or teachers can use daily storybook reading to discuss book-handling skills and directionality concepts that are particularly important for children who are unfamiliar with printed texts..

Teachers can also use repeated readings to give students multiple exposures to unfamiliar words or extended opportunities to look at books with predictable patterns, as well as provide support by modeling the behaviors associated with reading. Teachers can act as scaffolds during these storybook reading activities by adjusting their demands (e.g., asking increasingly complex questions or encouraging children to take on portions of the reading) or by reading more complex texts as students gain knowledge of beginning literacy components.

Strategic Integration

Many children with diverse literacy experiences have difficulty making connections between old and new information. Strategic integration can be applied to help link old and new learning. For example, in the classroom, strategic integration can be accomplished by providing access to literacy materials in classroom writing centers and libraries. Students should also have opportunities to integrate and extend their literacy knowledge by reading aloud, listening to other students read aloud and listening to tape recordings and videotapes in reading corners.

Primed Background Knowledge

All children bring some level of background knowledge (e.g., how to hold a book, awareness of directionality of print) to beginning reading. Teachers can utilize children's background knowledge to help children link their personal literacy experiences to beginning reading instruction, while also closing the gap between students with rich and students with impoverished literacy experiences. Activities that draw upon background knowledge include incorporating oral language activities (which discriminate between printed letters and words) into daily read-alouds, as well as frequent opportunities to retell stories, look at books with predictable patterns, write messages with invented spellings, and respond to literature through drawing.

Skill 1.3 Identify characteristics of emergent literacy development and strategies for promoting the acquisition of these skills

Emergent Literacy

Emergent literacy research examines early literacy knowledge and the contexts and conditions that foster that knowledge. Despite differing viewpoints on the relation between emerging literacy skills and reading acquisition, strong support is found in the literature for the important contribution that early childhood exposure to oral and written language makes to the facility with which children learn to read.

Reading for comprehension of factual material—content area textbooks, reference books, and newspapers—is closely related to study strategies in the middle/junior high. Organized study models, such as the SQ3R method, a technique that makes it possible and feasible to learn the content of even large amounts of text (survey, question, read, recite and review studying), teach students to locate main ideas and supporting details, recognize sequential order, distinguish fact from opinion and determine cause/effect relationships.

Instructional Strategies

1. Teacher-guided activities that require students to organize and to summarize information based on the author's explicit intent are pertinent strategies in middle grades. Evaluation techniques include oral and written responses to standardized or teacher-made worksheets.

2. Reading of fiction introduces and reinforces skills in inferring meaning from narration and description. Teacher-guided activities in the process of reading for meaning should be followed by cooperative planning of the skills to be studied and of the selection of reading resources. Many printed reading-for-comprehension instruments, as well as individualized computer software programs, exist to monitor the progress of acquiring comprehension skills.

3. Older middle school students should be given opportunities for more student-centered activities—individual and collaborative selection of reading choices based on student interest, small group discussions of selected works and greater written expression. Evaluation techniques include teacher monitoring and observation of discussions and written work samples.

4. Certain students may begin some fundamental critical interpretation, such as recognizing fallacious reasoning in news media, examining the accuracy of News reports and advertising explaining their reasons for preferring one Author's writing to another's. Development of these skills may require a more learning-centered approach, in which the teacher identifies a number of objectives and suggested resources from which the student may choose his course of study. Self-evaluation through a reading diary should be stressed. Teacher and peer evaluation of creative projects resulting from such study is encouraged.

5. Reading aloud before the entire class as a formal means of teacher evaluation should be phased out in favor of one-to-one tutoring or peer-assisted reading. Occasional sharing of favored selections by both teacher and willing students is a good oral interpretation basic.

Most reading programs conceptually separate the reading process into three major categories: sight word vocabulary, word attack skills and comprehension. These three areas constitute the basic questions that should be asked by a teacher when assessing a student's current level of functioning. From answers obtained, the pertinent questions are:

1. How large is the student's sight word vocabulary?
2. What kinds of word attack skills does the student employ?
3. How well developed are the student's comprehension skills?

Sight words are printed words that are easily identified by the learner. The selection of words to be learned will rely to some extent on the age and abilities of the student. Primary age students will use word lists composed of high-frequency words like basal readers, Dolch Word List.

Word attack skills are those techniques that enable a student to decode an unknown word so he can pronounce and understand it in the right context. Word attack skills are included in the areas of phonics, structural analysis, contextual and configuration clues and decoding.

Comprehension skills are categorized into levels of difficulty. The teacher should consider the following factors when analyzing a student's reading comprehension level (Schloss & Sedlak, 1986):

1. The past experience of the reader.
2. The content of the written passage.
3. The syntax of the written passage.
4. The vocabulary used in the written passage.
5. The oral language comprehension of the student.
6. The questions being asked to assess comprehension.

The major categories of reading skills, basic reading skills within these categories, and strategies for the development of each are listed. Suggestions for assisting the reader in improving silent and oral reading skills are also given. Some skills overlap categories.

Comprehension involves understanding what is read regardless of purpose or thinking skills employed. Comprehension can be delineated into categories of differentiated skills. Benjamin Bloom's taxonomy includes: knowledge, comprehension, application, analysis, synthesis and evaluation. Thomas Barrett suggests that comprehension categories be classified as: literal meaning, reorganization, inference, evaluation and appreciation. An overview of comprehension skills is presented in Skill 4 in this section. Strategies that might prove beneficial in strengthening a student's comprehension:

1. Asking questions of the student before he reads a passage. This type of directed reading activity assists the student in focusing attention on the information in the text that will help him to answer the questions.
2. Using teacher questions to assist the student in developing self-questioning skills covering all levels of comprehension.

Silent and Oral Reading Skills

Silent reading refers to the inaudible reading of words or passages. Since the act of reading is one on a covert basis, the accuracy of the reading process can only be inferred through questions or activities required of the student following his reading. What may be observed is attention given to the printed material, the eye movements as an indication of relative pace, and body language signifying frustration or ease of reading. Strategies that might assist the child in reading silently are:

1. Preparing activities or questions pertaining to the printed passage. Vary the activities so that some are asking specific comprehension questions and others are geared toward creative expression like art or written composition.
2. Allowing time for pleasurable reading, such as through an activity like sustained silent reading.

Language is the means whereby people communicate their thoughts, make requests and respond to others. Communication competence is an interaction of cognitive competence, social knowledge and language competence. Communication problems may result from in any or all of these areas, which directly impact the student's ability to interact with others. Language consists of several components, each of which follows a sequence of development.

Brown and colleagues were the first to describe language as a function of developmental stages rather than age (Reid, 1988, p. 44). He developed a formula to group the mean length of utterances (sentences) into stages. Counting the number of morphemes per 100 utterances, one can calculate a mean length of utterance, MLU. Total number of morphemes/100 = MLU, e.g., 180/100 = 1.8.

Summary of Brown's findings about MLU and language development:

Stage	MLU	Developmental Features
L	1.5-2.0	14 basic morphemes (e.g., in, on, articles and possessives).
LI	2.0-2.5	Beginning of pronoun use, auxiliary verbs.
LII	2.5-3.0	Language form approximate adult forms. Beginning of questions and negative statements.
Lv	3.0-3.5	Use of complex (embedded) sentences.
V	3.5-4.0	Use of compound sentences.

Components of Language
Language learning is composed of five components. Children progress through developmental stages through each component.

Phonology–the system of rules about sounds and sound combinations for a language. A phoneme is the smallest unit of sound that combines with other sounds to make words. A phoneme, by itself, does not have a meaning; it must be combined with other phonemes. Problems in phonology may be manifested as developmental delays in acquiring consonants or as reception problems, such as misinterpreting words because a different consonant was substituted.

Morphology–the smallest units of language that convey meaning. Morphemes are root words, or free morphemes that can stand alone (e.g., walk), and affixes (e.g., ed, s, ing). Content words carry the meaning in a sentence and functional words join phrases and sentences. Generally, students with problems in this area may not use inflectional endings in their words, may not be consistent in their use of certain morphemes or may be delayed in learning morphemes such as irregular past tenses.

Syntax–commonly known as grammar, govern how morphemes and words are correctly combined. Wood (1976) describes six stages of syntax acquisition (Mercer, p. 347).

1. **Stages 1 and 2—Birth to about 2 years**: child is learning the semantic system.
2. **Stage 3—Ages 2 to 3 years**: simple sentences contain subject and predicate.
3. **Stage 4—Ages 2 ½ to 4 years**: elements such as question words are added to basic sentences (e.g., where) and word order is changed to ask questions. The child begins to use "and" to combine simple sentences and the child begins to embed words within the basic sentence.
4. **Stage 5—About 3 ½ to 7 years**: the child uses complete sentences that include word classes of adult language. The child is becoming aware of appropriate semantic functions of words and differences within the same grammatical class.
5. **Stage 6—About 5 to 20 years**: the child begins to learn complex sentences and sentences that imply commands, requests and promises.

Syntactic deficits are manifested by the child using sentences that lack length or complexity for a child that age. The child may have problems understanding or creating complex sentences and embedded sentences.

Semantics—language content, i.e., objects, actions and relations between objects. As with syntax, Wood (1976) outlines stages of semantic development:

1 **Stage 1—Birth to about 2 years**: the child is learning meaning while learning his first words. Sentences are one-word, but the meaning varies according to the context. Therefore, "doggie" may mean, "This is my dog," or "There is a dog," or "The dog is barking."

2 **Stage 2—About 2 to 8 years**: the child progresses to two-word sentences about concrete actions. As more words are learned, the child forms longer sentences. Until about age 7, things are defined in terms of visible actions. The child begins to respond to prompts (e.g., pretty/flower), and at about age 8, the child can respond to a prompt with an opposite (e.g., pretty/ugly).

3 **Stage 3—Begins at about age 8**: the child's word meanings relate directly to experiences, operations and processes. Vocabulary is defined by the child's experiences, not the adult's. At about age 12, the child begins to give "dictionary" definitions and the semantic level approaches that of adults.

Semantic problems take the form of:

1 Limited vocabulary.

2 Inability to understand figurative language or idioms; interprets literally.

3 Failure to perceive multiple meanings of words and changes in word meaning from changes in context, resulting in incomplete understanding of what is read.

4 Difficulty understanding linguistic concepts (e.g., before/after), verbal analogies and logical relationships, such as possessives, spatial and temporal.

5 Misuse of transitional words, such as "although" and "regardless."

Pragmatics—commonly known as the speaker's intent, pragmatics is used to influence or control actions or attitudes of others. Communicative competence depends on how well one understands the rules of language, as well as the social rules of communication, such as taking turns and using the correct tone of voice.

Pragmatic deficits are manifested by failures to respond properly to indirect requests after age 8 (e.g., "Can't you turn down the TV?" elicits a response of "No" instead of "Yes" and the child turning down the volume). Children with these deficits have trouble reading cues that indicate the listener does not understand them. Whereas a person would usually notice this and adjust one's speech to the listener's needs, the child with pragmatic problems does not do this.

Pragmatic deficits are also characterized by inappropriate social behaviors, such as interruptions or monopolizing conversations. Children may use immature speech and have trouble sticking to a topic. These problems can persist into adulthood, affecting academic, vocational and social interactions. Problems in language development often require long-term interventions and can persist into adulthood. Certain problems are associated with different grade levels:

Preschool and Kindergarten—the child's speech may sound immature, the child may not be able to follow simple directions and the child often cannot name things such as the days of the week and colors. The child may not be able to discriminate between sounds and the letters associated with the sounds. The child might substitute sounds and have trouble responding accurately to certain types of questions. The child may play less with his peers or participate in non-play or parallel play.

Elementary School—problems with sound discrimination persist, and the child may have problems with temporal and spatial concepts (e.g., before/after). As the child progresses through school, he may have problems making the transition from narrative to expository writing. Word retrieval problems may not be very evident because the child begins to devise strategies such as talking around the word he cannot remember or using fillers and descriptors. The child might speak more slowly, have problems sounding out words, and get confused with multiple-meaning words. Pragmatic problems show up in social situations, such as failure to correctly interpret social cues and adjust to appropriate language, inability to predict consequences, and inability to formulate requests to obtain new information.

Secondary School—at this level, difficulties become more subtle. The child lacks the ability to use and understand higher-level syntax, semantics and pragmatics. If the child has problems with auditory language, he may also have problems with short-term memory. Receptive and/or expressive language delays impair the child's ability to learn effectively. The child often lacks the ability to organize/ categorize the information received in school. Problems associated with pragmatic deficiencies persist, and because the child is aware of them, he becomes inattentive, withdrawn or frustrated.

Skill 1.4   Recognize the nature of cultural, linguistic and ethnic diversity and how these characteristics and experiences can influence students as they learn to read

Consideration for ELL Learners

Given the demographics of our country, which is becoming increasingly pluralistic and has burgeoning numbers of citizens who are from ELL–English Language Learner backgrounds, the likelihood that currently, or at least within the next few years of your teaching career, you will be teaching at least one, if not more, children who are from a non-native English speaking background (even though they won't officially be classified as ELL students), is at least 75%, if not more. Therefore, as a conscientious educator, it is important that you understand the special factors involved in supporting their literacy development, which includes fostering progress in native language literacy as a perquisite for second language (English) reading progress.

Not all English phonemes are present in various ELL native languages. Some native language phonemes may and do conflict with English phonemes.

It is recommended that all teachers of reading, and particularly those who are working with ELL students, use meaningful, student-centered and culture-customized activities. These activities may include: language games, word walls and poems. Some of these activities might also, if possible, be initiated in the child's first language and then reiterated in English.

Reading and the ELL Learner

Research has shown that there is a positive and strong correlation between a child's literacy in his/her native language and his/her learning of English. The degree of native language proficiency and literacy is a strong predictor of English language development. Children who are literate and engaged readers in their native languages can easily transfer their skills to a second language (i.e., English).

What this means is that educators should not approach the needs of ELL learners in reading as the same. Those whose families are not from a focused oral literacy and reading culture in the native language will need additional oral language rhymes, read-alouds and singing as supports for reading skills development in both their native and the English language.

COMPETENCY 2.0 UNDERSTAND WORD ANALYSIS SKILLS AND STRATEGIES.

Skill 2.1 Demonstrate knowledge of phonemic awareness, concepts of print, and phonics and their roles in reading development

Phonemic awareness is the acknowledgement of sounds and words, for example, a child's realization that some words rhyme. Onset and rhyme, for example, are skills that might help students learn that the sound of the first letter "b" in the word "bad" can be changed with the sound "d" to make it "dad." The key in phonemic awareness is that when you teach it to children, it can be taught with the students' eyes closed. In other words, it's all about sounds, not about ascribing written letters to sounds. To be phonemically aware means that the reader and listener can recognize and manipulate specific sounds in spoken words. Phonemic awareness deals with sounds in words that are spoken. The majority of phonemic awareness tasks, activities, and exercises are ORAL.

Since the ability to distinguish between individual sounds, or phonemes, within words is a prerequisite to association of sounds with letters and manipulating sounds to blend words—a fancy way of saying "reading"—the teaching of phonemic awareness is crucial to emergent literacy (early childhood K-2 reading instruction). Children need a strong background in phonemic awareness in order for phonics instruction (sound-spelling relationship printed materials) to be effective. Theorist Marilyn Jager Adams, who researches early reading, has outlined five basic types of phonemic awareness tasks.

Task 1—the ability to hear rhymes and alliteration—for example, the children listen to a poem, rhyming picture book or song and identify the rhyming words heard, which the teacher might then record or list on an experiential chart.

Task 2—the ability to do oddity tasks (recognize the member of a set that is different [odd] among the group)—for example, the children look at the pictures of a blade of grass, a garden and a rose. The teacher asks starts with a different sound.

Task 3—the ability to orally blend words and split syllables—for example, the children can say the first sound of a word and then the rest of the word and then put it together as a single word.

Task 4—the ability to orally segment words—for example, the ability to count sounds. The children would be asked as a group to count the sounds in "hamburger."

Task 5—the ability to do phonics manipulation tasks—for example, replace the "r" sound in rose with a "p" sound.

The Role of Phonemic Awareness in Reading Development

Children who have problems with phonics generally have not acquired or been exposed to phonemic awareness activities usually fostered at home and in preschool to second grade. This includes extensive songs, rhymes and read – alouds.

Instructional methods that may be effective for teaching phonemic awareness can include:

- Clapping syllables in words.
- Distinguishing between a word and a sound.
- Using visual cues and movements to help children understand when the speaker goes from one sound to another.
- Incorporating oral segmentation activities which focus on easily-distinguished syllables rather than sounds.
- Singing familiar songs (e.g., Happy Birthday, Knick Knack Paddy Wack) and replacing key words with words with a different ending or middle sound (oral segmentation).
- Dealing children a deck of picture cards and having them sound out the words for the pictures on their cards or calling for a picture by asking for its first and second sound.

Knowledge of Phonemes

In everyday language, we attach affective meanings to words unconsciously; we exercise more conscious control of informative connotations. In the process of language development, the student must come not only to grasp the definitions of words, but also to become more conscious of the affective connotations and how his listeners process these connotations. Gaining this conscious control over language makes it possible to use language appropriately in various situations and to evaluate its uses in literature and other forms of communication.

The manipulation of language for a variety of purposes is the goal of language instruction. Advertisers and satirists are especially conscious of the effect word choice has on their audiences. By evoking the proper responses from readers/listeners, we can prompt them to take action.

A <u>phoneme</u> is the smallest contrastive unit in a language system and the representation of a sound. The phoneme has been described as the smallest meaningful psychological unit of sound. The phoneme is said to have mental, physiological, and physical substance: our brains process the sounds; the human speech organs produce the sounds; and the sounds are physical entities that can be recorded and measured. Consider the English words "pat" and "sat," which appear to differ only in their initial consonants. This difference, known as <u>contrastiveness</u> or <u>opposition</u>, is adequate to distinguish these words, and therefore the "p" and "s" sounds are said to be different phonemes in English. A pair of words, identical except for such a sound, is known as a <u>minimal pair</u>, and the two sounds are separate phonemes.

Where no minimal pair can exist to demonstrate that two sounds are distinct, it may be that they are <u>allophones</u>. Allophones are variant phones (sounds) that are not recognized as distinct by a speaker, and are not meaningfully different in the language, and so are perceived as being the same. An example of this would be the heavy sounding "l" when landed on at the end of a word like "wool," as opposed to the lighter sounding "l" when starting a word like "leaf." This demonstrates allophones of a single phoneme. While it may exist and be measurable, such a difference is unrecognizable and meaningless to the average English speaker. The real value is as a technique for teaching reading and pronunciation. Identifying phonemes for students and applying their use is a step in the process of developing language fluency.

Examples Of Common Phonemes Applied

Phoneme	Uses
/A/	a (table), a_e (bake), ai (train), ay (say)
/a/	a (flat)
/b/	b (ball)
/k/	c (cake), k (Key), ck (back)
/d/	d (door)
/E/	e (me), ee (feet), ea (leap), y (baby)
/e/	e (pet), ea (head)
/f/	f (fix), ph (phone)
/g/	g (gas)
/h/	h (hot)
/I/	i (I), i_e (bite), igh (light), y (sky)
/i/	i (sit)
/j/	j (jet), dge (edge), g (gem)
/l/	l (lamp)
/m/	m (map)
/n/	n (no), kn (knock)
/O/	o (okay), o_e (bone), oa (soap), ow (low)

/o/	o (hot)
/p/	p (pie)
/kw/	qu (quick)
/r/	r (road), wr (wrong), er (her), ir (sir), ur (fur)
/s/	s (say), c (cent)
/t/	t (time)
/U/	u (future), u_e (use), ew (few)
/u/	u thumb, a (about)
/v/	v (voice)
/w/	w (wash)
/gz/	x (exam)
/ks/	x (box)
/y/	y (yes)
/z/	z (zoo), s (nose)
/OO/	oo (boot), u (truth), u_e (rude), ew (chew)
/oo/	oo (book), u (put)
/oi/	oi (soil), oy (toy)
/ou/	ou (out), ow (cow)
/aw/	aw (saw), au (caught), al (tall)
/ar/	ar (car)
/sh/	sh (ship), ti (nation), ci (special)
/hw/	wh (white)
/ch/	ch (chest), tch (catch)
/th/	th (thick)
/th/	th (this)
/ng/	ng (sing)
/zh/	s (measure)

Choice of the medium through which the message is delivered to the receiver is a significant factor in controlling language. Spoken language relies as much on the gestures, facial expressions and tone of voice of the speaker as on the words he speaks. Slapstick comics can evoke laughter without speaking a word. Young children use body language overtly and older children more subtly, to convey messages. These refinements of body language are paralleled by an ability to recognize and apply the nuances of spoken language. To work strictly with the written word, the writer must use words to imply the body language.

By the time children begin to speak, they have begun to acquire the ability to use language to inform and manipulate. They have already used kinesthetic and verbal cues to attract attention when they seek some physical or emotional gratification. Children learn to apply names to objects and actions. They learn to use language to describe the persons and events in their lives and to express their feelings about the world around them.

Phonics Approach

Word recognition is taught through grapheme-phoneme associations, with the goal of teaching the student to independently apply these skills to new words. Phonics instruction may be synthetic or analytic. In the synthetic method, letter sounds are learned before the student goes on to blend the sounds to form words. The analytic method teaches letter sounds as integral parts of words.

The sounds are usually taught in the sequence: vowels, consonants, consonant blends at the beginning of words (e.g., bl and dr) and consonant blends at the end of words (e.g., ld and mp), consonant and vowel digraphs (e.g., ch and sh), and diphthongs (e.g., au and oy).

Critics of the phonics approach point out that the emphasis on pronunciation may lead to the student focusing more on decoding than comprehension. Some students may have trouble blending sounds to form words and others may become confused with words that do not conform to the phonetic "rules." However, advocates of phonics say that the programs are useful with remedial reading and developmental reading. Examples of phonics series are *Science Research Associates, Merrill Phonics* and DML's *Cove School Reading Program.*

Phonics

As opposed to phonemic awareness, the study of phonics must be done with the eyes open. It's the connection between the sounds and letters on a page. In other words, students learning phonics might see the word "bad" and sound each letter out slowly until they recognize that they just said the word.

Phonological awareness means the ability of the reader to recognize the sounds of spoken language. This recognition includes how these sounds can be blended together, segmented (divided up), and manipulated (switched around). This awareness then leads to phonics, a method for teaching children to read. It helps them "sound out" words.

Development of phonological skills may begin during the preschool years. Indeed, by the age of 5, a child who has been exposed to rhyme can recognize a rhyme. Such a child can demonstrate phonological awareness by filling in the missing rhyming word in a familiar rhyme or rhymed picture book.

You teach children phonological awareness when you teach them the sounds made by the letters and the sounds made by various combinations of letters and to recognize individual sounds in words.

Phonological awareness skills include:
1. Rhyming and syllabification.
2. Blending sounds into words—such as pic-tur-bo-k.
3. Identifying the beginning or starting sounds of words and the ending or closing sounds of words.
4. Breaking words down into sounds—also called "segmenting" words.
5. Recognizing other smaller words in the big word by removing starting sounds—such as "hear" to ear.

Skill 2.2   Demonstrate knowledge of structural analysis skills, including the use of base words, roots, prefixes, suffixes and inflections

Development of Word Analysis Skills and Strategies
Strategy One: Word Study Group (A Balanced Literacy Approach detailed in Sharon Taberski's *On Solid Ground* [2000]).

This involves the teacher taking time to meet with children from grades 3-6 in a small group of no more than 6 children for a word study session. Taberski suggests that this meeting take place next to the Word Wall (see Spelling Wall on p 20). The children selected for this group are those who need to focus more on the relationship between spelling patterns and their consonant sounds.

It is important that this not be a formalized traditional reading group that meets at a set time each week or biweekly. Rather the group should be spontaneously formed by the teacher based on the teacher's quick inventory of the selected children's needs at the start of the week. Taberski has templates in her book of *Guided Reading Planning Sheets*. These sheets are essentially targeted word and other skills sheets with her written and dated observations of children who are in need of support to develop a given skill (kid watching—see Dictionary of Terms).

The teacher should try to meet with this group for at least two consecutive twenty-minute periods per day. Over those two meetings, the teacher can model a Making Words Activity. Once the teacher has modeled making words the first day, the children would then make their own words. On the second day, the children would "sort" their words.

Other topics for a word study group within the framework of the Balanced Literacy Approach that Taberski advocates are: inflectional endings, prefixes and suffixes and/or common spelling patterns.

It should be noted that theorists would classify this activity as a structural analysis activity because the structural components (i.e., prefixes, suffixes and spelling patterns) of the words are being studied.

Strategy Two: Discussion Circles (A Balanced Literacy Approach from the work of J. David Cooper, *Literacy*: *Helping Children Construct Meaning* [2004])

Cooper believes that children should not be "taught" vocabulary and structural analysis skills. Flesch and E.D. Hirsch, who are key theorists of the Phonics approach and advocates of Cultural Literacy (a term coined and associated with E. D. Hirsch), believe that specific vocabulary words at various grade and age levels need to be mastered and MUST be explicitly taught in schools. As far as J. David Cooper is concerned, all the necessary and meaningful (for the child and ultimately adult reader) vocabulary can't possibly be taught in schools (no apologies to Hirsch). To Cooper, it is far more important that the children be made aware of and become interested in learning words by themselves. Cooper feels that through the child's reading and writing, he or she develops a love for and a sense of "ownership" of words. All of Cooper's suggested Structural Analysis word strategies are therefore designed to foster the child's love of words and a desire to "own" more of them through reading and writing.

Discussion Circles is an activity which fits nicely into the Balanced Literacy Lesson Format as part of a SHARE (see Dictionary of Terms). This activity works well from grades 3-6 and beyond. After the children conclude a particular text, Cooper suggests that they get together in discussion circles to respond to the book. Among the prompts, the teacher-coach might suggest that the children focus on words of interest they encountered in the text. These can also be words that they heard if the text was read aloud. Children can be asked to share something funny or upsetting or unusual about the words they have read. Through this focus on children's response to words as the center of the discussion circle, peers become more interested in word study.

Strategy Three: Banking, Booking and Filing It (Making Words My Own)
Children can literally realize the goal of making words their own and exploring word structures through creating concrete objects or displays that demonstrate to the children themselves and to others the words they own. Children can create and maintain their own files of words they have learned or are interested in learning.

The children can categorize the files according to their own interests. They should be encouraged to develop files using science, history, physical education, fine arts, dance and technology content. Newspapers and web resources, which the teacher has approved, are excellent sources for such words. In addition, this provides the teacher with the opportunity to instruct the child in appropriate age- and grade-level research skills. Even children in grades 2 and 3 can begin simplified bibliographies and webliographies for their "found" words. Children can learn how to annotate and note the page of a newspaper, book or URL for a particular word.

They can also copy down the word as it appears in the text (print or electronic); if appropriate, the child can place the particular words found for a given topic or content in an actual bank of the child's own making. The words can be printed on cardboard emblems. This allows for differentiated word study and nurtures those children who are kinesthetic and spatial learners. Of course, children can also choose to create their own word books, which include their specialized vocabulary and descriptions of how they identified or hunted down their words. Richard Scarry's *Watch Out!* books can be anchor books to inspire this structural analysis activity.

ELL learners can share their accounts in their native language first and then translate (with the help of the teacher) these accounts into English with both the native language and the English language versions of the word exploration posted.

Strategy Four: <u>Write Out Your Words; Write With Your Words.</u>
Ownership of words can be demonstrated by having the children use them as part of their writings. The children can author a procedural narrative (a step-by-step description) of how they went about their word searches to compile the words they found for any of the activities. If the children are in grades K-1, or if the children are struggling readers and writers, their procedural narratives can be dictated. Then, the teacher can post them.

As with the previous strategy, ELL learners can share their accounts in their native language first and then translate (with the help of the teacher) these accounts into English with both the native language and the English language versions of the word exploration posted.

Special needs children may model a word box on a specific holiday theme, genre or science/social studies topic with the teacher. Initially, this can be done as a whole class. As the children become more confident, they can work with peers or with a paraprofessional to create their own individual or small team/pair word boxes.

Special needs children can storyboard (with the support of a paraprofessional, their teacher, or a resource specialist) a class or individual or small team word group. They can also narrate their story of how they all found the words by using a tape recorder.

Strategy Five: **Come and See Them/The Words are Here!** (**Word Study Museum within the Classroom**).
This strategy, which I do as part of my Museum within a School Residency in NYC and Westchester schools, has been presented in detail so that teachers within their own classrooms can use it. In addition, the way the activity is described and the mention at the end of the description of how the activity can address family literacy, ELL and special needs children's talents, provides an example of other audiences a teacher should consider in curriculum design.

Almost every general education teacher and reading specialist will have to differentiate instruction to address the needs of special education and ELL learners even though "officially" specialists or teachers are not "teaching" these populations. Family or shared literacy is a major component of all literacy instruction.

Within their classrooms, children can create either single or multiple exhibits in museum style to celebrate their word study. They can build actual representations of the type of study they have done, including word trees (made out of cardboard or foam board), elaborate word boxes and games, word history timelines or murals, and word study maps. They can develop online animations, Kids Spiration graphic organizers, quick movies, digital photo essays and PowerPoint presentations to share the word they have identified. The classroom, gym, or cafeteria will be transformed into a gallery space. Children can author brochure descriptions for their individual, team, or class exhibits. Some children can volunteer to be tour guides or docents for the experience. Other children can work to create a banner for the Museum. The children can name the Museum themselves and send out invitations to its opening. Invitations can be sent to parents, community, staff members and peer or younger classes.

Depending on their age and grade level, children can also develop interactive games and quizzes focused on particular exhibits. An artist, or a team of class artists, can design a poster for the exhibit, while other children may choose to build the exhibits. Another small group can work on signage and a catalogue or register of objects within the exhibit. Greeters who will welcome parents and peers to the exhibit can be trained and can develop their own scripts.

If the children are in grades 4-6, they can also develop their own visitor feedback forms and design word-themed souvenirs. The whole museum within the school or classroom can be captured digitally or with a regular camera. The record of this event can be hung near the word walls. Of course, the children can use many of their newly-recognized and owned words to describe the event.

The Word Study Museum activity can be used with either a phonics-based or a balanced literacy approach. It promotes additional writing, researching, discussing and reading about words.

It is also an excellent family literacy strategy in that families can develop their own Word Exhibits at home, and it models many easily-adapted models for family use. Don't throw out that used paper towel cardboard roll, for it could easily become a word tree! Hang on to that empty family cereal box; it can become a magic word box to store all a child's newspaper "found" weather words!

This activity can also support and celebrate special needs learners. It can be presented in dual languages by children who are ELL learners and fluent in more than a single language.

Use of Semantic and Syntactic Cues

Semantic Cues
Prompts that the teacher can use which will alert the children to semantic cues include:

1. You said (child's statement and incorrect attempt). Does that make sense to you?
2. If someone said (repeat the child's attempt), would you know what he or she meant?
3. You said (child's incorrect attempt). Would you write that?

Children need to use meaning to predict what the text says so that the relevant information can prompt the correct words to surface as they identify the words. If children come to a word they can't immediately recognize, they need to try to figure it out using their past reading (or being read to) experiences, background knowledge and what they can deduce so far from the text itself.

Syntactic Clues
1. You said (child's incorrect attempt). Does that sound right?
2. You said (child's incorrect attempt). Can we say it like that?

Identification of Common Morphemes, Prefixes and Suffixes
This aspect of vocabulary development is to help children look for structural elements within words, which they can use independently to help them determine meaning.

Some teachers choose to directly teach structural analysis. In particular, those who teach by following the phonics-centered approach for reading do this. Other teachers, who follow the balanced literacy approach, introduce the structural components as part of mini-lessons that are focused on the students' reading and writing.

Structural analysis of words, as defined by J. David Cooper (2004), involves the study of significant word parts. This analysis can help the child with pronunciation and constructing meaning.

The term list below is generally recognized as the key structural analysis components.

Root Words—a word from which another word is developed. The second word can be said to have its "root" in the first. This structural component nicely lends itself to a tree with roots illustration, which can make the meaning relevant for children. Children may also want to literally construct root words using cardboard trees and/or actual roots from plants to create word family models.

ELL learners can construct these models for their native language root word families, as well for the English language words they are learning. ELL learners in the 5th and 6th grade may even appreciate analyzing the different root structures for contrasts and similarities between their native language and English.

Special needs learners can work in small groups or individually with a paraprofessional on building root word models.

Base Words—stand-alone linguistic units, which cannot be deconstructed or broken down into smaller words; for example, in the word "re-tell," the base word is "tell."

Contractions—shortened forms of two words, in which a letter or letters have been deleted. These deleted letters have been replaced by an apostrophe.

Prefixes—beginning units of meaning which can be added (the vocabulary word for this type of structural adding is "affixed") to a base word or root word. They cannot stand alone. They are also sometimes known as "bound morphemes," meaning that they cannot stand alone as a base word.

Suffixes—ending units of meaning which can be "affixed" or added on to the ends of root or base words. Suffixes transform the original meanings of base and root words. Like prefixes, they are also known as "bound morphemes" because they cannot stand alone as words.

Compound Words—Occur when two or more base words are connected to form a new word. The meaning of the new word is in some way connected with that of the base word.

Inflectional Endings—types of suffixes that impart a new meaning to the base or root word. These endings in particular change the gender, number, tense or form of the base or root words. Just like other suffixes, these are also termed "bound morphemes."

Structural Analysis—splitting words into parts to discover the meaning of unknown words.

Learning how to distinguish among and to correctly define these structural word components is seemingly daunting for young children; however, they actually can easily accomplish memorizing these set definitions, which is the first necessary step for correctly using them as they construct the meaning. How so? Well, pleasure in structural analysis is just a melodic song away.

Use a familiar song, which is actually a definition of sing-along, e.g., *Do-Re-Mi* from *The Sound of Music*, or use any children's song that is regularly used in the classroom.

Model for the children how the familiar song, *Do-Re-Mi*, can be "changed" to be the "sung" definitions of these structural components.

For example:
- "Re," a prefix, at the beginning of a word.
- "Ful," a suffix, when someone is fearful.
- "Ed," an inflectional at the end of walk; it means he walked in the past.
- "Don't," a contraction made up of do and not.
- That will bring us back to …

Once the teacher does the opening stanza, the children can then be challenged to come up with the next stanza's lines. The teachers will set the structural component for the line, e.g., compound words. Then, the children as either a whole class, in small groups, or as a guided writing activity will author a line to share a compound word and explain what it is. Once this is successfully done, the child or group of children who wrote the correct lyric can select another structural component. They can challenge other class members to complete the next line and the structural song writing can continue for the time allotted to vocabulary development or writing workshop.

This activity can develop into a structural song writing lyric wall, center, and/or sound recording. The teacher, or one of the children (if the children are on grade three level or above), can write down each lyric line contributed and then routinely sing it with small groups or the whole class as practice for reviewing structural components or just for fun. The songs can be shared with other classes. They can also be used as student-centered (written by and for students) exercises for a structural analysis center, where peers will do activities in word study using work actually done by their classmates.

ELL learners can do these types of songs using songs which are familiar to them from their native language or in a dual language version.

Using singing to help support children in necessary structural analysis definitions also differentiates instruction and helps the teacher to draw children whose learning styles and strengths are auditory and musical into the circle of engaged readers and writers.

Knowledge of Greek and Latin Roots that Form English Words
Knowledge of Greek and Latin roots, which comprise English words, can measurably enhance children's reading skills and can also enrich their writing.

Strategy One: Word Webs
Sharon Taberski (2000) does not advocate teaching Greek and Latin derivatives in the abstract to young children. However, when she comes across (as is common and natural) specific Greek and Latin roots in her readings with and to children, she uses that opportunity to introduce children to these rich resources.

For example, during readings on rodents (a favorite of first and second graders), Taberski draws her class's attention to the fact that beavers gnaw at things with their teeth. She then connects the "dent" root or derivative to the children's lives, other words they are familiar with, or their experiences. The children then volunteer "dentist," "dental," "denture" and etc. Taberski begins to place these in a graphic organizer or word web.

When she has tapped the extent of the children's prior knowledge of "dent" words, she shares with them the fact that "Dens/dentis" is the Latin word for teeth. Then, she introduces the word "indent," which she has already previewed with them as part of their conventions of print study. She helps them to see that the "indenting" of the first line of a paragraph can even be related to the "teeth" Latin root in that it looks like a "print" bite was taken out of the paragraph.

Taberski displays the word web in the Word Wall Chart section of her room. The class is encouraged throughout a week's time to look for other words to add to the web. Taberski stresses that for her, as an elementary teacher of reading and writing, the key element of the Greek and Latin word root web activity is the children's coming to understand that if they know what a Greek or Latin word root means, they can use that knowledge to figure out what other words mean. She feels the key concept is to model and demonstrate for children how fun and fascinating Greek and Latin root study can be.

Strategy Two: Greek and Latin Root Word Webs Using the Internet
Older children in grades 3-6 can build on this initial print activity by searching online for additional words for a particular Greek or Latin root that has been introduced in class.

They can easily do this in a way that authentically ties in with their own interests and experiences by reading reviews for a book which has been a read-aloud online or by just reading the summaries of the day's news and printing out those words which appear in the stories online that share the root discussed.

The children can be encouraged to circle or cut out these online identified instances of their Latin or Greek root and also to document the exact date and URL for the citation. These can be posted as part of their own online web in the word wall section study area. If the school or class has a website or webpage, the children can post this data there as a special Greek and Latin root word page.

Expanding the concept of the Greek and Latin word web from the printed page to the World Wide Web, nicely inculcates the child in the habits of lifelong reading and researching online. This beginning expository research will serve them well in upper elementary subject content area work and beyond.

Use of Syllabification as a Word Identification Strategy

Strategy: Clap Hands, Count those Syllables as They Come!! (Taberski, 2000)
The objective of this activity is for children to understand that every syllable in a polysyllabic word can be studied for its spelling patterns in the same way that monosyllabic words are studied for their spelling patterns.

The easiest way for the K-3 teacher to introduce this activity to the children is to share a familiar poem from the poetry chart (or to write out a familiar poem on a large experiential chart).

First, the teacher reads the poem with the children. As they are reading it aloud, the children clap the bats of the poem, and the teacher uses a colored marker to place a tic (/) above each syllable.

Next, the teacher takes letter cards and selects one of the polysyllabic words from the poem which the children have already "clapped" out.

The children use letter cards to spell that word on the sentence strip holder or it can be placed on a felt board or up against a window on display. Together, the children and teacher divide the letters into syllables and place blank letter cards between the syllables. The children identify spelling patterns they know.

Finally, and as part of continued small group syllabification study, the children identify other polysyllabic words they clapped out from the poem. They make up the letter combinations of these words. Then, they separate them into syllables with blank letter cards between the syllables.

Children who require special support in syllabification can be encouraged to use lots of letter cards to create a large butcher paper syllabic (in letter cards with spaces) representation of the poem or at least a few lines of the poem. They can be told that this is for use as a teaching tool for others. In this way, they authenticate their study of syllabification with a real product that can actually be referenced by peers.

Techniques for Identifying Compound Words

Use of Context Cues—these clues (e.g., semantic, syntactic) help students identify words and verify the pronunciation and the meaning of words.

Semantic Feature Analysis—this technique for enhancing vocabulary skills by using semantic cues is based on the research of Johnson and Pearson (1984) and Anders and Bos (1986). It involves young children in setting up a feature analysis grid of various subject content words, which is an outgrowth of their discussion about these words.

For instance, Cooper (2004) includes a sample of a Semantic Features Analysis Grid for Vegetables:

Vegetables	Green	Have Peels	Eat Raw	Seeds
Carrots	-	+	+	-
Cabbage	+	-	+	-

Note: the use of the + for yes, - for no, and possible use for + and - if a vegetable like squash could be both green and yellow. Make this grid very accessible for young readers and very easily done by them on their own as part of their independent word analysis.

Teachers of children in grade one and beyond can design their own semantic analysis grids to meet their students' needs and to align with the topics the kids are learning. The steps to create semantic analysis grids are as follows:

1. Select a category or class of words (e.g., planets, rodent family members, winter words, weather words).

2. Use the left side of the grid to list at least three, if not more, items that fit this category. The number of actual items listed will depend on the age and grade level of the children, three or four items is fine for K-1 and up, while ten to fifteen items may be appropriate for grades 5 and 6.

3. Brainstorm with the children, or if better suited to the class, the teacher may list features that the items have in common. As can be noted from the example excerpted from Cooper's *Literacy: Helping Children Construct Meaning* (2004), these common features, such as vegetables' green color, peels and seeds are usually pretty easy to identify.

4. Show the children how to insert +, -, and even?, (if they are not certain) notations on the grid. The teacher might also explore with the children the possibility that an item could get both a + and a -. For example, a vegetable like broccoli might be eaten cooked or raw, depending on taste, and squash can be green or yellow.

Whatever the length of the grid when first presented to the children (perhaps as a semantic cue lesson in and of itself tied in to a text being read in class), make certain that the grid as presented and filled out is not the end of the activity.

Children can use it as a model for developing their own semantic features grid and share them during the share time with the whole class. Child developed grids can become part of a Word Work center in the classroom or even be published in a Word Study Games book by the class as a whole. Such a publication can be shared with parents during open school week and evening visits and with peer classes.

Contextual Redefinition

This strategy supports children to use the context more effectively by presenting them with sufficient context BEFORE they begin reading. It models for the children the use of contextual clues to make informed guesses about word meanings.

To apply this strategy, the teacher should first select unfamiliar words for teaching. No more than two or three words should be selected for direct teaching. The teacher should then write a sentence in which there are sufficient clues supplied for the child to successfully figure out the meaning. Among the types of context clues the teacher can use are: compare/contrast, synonyms and direct definition.

Then, the teacher should present the words by themselves on the experiential chart or as letter cards. Have the children pronounce the words. As they pronounce them, challenge them to come up with a definition for each word. After more than one definition is offered, encourage the children to decide as a whole group what the definition is. Write down their agreed upon definition with no comment as to its true meaning.

Next, share with the children the contexts (sentences the teacher wrote with the words and explicit context clues). Ask that the children read the sentences aloud. Then have them come up with a definition for each word. Make certain that as they present their definitions, the teacher does not comment. Ask that they justify their definitions by making specific references to the context clues in the sentences. As the discussion continues, direct the children's attention to their previously agreed upon definition of the word, facilitate them in discussing the differences between their guesses about the word when they saw only the word itself and their guesses about the word when they read it in context; finally, have the children check their use of context skills to correctly define the word by using a dictionary.

This type of direct teaching of word definitions is useful when the children have dictionary skills and the teacher is aware of the fact that there are not sufficient clues about the words in the context to help the students define them. In addition, struggling readers and students from ELL backgrounds may benefit tremendously from being walked through this process that highly proficient and successful readers apply automatically.

By using this strategy, the teacher can also "kid watch" and note the students' prior knowledge as they guess the word in isolation. The teacher can also actually witness and hear how various students use context skills.

Through their involvement in this strategy, struggling readers gain a feeling of community as they experience the ways in which their struggles and guesses resonate in other peers' responses to the text. They are also getting a chance to be "walked through" this maze of meaning and learning how to use context clues in order to navigate it themselves.

Extending a Reader's Understanding of Familiar Words

Dictionary Use
Dictionaries are useful for spelling, writing and reading. It is very important to initially expose and habituate students to enjoy using the dictionary.

Cooper (2004) suggests that the following be kept in mind as the teacher of grades K-6 introduces and then habituates children in what is to be hoped will be a lifelong fascination with the dictionary and with vocabulary acquisition.

Requesting or suggesting that children look up a word in the dictionary should be an invitation to a wonderful exploration, not a punishment or busy work that has no reference to their current reading assignment. Do not routinely require children to look up every new spelling word in the dictionary (This is Cooper's view and many other theorists would disagree with him here.).

Model the correct way to use the dictionary for children even as late as the third through sixth grade. Many have never been taught proper dictionary skills. The teacher needs to demonstrate to the children that, as an adult reader and writer, he or she routinely and happily uses the dictionary and learns new information that makes him or her better at reading and writing.

Cooper believes in beginning dictionary study as early as kindergarten and this is now very possible because of the proliferation of lush picture dictionaries, which can be introduced at that grade level. He also suggests that children not only look at these picture dictionaries, but also begin to make dictionaries of their own at this grade level, filled with pictures and beginning words. As children join the circle of lexicographers, they will begin to see themselves as compilers and users of dictionaries. Of course, this will support their ongoing vocabulary development.

In early grade levels, use of the dictionary can nicely complement the children's mastery of the alphabet. They should be given whole class and small group practice in locating words.

As the children progress with their phonetic skills, the dictionary can be used to show them phonetic re-spelling using the pronunciation key.

Older children in grades 3 and beyond need explicit teacher demonstrations and practice in the use of guidewords. They also need to begin to learn about the hierarchies of various word meanings. In the upper grades, children should also explore using special content dictionaries and glossaries in the backs of their books.

Key Words
Cooper (2004) feels that it is up to the teacher to preview the content area text to identify the main ideas. Then the teacher should compile a list of terms related to the content thrust. These terms and words become part of the key concepts list.

Next, the teacher sees which of the key concept words and terms are already defined in the text. These will not require direct teaching. Words for which children have sufficient skills to determine their meaning, through base, root, prefixes or suffixes, also will not require direct teaching.

Instruction in the remaining key words, which should not be more than two or three key words, can be provided before, during or after reading. If students have previewed the content area and identified those words they need support with, the instruction should be provided before reading. Instruction can also easily be provided as part of guided reading support. After reading support is indicated, the text offers the children an opportunity to enrich their own vocabularies.

Having children work as a whole class or in small groups on a content-specific dictionary for a topic regularly covered in their grade level social studies, science or mathematics curriculum offers an excellent collaborative opportunity for children to design a dictionary/word resource that can celebrate their own vocabulary learning. Such a resource can then be used with the next year's classes as well.

Development of Vocabulary Knowledge and Skills in Individual Students (e.g., English Language Learners, struggling readers through highly proficient readers) Using the Semantic Feature Analysis Grid

Highly proficient readers can be asked to help on-grade peers, or better yet, younger peers, with their word analysis skills by having them work with these struggling readers on filling out teacher developed semantic analysis grids. Some 5th and 6th grade highly proficient readers may also evidence the aptitude and desire to create their own semantic analysis grids for their peer or younger peer tutees. In this way, highly proficient readers can gain insights into the field of teaching reading at an early age, and younger struggling readers can have the edge taken off their struggles by working with a peer or an older student. For both individuals, the experience is one that promotes and celebrates word analysis skills and nurtures the concept of a literate and caring community of readers.

ELL students can also add in deliberate items to the categories to reflect their cultures. For instance, Latino children can add in plantains and guava to the fruits their non-Latino peers might list. This provides the ELL learners with an opportunity to enrich the knowledge base of their peers' subject category inventory and puts them in a positive spotlight. The easy notations on the grid make it accessible for even ELL children with limited English language writing and speaking capacities.

Special needs learners can benefit from the grid. Teachers, paraprofessionals, and tutors can develop it and the children themselves can notate it. They can also illustrate it. It can be posted or kept in the word center. The grid provides these learners, who are often spatial learners, with a concrete demonstration of their word analysis achievement.

Biemiller's research indicates that the listening vocabulary for a 6th grader who tests at the 25th percentile in reading is equivalent to that attained by the 75th percentile 3rd grader. This deficit in vocabulary presents a formidable challenge for the 6th grader to succeed, not only on reading tests, but also in various content subjects in elementary school and beyond.

Comments

Definitions are included because the structural analysis components are explicitly taught in schools that advocate the phonics-centered approach and are also incorporated into the word work component of the schools that advocate the balanced literacy approach for instruction.

Definition questions, that are multiple choice questions which have only a single right answer because they are testing whether the teacher candidate has memorized the appropriate content usage of the terms, constitute for no less than 15% of the multiple-choice questions on the test. Therefore, by taking the time to memorize these easy definitions, scores are more likely to improve.

What about the use of these concepts to engage children in successful reading? One activity was also detailed above as far as root families, and a few more will be provided further on. Some of you may want to know why some of the activities are presented in such detail. Again, this is deliberate, and these activities have been bolded for easy identification. Often, the constructed response questions of the foundations of reading tests and certification tests ask the teacher to explain how a certain concept would be taught in a given grade for a certain student population. This type of constructed response question is simple for a teacher who is already teaching that concept to precisely that group of students in precisely that grade. There are a certain number of working educators who take these tests to get additional certification or to be become certified, so for them, these detailed, "How would you teach" _____ questions are a breath of tension-free air.

However, as both a trainer of working teachers in elementary schools and a graduate education educator, I know first-hand the tension level caused by these constructed response questions for the graduate education student who has never set foot in an elementary school since the day he or she left there as a child. I also know how unnerving many educators who are career changers find the challenge of describing how they would teach something they can easily "do" themselves to children on the elementary level. Indeed, these constructed response questions even upset experienced, currently teaching educators who may work full time as kindergarten or special needs instructors and are suddenly being asked how they would differentiate (memorize that key in vogue education term) instruction to support children from an ELL background or to align with the US history theme mandated for fifth graders.

If the question doesn't focus on grades even the most experienced teacher candidate has taught, he or she can come up high and dry as far as explaining how to teach an unfamiliar concept to a given unfamiliar student population. Therefore, the detailed activities, which have been deliberately strewn throughout the guide, are **CONSTRUCTED RESPONSE** models, which teacher candidates are invited, enjoined, and URGED to review once and again before the examination. It is hoped that if the constructed response is a call for a "HOW WOULD YOU TEACH ____ to _____," and you haven't taught or haven't taught that to the designated population, you can easily use my experiences with my best wishes and hopes that they will work for you as they have for me.

Skill 2.3   Demonstrate knowledge of the use of syllabication as a word identification strategy.

(See skill 2.2.)

Skill 2.4   Demonstrate knowledge of sight words and their use as a word identification strategy.

Word recognition involves the ability to recognize words according to the arrangement of printed symbols. <u>Strategies</u> that can be used to aid students in word recognition are:

1. Make a picture dictionary. The student compiles a scrapbook that is indexed with the letters of the alphabet. This type of activity has an advantage over commercial picture dictionaries since the student collects pictures of words he is learning.

2. Use picture cards. The student pronounces the word that is represented by the picture.

3. Make a tachistoscope. Cut a window in the center of a sturdy card or piece of oak tag. Make up word cards with basic sight vocabulary words listed on them. Flash the words one at a time in the window box. The length of time exposure can vary.

Sight vocabulary refers to the total stock of words that are recognized by sight. <u>Strategies</u> for developing sight vocabulary fall into two sub-categories: basic sight words and other sight words.

1. <u>Basic sight words</u> refer to high frequency words that appear most often in print and are included in basic word lists like Dolch Word List. Continual exposure to basic word lists should help to increase the number of basic sight words mastered by the student.

2. <u>Other sight words</u> are high frequency words that vary from basal reader to basal reader and include all words known instantly or without the use of word-attack skills. Frequent reading experiences will help to increase the number of other sight words a student recognizes.

Skill 2.5   Demonstrate knowledge of strategies for promoting the development of word analysis skills in individual students

Decoding, Word Recognition and Spelling

Word analysis (a.k.a. phonics or decoding) is the process readers use to figure out unfamiliar words based on written patterns. Word recognition is the process of automatically determining the pronunciation and some degree of the meaning of an unknown word. In other words, fluent readers recognize most written words easily and correctly, without consciously decoding or breaking them down. These elements of literacy below are skills readers need for word recognition.

To decode means to change communication signals into messages. Reading comprehension requires that the reader learn the code within which a message is written and be able to decode it to get the message. Encoding involves changing a message into symbols. Examples include encoding oral language into writing (spelling),encoding an idea into words, or encoding a mathematical or physical idea into appropriate mathematical symbols.

Although effective reading comprehension requires identifying words automatically (Adams, 1990, Perfetti, 1985), children do not have to be able to identify every single word or know the exact meaning of every word in a text to understand it. Indeed, Nagy (1988) says that children can read a work with a high level of comprehension even if they do not fully know as many as 15 percent of the words within a given text. Children develop the ability to decode and recognize words automatically. They then can extend their ability to decode to multi-syllabic words.

Spelling instruction should include words misspelled in daily writing, generalizing spelling knowledge and mastering objectives in progressive phases of development. The developmental stages of spelling are:

1) **Pre-phonemic spelling**—children know that letters stand for a message, but they do not know the relationship between spelling and pronunciation.

2) **Early phonemic spelling**—children are beginning to understand spelling. They usually write the beginning letter correctly, with the rest consonants or long vowels.

3) **Letter-name spelling**—some words are consistently spelled correctly. The student is developing a sight vocabulary and a stable understanding of letters as representing sounds. Long vowels are usually used accurately, but silent vowels are omitted. Unknown words are spelled by the child attempting to match the name of the letter to the sound.

4) **Transitional spelling**—this phase is typically entered in late elementary school. Short vowel sounds are mastered and some spelling rules known. They are developing a sense of which spellings are correct and which are not.

5) **Derivational spelling**—this is usually reached from high school to adulthood. This is the stage where spelling rules are being mastered.

Word-Attack Skills

Phonics instruction helps the student with pronunciation of printed symbols. Strategies include two basic approaches: analytic and synthetic.

1. The *analytic* approach is that of beginning with a pool of 75 to 100 sight words from which letter sounds are taught.

2. The *synthetic* approach emphasizes the blending of sounds and the teaching of sounds for certain letters.

Structural analysis involves the use of structural cues to decode derived and inflected words. The term refers to larger parts of words that bear meaning, such as root words, suffixes, prefixes, word endings, apostrophes, plus "s" to show possession, contractions and compound words. Strategies useful in strengthening the ability to analyze the structure of words are:

1. Presenting a list of words with variant endings and having the student circle the root word.

2. Giving the student a list of words and a list of endings and asking him to make up as many real words as he can using the endings.

3. Writing two identical sentences but leaving a space for a prefix to be added to one of the words. For example, "Tom tied his shoes. Tom tied his shoes." Ask the student to add a prefix that would make the new sentence mean the opposite of the first one.

4. Writing a sentence on the blackboard with a derived form of a word in it. Show the student how the suffixes change the meaning as well as the part of speech. For example, the verb "fear" may be changed to the adjective "fearsome." "I fear that scary man," tells about the feeling of the speaker. "That scary man is fearsome," Tells about the scary man.

Context cueing refers to the clues or hints a student receives from a word by the way it is used in the context of a sentence. Another kind of context cue is the use of pictures of illustrations corresponding with the written words or passages. Strategies that might enhance the use of context clues include:

1. Providing sentences such as, "The farmer drove his truck down the country (road)." Query students about possible answers.
2. Supplying pictures illustrating the reading passage. Have the reader tell what the omitted word might be.

Configuration is the use of the shape of a word and its distinctive features to identify or distinguish it from other words. Distinctive features refer to the length of the words, the use of capital and lower-case letters, the presence of double letters, and ascending and descending parts of letters. Strategies for using configuration clues include:

1. Drawing a solid line with right angles around the outer parts of letters that form the word to produce a visible contour or shape, such as "youth."
2. Having the students first discriminate words in which the distinctive features are dissimilar, such as "go," "book" and "elephant."
3. Having the students later distinguish words in which the distinctive features are similar, such as "hot," "hat" and "hit". This is a harder task.

Decoding is the process of deciphering the identity, like pronunciation of an unfamiliar word, on the basis of its arrangement of symbols, like letters. Reliance is made on grapheme-phoneme correspondence. Strategies appropriate for the development of decoding skills include:

1. Having the student correspond speech sounds (phonemes) with letters (graphemes) in the alphabet. This can be done during instructional lessons or during informal practice activities.
2. Telling the student to break the word into parts and pronounce each component.
3. Covering parts of the words and asking the student to decode each component.
4. Locating sounds in the word the student are misreading. Isolate the letter, or combination of letters, and ask the student to tell you the sounds that is made by those particular graphic symbols.

Word study skills teach students how to recognize words upon sight or learn to use effective decoding practices. <u>Strategies</u> include activities used in word attack skills, structural analysis, sight vocabulary, decoding skills and phonetic analysis. Some suggestions for increasing students' total stock of vocabulary include:

1. Showing a learner a sight word on a flash card and saying, "This word is _____," and then asking the learner, "What word is this?"

2. Pointing out distinctive features of a word through the use of configuration cues.

3. Introducing word families and teaching substitutions of sounds.

4. Emphasizing root words and the different words that can be obtained through addition of prefixes, suffixes and inflectional endings.

5. Providing practice in recognizing and saying the most commonly used high-frequency words.

6. Using pools of known words to learn compound words.

7. Using reinforcement and continuous charting of progress.

8. Timing the recognition of words.

9. Controlling vocabulary through presentation devices, such as Language Master, teaching machines and computer software.

COMPETENCY 3.0 UNDERSTAND VOCABULARY DEVELOPMENT.

Skill 3.1 Demonstrate understanding of the relationship between oral and written vocabulary and reading comprehension

The National Reading Panel has put forth the following conclusions about vocabulary instruction.

1. There is a need for direct instruction of vocabulary items required for a specific text.

2. Repetition and multiple exposures to vocabulary items are important. Students should be given items that will be likely to appear in many contexts.

3. Learning in rich contexts is valuable for vocabulary learning. Vocabulary words should be those that the learner will find useful in many contexts. When vocabulary items are derived from content learning materials, the learner will be better equipped to deal with specific reading matter in content areas.

4. Vocabulary tasks should be restructured as necessary. It is important to be certain that students fully understand what is asked of them in the context of reading rather than focusing only on the words to be learned.

5. Vocabulary learning is effective when it entails active engagement in learning tasks.

6. Computer technology can be used effectively to help teach vocabulary.

7. Vocabulary can be acquired through incidental learning. Much of a student's vocabulary will have to be learned in the course of doing things other than explicit vocabulary learning. Repetition, richness of context, and motivation may also add to the efficacy of incidental learning of vocabulary.

8. Dependence on a single vocabulary instruction method will not result in optimal learning. A variety of methods were used effectively with emphasis on multimedia aspects of learning, richness of context in which words are to be learned, and the number of exposures to words that learners receive.

The Panel found that a critical feature of effective classrooms is the instruction of specific words that includes lessons and activities where students apply their vocabulary knowledge and strategies to reading and writing. Included in the activities were discussions where teachers and students talked about words, their features, and strategies for understanding unfamiliar words.

There are many methods for directly and explicitly teaching words. In fact, the Panel found twenty-one methods that have been found effective in research projects. Many emphasize the underlying concept of a word and its connections to other words, such as semantic mapping and diagramming that use graphics. The keyword method uses words and illustrations that highlight salient features of meaning. Visualizing or drawing a picture, either by the student or by the teacher, was found to be effective. Many words cannot be learned in this way, of course, so it should be used as only one method among others. Effective classrooms provide multiple ways for students to learn and interact with words. The Panel also found that computer-assisted activities can have a very positive role in the development of vocabulary.

Skill 3.2   Demonstrate understanding of the development of vocabulary knowledge and skills in students with disabilities

If there were two words that can be synonymous with reading comprehension as far as the balanced literacy approach is concerned, they would be "Constructing Meaning."

Cooper, Taberski, Strickland and other key theorists and classroom teachers conceptualize the reader as designating a specific meaning to the text using both clues in the text and his/her own prior knowledge. Comprehension for the balanced literacy theorists is a strategic process.

The reader interacts with the text and brings his/her prior knowledge and experience to it or LACK of prior knowledge and experience to it. Writing is interlaced with reading and is a mutually integrative and supportive parallel process. Hence the division of literacy learning by the balanced literacy folks into reading workshop and writing workshop, with the same anchor, readings or books, being used for both.

Consider the sentence, "The test booklet was white with black print, but very scary looking."

According to the idea of constructing meaning as the reader reads this sentence, the schemata (generic information stored in the mind) of tests was personally activated by the author's ideas that tests are scary. Therefore, the ultimate meaning that the reader derives from the page is from the reader's own responses and experiences with the ideas the author presents. The reader constructs a meaning that reflects the author's intent and also the reader's response to that intent.

It is also to be remembered that readings, for the most part, are fairly lengthy passages, comprised of paragraphs which in turn are comprised of more than one sentence. With each successive sentence, and every new paragraph, the reader refocuses. The schemata are reconsidered, and a new meaning is constructed.

Language development is definitively paralleled along the physiological development of the learner. The cognitive processes that occur during the physical development have been documented in the writings of Piaget and Kohlberg's cognitive learning theories.

Skill 3.3 Demonstrate understanding of the importance of frequent, extensive, varied reading experiences in vocabulary development

The Relationship between Oral and Written Vocabulary Development and Reading Comprehension
Biemiller's (2003) research documents that those children entering 4th grade with significant vocabulary deficits demonstrate increasing reading comprehension problems. Evidence shows that these children do not catch up, but rather continue to fall behind.

Strategy One: Word Map Strategy
This strategy is a good one for children grades 3-6 and beyond. The target group of children for this strategy includes those who need to improve their independent vocabulary acquisition abilities. The strategy is essentially teacher-directed learning where children are "walked through" the process. They are helped by the teacher to identify the type of information that makes a definition. They are also assisted in using context clues and background understanding to construct meaning.

The word map graphic organizer is the tool teachers use to complete this strategy with children. Word map templates are available online from the Houghton Mifflin web site and from ReadWriteThink, the web site of the NCTE (see webliography section). The word map helps the children to visually represent the elements of a given concept.

The children's literal articulation of the concept can be prompted by three key questions: What is it? What is it like? What are some examples?

For instance, the word "oatmeal" might yield a word map with "What is it?" in a rectangular box with the definition, a hot cereal you eat in the morning. The "What is it like?" box may contain the words hot, mushy and salty. The "What are some examples?" box might include instant oatmeal you make in a minute, apple-flavor oatmeal or Irish Oatmeal.

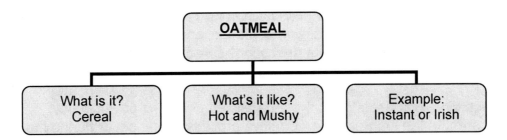

The procedure to be used in sharing this strategy with children is to select three concepts the children are familiar with. Then, show them the template of a word map. Tell them that the three questions asked on the map and the boxes to fill in beneath them, help readers to see what they need to know about a word. The teacher of balanced literacy program will also mention that these same three things are necessary for writers to know when they write about a word.

Next, help the children to complete at least two word maps for two of the three concepts that were pre-selected. Then have the children select a concept of their own to map either independently or in a small group. As the final task for this first part of the strategy, have the children, in teams or individually, write a definition for at least one of the concepts using the key things about it listed on the map. Have the children share these definitions aloud and talk about how they used the word maps to help them with the definitions.

For the next part of this strategy, the teacher should pick up an expository text or a textbook the children are already using to study mathematics, science or social studies. The teacher should either locate a short excerpt where a particular concept is defined or use the content to write model passages of definitions on his/her own.

After the passages are selected or authored, the teacher should duplicate them. Then, they should be distributed to the children, along with blank word map templates. The children should be asked to read each passage and then to complete the word map for the concept in each passage.

Finally, have the children share the word maps they have developed for each passage. Give them a chance to explain how they used the word in the passage to help them fill out their word map. End by telling them that the three components of the concept—class, properties, examples—are just three of the many components for any given concept.

This strategy has assessment potential for the teacher because the teacher can literally see how the students understand specific concepts by looking at their maps and hearing their explanations. The maps the students develop on their own demonstrate whether they have really understood the concepts in the passages.

This strategy serves to ready students for independently inferring word meanings. By using the word map strategy, children develop concepts of what they need to know to begin to figure out an unknown word on their own. It assists the children in grades 3 and beyond to connect prior knowledge with new knowledge.

This word map strategy can be adapted by the teacher to suit the specific needs and goals of instruction. Illustrations of the concept and comparisons to other concepts can be included in the word mapping for children grades 5 and beyond. This particular strategy is one that can be used with a research theme in the social studies content areas.

Strategy Two: Preview in Context
This is a direct teaching strategy that allows the teacher to guide the students as they examine words in their context prior to reading a passage.

Before beginning the strategy, the teacher selects only two or three key concept words. Then the teacher reads the text carefully to identify passages within the text that evidence strong context clues for the word.

The teacher then presents the word and the context to the children. As the teacher reads aloud, the children follow along. Once the teacher has finished the read aloud, the children re-read the material silently.

After the silent re-reading, the children will be facilitated or coached by the teacher to a definition of one of the key words selected for study. This is done through a child-centered discussion. As part of the discussion, the teacher asks questions which get the children to activate their prior knowledge and to use the contextual clues to figure out the correct meaning of the selected key concept words. Make certain that the definition of the key concept word is finally made by the children.

Next, help the children to begin to expand the word's meaning, do this by having them consider the following for the given key concept word: synonyms, antonyms and other contexts or other kinds of stories/texts where the word might appear. This is the time to have the children check their responses to the challenge of identifying word synonyms and antonyms by having them go to the thesaurus or the dictionary to confirm their responses. In addition, have the children place the synonyms or antonyms they find in their word boxes or word journals. The recording of their findings will guarantee them ownership of the words and deepen their capacity to use contextual clues.

The main point to remember in using this strategy is that it should only be used when the context is strong. It will not work with struggling readers who have no prior knowledge. Through listening to the children's responses as the teacher helps them to define the word and its potential synonyms and antonyms, the teacher can assess their ability to successfully use context clues. The key to this simple strategy is that it allows the teacher to draw the child out and to grasp, through the child's responses, the individual child's contextual clue process. The more talk from the child, the better.

The Role of Systematic, Noncontextual Vocabulary Strategies

Hierarchical and Linear Arrays

The very complexity of the vocabulary used in this strategy description may be unnerving for the teacher. Yet this strategy, included in the Cooper (2004) literacy instruction, is really very simple once it is explicitly outlined for children.

This strategy is best used after reading since it will help the children to expand their word banks.

Contextual Vocabulary Skills

Vocabulary Self-Collection is a strategy in which children, even on the emergent level from grade 2 and up, take responsibility for their learning. It is also, by definition, a student-centered strategy that demonstrates student ownership of their chosen vocabulary.

This strategy is one that can be introduced by the teacher early in the year, perhaps even the first day or week. The format for self-collection can then be started by the children. It may take the form of a journal with photocopied template pages and can be continued throughout the year.

To start, ask the children to read a required text or story. Invite them to select one word for the class to study from this text or story. The children can work individually, in teams, or in small groups. The teacher can also do the self-collecting so that this becomes the joint effort of the class community of literate readers. Tell the children that they should select words that particularly interest them or that are unique in some way.

After the children have had time to make their selections and to reflect on them, make certain that they have time to share them with their peers as a whole class. When each child shares the word that he or she has selected, have them provide a definition for the word. Each word that is given should be listed on a large experiential chart or even in a Big Book format, if that is age and grade appropriate. The teacher should also share the word he or she selected and provide a definition. The teacher's definition and sharing should be somewhere in the middle of the children's recitations.

The dictionary should be used to verify the definitions. When all the definitions have been checked, a final list of child-selected (and single teacher-selected) words should be made.

Once this final list has been compiled, the children can record it in their word journals or they may opt to record only those words they find interesting in their individual journals. It is up to the teacher at the onset of the vocabulary self-collection activity to decide whether the children have to record all the words on the final list or can eliminate some. The decision made at the beginning by the teacher must be adhered to throughout the year.

To further enhance this strategy, children, particularly those in grades 3 and beyond, can be encouraged to use their collected words as part of their writings or to record and clip the appearance of these words in newspaper stories or online. This type of additional recording demonstrates that the child has truly incorporated the word into his/her reading and writing. It also habituates children to be lifelong readers, writers, and researchers.

One of the nice things about this simple, but versatile strategy is that it works equally well with either expository or narrative texts. It also provides children with an opportunity to use the dictionary.

Assessment is built into the strategy. As the children select the word for the list, they share how they used contextual clues and through the children's response to the definitions offered by their peers, their prior knowledge can be assessed.

What is most useful about this strategy is that it documents that children can learn to read and write by reading and writing. The children take ownership of the words in the self-collection journals, and that can also be the beginning of writer observation journals as they include their own writings. They also use the word lists as a start for writers' commonplace books. These books are filled with newspaper, magazine and functional document clippings using the journal words.

This activity is a good one for demonstrating the balanced literacy belief that vocabulary study works best when the words studied are child centered.

The Relationship between Oral Vocabulary and the Process of Identifying and Understanding Written Words
One way to explore the relationship between oral vocabulary and the comprehension of written words is through the use of Oral Records (which are discussed at length in the appendix).

In *On Solid Ground: Strategies for Teaching Reading K-3*, Sharon Taberski (2000) discusses how oral reading records can be used by the K-3 teacher to assess how well children are using cueing systems. She notes that the running record format can also show visual depictions for the teacher of how the child "thinks" as the child reads. The notation of miscues, in particular, shows how a child "walks through" the reading process. They indicate if and in what ways the child may require "guided" support in understanding the words he or she reads aloud (oral language).

By using the term "hierarchical and linear" arrays, Cooper really is talking about how some words are grouped based on associative meanings. The words may have a "hierarchical" relationship to one another. For instance, an undergraduate or a first grader is lower in the school hierarchy than the graduate student and second grader. Within an elementary school, the fifth grader is at the top of the hierarchy, and the preschool or kindergartener is at the bottom of the hierarchy. By the way, the terms for this strategy obviously need not be explained in this detail to K-3 children, but might be shared with some grade- and age-appropriate modifications with children in grades 3 and beyond. It will enrich their vocabulary development and ownership of arrays they create.

Words can have a linear relationship to one another in that they run a spectrum from bad to good. For example, from K-3 experiences, bad, better, good, best/perfect.

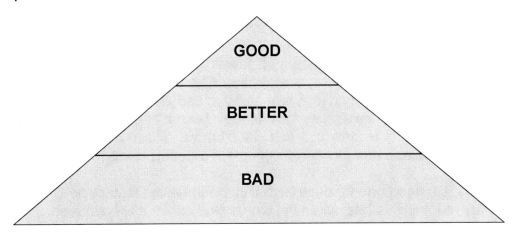

Once you get past the seemingly daunting vocabulary words, the arrays turn out to be another neat, graphic organizer tool that can help children "see" how words relate to one another.

To use this graphic organizer tool, the teacher should pre-select a group of words from a read aloud or from the children's writing. Show the children how the array will look using arrows for the linear array and just straight lines for the hierarchy. In fact, invite some children up to draw the straight hierarchy lines as it is presented, so they have a role in developing even the first hierarchical model.

Do one hierarchy array and one linear array with the pre-selected word with the children. Talk them through filling out (or helping the teacher to fill out) the array. After the children have had their own successful experience with arrays, they can select the words from their independent texts or familiar, previously read favorites to study. They will also need to decide which type of array, hierarchical or linear, is appropriate. For 5th and 6th graders, this choice can and should be voiced using the now "owned" vocabulary words "hierarchical array" and "linear array."

(See also Skill 2.2.)

Skill 3.4   Identify strategies for promoting oral language development and listening comprehension (e.g., read-alouds)

Learning approach
Early theories of language development were formulated from learning theory research. The assumption was that language development evolved from learning the rules of language structures and applying them through imitation and reinforcement. This approach also assumed that language, cognitive and social developments were independent of each other. Thus, children were expected to learn language from patterning after adults who spoke and wrote Standard English. No allowance was made for communication through child jargon, idiomatic expressions or grammatical and mechanical errors resulting from too strict adherence to the rules of inflection (childs instead of children) or conjugation (runned instead of ran). No association was made between physical and operational development and language mastery.

Linguistic approach
Studies spearheaded by Noam Chomsky in the 1950s formulated the theory that language ability is innate and develops through natural human maturation as environmental stimuli trigger acquisition of syntactical structures appropriate to each exposure level. The assumption of a hierarchy of syntax downplayed the significance of semantics. Because of the complexity of syntax and the relative speed with which children acquire language, linguists attributed language development to biological rather than cognitive or social influences.

Cognitive approach

Researchers in the 1970s proposed that language knowledge derives from both syntactic and semantic structures. Drawing on the studies of Piaget and other cognitive learning theorists, supporters of the cognitive approach maintained that children acquire knowledge of linguistic structures after they have acquired the cognitive structures necessary to process language. For example, joining words for specific meaning necessitates sensory motor intelligence. The child must be able to coordinate movement and to recognize objects before she can identify words to name the objects or word groups to describe the actions performed with those objects. Children must have developed the mental abilities for organizing concepts, as well as concrete operations, predicting outcomes, and theorizing, before they can assimilate and verbalize complex sentence structures, choose vocabulary for particular nuances of meaning, and examine semantic structures for tone and manipulative effect.

Socio-cognitive approach

Other theorists in the 1970s proposed that language development results from sociolinguistic competence. Language, cognitive and social knowledge are interactive elements of total human development. Emphasis on verbal communication as the medium for language expression resulted in the inclusion of speech activities in most language arts curricula.

Unlike previous approaches, the socio-cognitive allowed that determining the appropriateness of language in given situations for specific listeners is as important as understanding semantic and syntactic structures. By engaging in conversation, children at all stages of development have opportunities to test their language skills, receive feedback and make modifications. As a social activity, conversation is as structured by social order as grammar is structured by the rules of syntax. Conversation satisfies the learner's need to be heard and understood and to influence others. Thus, his choices of vocabulary, tone and content are dictated by his ability to assess the language knowledge of his listeners. He is constantly applying his cognitive skills to using language in a social interaction. If the capacity to acquire language is inborn, without an environment in which to practice language, a child would not pass beyond grunts and gestures as did primitive man.

Of course, the varying degrees of environmental stimuli to which children are exposed at all age levels create a slower or faster development of language. Some children are prepared to articulate concepts and recognize symbolism by the time they enter fifth grade because they have been exposed to challenging reading and conversations with well-spoken adults at home or in their social groups. Others are still trying to master the sight recognition skills and are not yet ready to combine words in complex patterns.

When students practice fluency, they practice reading connected pieces of text. In other words, instead of looking at a word as just a word, they might read a sentence straight through. The point of this is that in order for the student to comprehend what she is reading, she would need to be able to "fluently" piece words in a sentence together quickly. If a student is NOT fluent in reading, he or she would sound each letter or word out slowly and pay more attention to the phonics of each word. A fluent reader, on the other hand, might read a sentence out loud using appropriate intonations. The best way to test for fluency, in fact, is to have a student read something out loud, preferably a few sentences in a row—or more. Sure, most students just learning to read will probably not be very fluent right away, but with practice, they will increase their fluency. Even though fluency is not the same as comprehension, it is said that fluency is a good predictor of comprehension. Think about it: if you're focusing too much on sounding out each word, you're not going to be paying attention to the meaning.

During the preschool years, children acquire cognitive skills in oral language that they apply later on to reading comprehension. Reading aloud to young children is one of the most important things that an adult can do because they are teaching children how to monitor, question, predict and confirm what they hear in the stories. Reid (1988) described four metalinguistic abilities that young children acquire through early involvement in reading activities:

1. **Word Consciousness**—children who have access to books can first tell the story through the pictures. Gradually, they begin to realize the connection between the spoken words and the printed words. The beginning of letter and word discrimination begins in the early years.

2. **Language and Conventions of Print**—during this stage, children learn the way to hold a book, where to begin to read, the left to right motion, and how to continue from one line to another.

3. **Functions of Print**—children discover that print can be used for a variety of purposes and functions, including entertainment and information.

4. **Fluency**—through listening to adult models, children learn to read in phrases and use intonation.

Mercer and Mercer divide the reading experience into two basic processes: word recognition and word and idea comprehension. Reading programs may differ in how and when these skills are presented.

Word Recognition	Word And Idea Comprehension
Configuration	Vocabulary Development
Content Analysis	Literal Comprehension
Sight Words	Inferential Comprehension
Phonics Analysis	Evaluation or Critical Reading
Syllabication	Appreciation
Structural Analysis	
Dictionary Analysis	

Silent and Oral Reading Skills

Silent reading refers to the inaudible reading of words or passages. Since the reading act is one on a covert basis, the accuracy of the reading process can only be inferred through questions or activities required of the student following his reading. What may be observed is attention given to the printed material, the eye movements, an indication of relative pace, and body language signifying frustration, or ease of reading. <u>Strategies</u> that might assist the child in reading silently are:

1. Preparing activities or questions pertaining to the printed passage. Vary the activities so that some are asking specific comprehension questions and others are geared toward creative expression, like art or written composition.

2. Allowing time for pleasurable reading, such as through an activity like sustained silent reading.

Skill 3.5   Identify strategies for teaching content-area vocabulary

Strategies for Integrating Language Arts Skills Across the Content Areas
Traditionally, language arts are considered to cover the skills of reading, writing, speaking, listening and study of literature. Although the language arts areas of reading (literature), speech and English are subjects in their own rights, language arts skills may be incorporated into every content area subject. Reading Students read a variety of materials for enjoyment and to gain new information. In the content areas of science and social studies, students may read a textbook or read information from other print and electronic sources.

In particular, the reading strategies of summarization, question answering, question generating, use of graphic organizers, use of text structure and marking, comprehension monitoring, and discussion are useful in science, mathematics and social studies.

- **Writing Students**—may be asked to answer questions with short or extended response, write notes during teaching, or write reports to demonstrate understanding of the material being taught.

- **Speaking Students**—use the language arts skills of speaking when they give oral presentations or participate in discussions.

- **Listening Students**—also use listening skills when attending to the oral presentations of other students, their teachers or guest speakers. Listening is also important during classroom discussions.

The Study of Literature transcends basic reading skills to a source for gathering information about a time in history, a culture, a geographic area, a vocation or career and etc.

To integrate language arts skills across content areas for the student with special needs when the special education or inclusion classroom has students with a variety of ability levels different assignments (appropriate for the individual student) may be given.

Oral presentations or verbally answering the questions on a test may offer a more appropriate way of demonstrated learning for some learning disabled students.

Special education students who have significant delays in reading skills may be able to listen to a literature selection to gain information about something like a certain weather type. An example of this would be Betsy Byars' book *Tornado*.

Additionally, as special education students use knowledge of text structures, for example, they are better able to approach text which may be at a difficult reading level for them and find needed answers for class assignments.

Special education students may use a graphic organizer to show learned information or to set up information from research that may later be used in report writing.

Using a combination of language arts activities across content areas can provide differentiated instruction for students with special needs.

COMPETENCY 4.0   UNDERSTAND READING COMPREHENSION SKILLS.

Skill 4.1   Demonstrate knowledge of various reading comprehension strategies and study skills and factors that affect reading comprehension

Use of Comprehension Strategies Before, During and After Reading
Cooper (2004), Taberski (2000), Cox (2005), and other researchers recommend a broad array of comprehension strategies before, during and after reading.

Cooper (2004) suggests a broad range of posters and explicit instruction in class so that children have prompts to monitor their own reading—for example, My Strategic Reading Guide:

1. Do I infer/predict important information, use what I know, think about what may happen, or what I want to learn?
2. Identify important information about the story elements.
3. Self-question, generate questions and search for the answers.
4. Monitor-Ask: Does this make sense to me? Does this help me meet my purpose in reading?
5. If lost, what should I do? Try fix-ups: re-read, read further ahead, look at the illustrations, ask for help and think about the words.
6. Evaluate what I have read.
7. Summarize: Think about how the parts of the stories that I was rereading came together.

The story maps previously discussed in connection with Taberski represent her comprehension strategies for predicting and visualizing.

Storyboard panels, which are used by comic strip artists and by those artists who do advertising campaigns, as well as television and film directors, are perfect for engaging children K-6 in a variety of comprehension strategies before, during, and after reading. They can storyboard the beginning of a story, read aloud, and then storyboard its predicted middle or end. Of course, after they experience or read the actual middle or ending of the story, they can compare and contrast what they produced with its actual structure. They can play familiar literature identification games with a buddy or as part of a center by storyboarding one key scene or characters from a book and challenging a partner or peer to identify the book and characters correctly.

Development of the Reading Comprehension Skills and Strategies of Individual Students

ELL Learners bring to their classrooms different prior knowledge concerns than their native English Language speaking peers. Some of the ELL students have extensive prior knowledge in their native language and can read well on or above their chronological age level in their native language.

Other ELL learners come to the United States from cultures where reading was not emphasized or circumstances did not allow their families time to take advantage of native language literacy opportunities.

Even if a teacher is not technically an ELL teacher, it is likely, given the demographics of the 21st Century, that children from ELL backgrounds will be part of regular education classrooms.

Rigg and Allen (1999) offer the following five principles regarding the literacy development and prior knowledge of ELL-second language learners:

- They are foremost people like any others.
- In learning a language, you learn to do the things you want to do with people who are speaking that language.
- A second language, like the first, does not develop linearly, but rather globally.
- Language can develop in rich contexts.
- Literacy develops parallel to language; therefore, as speaking and listening for second language develop, so do writing and reading.

As far as retelling, it needs to be noted that English Language Learners have the problem of not bringing rich oral English vocabulary to the stories they are decoding. Therefore, they often "sound the stories out" well, but cannot explain what they are about because they do not know what the words mean.

Relationship between Word Analysis Skills and Reading Comprehension

The explicit teaching of word analysis requires that the teacher pre-select words from a given text for vocabulary learning. These words should be chosen based on the storyline and main ideas of the text. The educator may even want to create a story map for a narrative text or develop a graphic organizer for an expository text.

Once the story mapping and/or graphic organizing have been done, the educator can compile a list of words that relate to the storyline and/or main ideas. Next, the educator should decide which key words are already well defined in the text. Obviously, these will not need explicit class review. Identify the words that the child can determine through use of prefixes, suffixes, or base words. Again, these words will not require direct teaching.

Then reflect on the words in relation to the children's background, prior knowledge base and language experiences (including native language/dialect words).

Based on the above steps, decide which words need to be taught. The number of words that require explicit teaching should only be two or three. If the number is higher than that, the children need guided reading, and the text needs to be broken down into smaller sections for teaching. When broken down into smaller sections, each text section should only have two to three words that require explicit teaching.

Some researchers, including Tierney and Cunningham, believe that a few words should be taught as a means of improving comprehension. It is up to the educator whether the vocabulary selected for teaching needs review before reading, during reading or after reading.

Introduce vocabulary BEFORE READING if:
- Children are having difficulty constructing meaning on their own. Children themselves have previewed the text and indicated words they want to know.
- The teacher has seen that there are words within the text which are definitely keys necessary for reading comprehension.
- The text itself, in the judgment of the teacher, contains concepts which may be difficult for the children to grasp.

Introduce vocabulary DURING READING if:
- Children are already doing guided reading.
- The text has words that are crucial to its comprehension, and the children will have trouble comprehending it if they are not helped with the text.

Introduce vocabulary AFTER READING if:
- The children themselves have shared words which they found difficult or interesting.
- The children need to expand their vocabulary.
- The text itself is one that is particularly suited for vocabulary building.

Strategies that can be used to support word analysis as a vehicle for enhancing and enriching reading comprehension include:

- Use of a graphic organizer such as a word map
- Semantic mapping
- Semantic feature analysis
- Hierarchical and linear arrays
- Preview in context
- Contextual redefinition
- Vocabulary self-collection
- (See Directory of Word Terms and Phrases)

Skill 4.2 **Demonstrate knowledge of literal comprehension skills (e.g., recognizing facts and opinions, sequence of events, main ideas or supporting details in a text)**

Literal Comprehension focuses on ideas and information that are explicitly stated in the details of the reading selection.

A. <u>Recognition</u> requires the student to locate or identify ideas or information explicitly stated in the reading selection.

1. Recognition of setting: Where did the three bears live?
2. Recognition of main ideas: Why did the three bears go out for a walk?
3. Recognition of sequence: Whose porridge was too hot? Whose porridge did Goldilocks taste first?
4. Recognition of comparisons: Whose porridge was too hot? Too cold? Just right?
5. Recognition of cause-and-effect relationships: Why didn't Papa Bear's and Mama Bear's chairs break into pieces like Baby Bear's chair?
6. Recognition of character traits: Which words can you find to describe Goldilocks?

In any of the above cases, the teacher may provide the answers herself, or she may state the answer without the question and have the child show her in the pictures, or read in the text, the part of the story pertaining to her statement. The objective is to test the child's literal comprehension and not his memory.

B. <u>Recall</u> requires the student to produce from memory ideas and information explicitly stated in the reading selection.

1. Recall of details: What were the names of the three bears?
2. Recall of main ideas: Why did Goldilocks go into the bears' house?
3. Recall of a sequence: In order, name the things belonging to the three bears that Goldilocks tried.

4. Recall of comparisons: Whose bed was too hard? Too soft? Just right?

5. Recall of cause-and-effect relationships: Why did Goldilocks go to sleep in Baby Bear's bed?

6. Recall of character traits: What words in the story described each of the three bears?

Skill 4.3 **Demonstrate knowledge of inferential comprehension skills (e.g., summarizing; drawing conclusions; making generalizations from given information; drawing inferences about character, setting or cause-and-effect relationships in an excerpt)**

Inferential Comprehension is demonstrated by the student when he "uses the ideas and information explicitly stated in the selection, his intuition, and his personal experiences as a basis for conjectures and hypotheses," according to Barrett (cited in Ekwall & Shanker, 1983, p. 67).

1. Inferring supporting details: Why do you think Goldilocks found Baby Bear's things to be just right?

2. Inferring main ideas: What did the bear family learn about leaving their house unlocked?

3. Inferring sequence: At what point did the bears discover that someone was in their house?

4. Inferring comparisons: Compare the furniture mentioned in the story. Which was adult size and which was a child's size?

5. Inferring cause-and-effect relationships: What made the bears suspect that someone was in their house?

6. Inferring character traits: Which of the bears was the most irritated by Goldilocks' intrusion?

7. Predicting outcomes: Do you think Goldilocks ever went back to visit the bears' house again?

8. Interpreting figurative language: What did the author mean when he wrote, "The tress in the deep forest howled a sad song in the wind?"

Skill 4.4 **Demonstrate knowledge of interpretive and evaluative comprehension skills (e.g., analyzing an author's purpose or point of view; evaluating the use of language or illustration to portray characters, develop plot or elicit an emotional reaction)**

Evaluation requires the student to make a judgment by comparing ideas presented in the selection with external criteria provided by the teacher, or by some other external source, or with internal criteria provided by the student himself.

1. Judgment of reality or fantasy: Do you suppose that the story of *The Three Bears* really happened? Why or why not?

2. Judgment of fact or opinion: Judge whether Baby Bear's furniture really was just right for Goldilocks. Why or Why not?

3. Judgment of adequacy and validity: Give your opinion as to whether it was a good idea for the bears to take a walk while their porridge cooled.

4. Judgment of appropriateness: Do you think it was safe for Goldilocks to enter an empty house?

5. Judgment of worth, desirability, and acceptability: Was Goldilocks a guest or an intruder in the bears' home?

Appreciation deals with the psychological and aesthetic impact of the selection on the reader.

1. Emotional response to the content: How did you feel when the three bears found Goldilocks asleep in Baby Bear's bed?

2. Identification with characters or incidents: How do you suppose Goldilocks felt when she awakened and saw the three bears?

3. Reaction to the author's use of language: Why do you think the author called the bears Papa, Mama, and Baby instead of Mr. Bear, Mrs. Bear and Jimmy Bear?

COMPETENCY 5.0 **UNDERSTAND THE ROLE OF LITERATURE AND OTHER RESOURCES IN INSTRUCTION TO PROMOTE LITERACY DEVELOPMENT.**

Skill 5.1 **Demonstrate knowledge of literature for children and young adults**

Children's literature is a genre of its own and emerged as a distinct and independent form in the second half of the 18th century. *The Visible World in Pictures*, by John Amos Comenius, a Czech educator, was one of the first printed works and the first picture book. For the first time, educators acknowledged that children are different from adults in many respects.

Modern educators acknowledge that introducing elementary students to a wide range of reading experiences plays an important role in their mental/social/psychological development. Some of the most common forms of literature specifically for children follow:

- **Traditional Literature**—traditional literature opens up a world where right wins out over wrong, where hard work and perseverance are rewarded, and where helpless victims find vindication—all worthwhile values that children identify with even as early as kindergarten. In traditional literature, children will be introduced to fanciful beings, humans with exaggerated powers, talking animals and heroes that will inspire them. For younger elementary children, these stories in Big Book format are ideal for providing predictable and repetitive elements that can be grasped by these children.

- **Folktales/Fairy Tales**—some examples of these tales are: *The Three Bears, Little Red Riding Hood, Snow White, Sleeping Beauty, Puss-in-Boots, Rapunzel* and *Rumpelstiltskin*. Adventures of animals or humans and the supernatural characterize these stories. The hero is usually on a quest and is aided by other-worldly helpers. More often than not, the story focuses on good and evil and reward and punishment.

- **Fables**—animals that act like humans are featured in these stories and usually reveal human foibles or sometimes teach a lesson. Example: *Aesop's Fables*.

- **Myths**—these stories about events from the earliest times, such as the origin of the world, are considered true in their own societies.

- **Legends**—these are similar to myths except that they tend to deal with events that happened more recently. Example: *Arthurian legends*.

- **Tall Tales**—examples: *Paul Bunyan, John Henry* and *Pecos Bill*. These are purposely-exaggerated accounts of individuals with superhuman strength.

- **Modern Fantasy:** Many of the themes found in these stories are similar to those in traditional literature. The stories start out based in reality, which makes it easier for the reader to suspend disbelief and enter worlds of unreality. Little people live in the walls in *The Borrowers*, and time travel is possible in *The Trolley to Yesterday*. Including some fantasy tales in the curriculum helps elementary-grade children develop their senses of imagination. These often appeal to ideals of justice and issues having to do with good and evil; and because children tend to identify with the characters, the message is more likely to be retained.

- **Science Fiction**–robots, spacecraft, mystery and civilizations from other ages often appear in these stories. Most presume advances in science on other planets or in a future time. Most children like these stories because of their interest in space and the "what if" aspect of the stories. Examples: *Outer Space and All That Junk* and *A Wrinkle in Time*.

- **Modern Realistic Fiction**–these stories are about real problems that real children face. By finding that others share their hopes and fears, young children can find insight into their own problems. Young readers also tend to experience a broadening of interests as the result of this kind of reading. It's good for them to know that a child can be brave and intelligent and can solve difficult problems.

- **Historical Fiction**–*Rifles for Watie* is an example of this kind of story. Presented in a historically accurate setting, it's about a young boy (16 years) who serves in the Union army. He experiences great hardship but discovers that his enemy is an admirable human being. It provides a good opportunity to introduce younger children to history in a beneficial way.

- **Biography**–reading about inventors, explorers, scientists, political and religious leaders, social reformers, artists, sports figures, doctors, teachers, writers and war heroes help children to see that one person can make a difference. They also open new vistas for children to think about when they choose an occupation to fantasize about.

- **Informational Books**–these are ways to learn more about something you are interested in or something that you know nothing about. Encyclopedias are good resources, of course, but a book like *Polar Wildlife* by Kamini Khanduri shows pictures and facts that will capture the imaginations of young children.

Skill 5.2   Identify characteristics of varied literary genres (e.g., folktale, myth, poetry and fiction)

(See Skill 5.1.)

Skill 5.3   Identify various tools to estimate the readability of a text

Tools To Help You Teach the Foundations of Reading and Succeeding in Constructed Response Certification Examinations

Appendix 1—The Record of Reading Behavior—A close-up look at a key assessment tool:

Often in the constructed response question on foundations of education certification test or on a general elementary certification test, the educator is asked to analyze a record of reading behavior or to construct an appropriate one from dates given in an anecdote. Furthermore, with the current climate of intense accountability, it is a good idea for new teachers and for career changers to examine closely the basic elements of the record of reading behavior.

While there are various acceptable formats for emergent literacy assessment used throughout the country, the one selected for use here is based on the work of Marie Clay and Kenneth Goodman. These two are key researchers in the close observation and documentations of children's early reading miscues (reading mistakes).

It is important to emphasize that the teacher should not just "take the Record of Reading Behavior" and begin filling it out as the child reads from a random book prior to the beginning of the observation. There are specific steps for taking the record and analyzing its results.

1. **Select a text**–if you want to see if the child is reading on instructional level, choose a book that the child has already read. If the purpose of the test is to see whether the child is ready to advance to the next level, choose a book from that level which the child has not yet seen.

2. **Introduce the text**–if the book is one that has been read, you do not need to introduce the text, other than by saying the title. But if the book is new to the child, you should briefly share the title and tell the child a bit about the plot and style of the book.

3. **Take the record**–generally, with emergent readers in grades 1-2, there are only 100-150 words in a passage used to take a record. Make certain that the child is seated beside you so that you can see the text as the child reads it.

If desired, you may want to photocopy the text in advance for yourself, so you can make direct notations on your text while the child reads from the book. After you introduce the text, make certain that the child has the chance to read the text independently. Be certain that you do not "teach" or help the child with the text, other than to supply an unknown word that the child requests you to supply. The purpose of the record is to see what the child does on his or her own.

As the child reads the text, you must be certain to record the reading behaviors the child exhibits using the following notations. In taking the record, keep in mind the following:

- Allow enough time for the child to work independently on a problem before telling or supplying the word. If you wait too long, you could run the risk of having the child lose the meaning and his/her interest in the story as he or she tries to identify the unknown word.

- It is recommended that when a child is way off track, you tell him or her to "Try that again" (TTA).

- If a whole phrase is troubling, put it into square brackets and score it as only one error.

The notation for filling out the Record of Reading behavior involves noting the child's response on the top and the actual text below.

Comprehension Check

This can and should be done by inviting the child to retell the story. This retelling can then be used by you to ask further questions about characters, plot, setting and purpose, which allows you to observe and to record the child's level of comprehension.

Calculating the Reading Level and the Self-correction Rate

The key to Foundations of Reading is to "Do the Math." Calculating the reading level lets you know if the book is at the level from which the child can read it independently or comfortably with guidance or if the book is at a level where reading it frustrates the child.

Generally, an accuracy score of 95-100% suggests that the child can read the text and other books or texts on the same level.

An accuracy score of 90-94% indicates that the text and texts likely will present challenges to the child, but with guidance from you, a tutor or parent, the child will be able to master these texts and enjoy them.

However, an accuracy score of less than 89% tells you that the material you have selected for the child is too hard for the child to control alone. Such material needs to be shared with the child in a Shared Reading situation or read to the child.

Keeping Score on the Record

Insertions, omissions, substitutions and teacher-told responses all count as errors. Repetitions are not scored as errors. Corrected responses are scored as self-corrections.

No penalty is given for a child's attempts at self-correction that result in a finally correct response, but the attempts should be noted. Multiple unsuccessful attempts at a word score as one error only.

The lowest score for any page is zero. If a child omits a line or lines, each word omitted is counted as an error. If the child omits a page, deduct the number of words omitted from the total number of words that you have used for the record.

Calculating the Reading Level
Note the number of errors made on each line on the Record of Reading Behavior in the column marked E (for Error).

Total the number of errors in the text and divide this number into the number of words that the child has read. This will give you the error rate.

If a child read a passage of 100 words and made 10 errors, the error rate would be 1 in 10. Convert this to an accuracy percentage.

Calculating the Self Correction Rate
Total all the self-corrections. Next, add the number of errors to the number of self-corrections and divide by the number of self-corrections.

A self-correction rate of 1 in 3 to 1 in 5 is considered good. This rate indicates that the child is able to help himself or herself as problems are encountered in reading.

Analyzing the record
This record should assist the educator in developing a detailed, date-specific picture of the child's progress in reading behavior. It should be used to help the educator individualize instruction for the specific child.

As the errors are reviewed, consider whether the child made the error because of semantics (cues from meaning), syntactic (language structure) or visual information difficulties.

As self-corrections are analyzed, consider what led the child to make that self-correction.

Check out and consider what cues the child does use effectively and which the child does not use well.

Consider the ways in which the child tackles an unknown word. Characterize that behavior and consider how the teacher can assist the child with this issue.

If a child can retell at least three quarters of a story, this is considered adequate for retelling.

Analysis of Reading Behavior Records can and should support the educator in designing appropriate mini-lessons and strategies to help the child with his/her recorded errors and miscues.

Matching young children with "just right" books fosters their reading independently, no matter how young they are. The teacher needs to have an extensive classroom library of books. Books that emergent readers and early readers can be matched with should have fairly large print, appropriate spacing so that the reader can easily see where words begin and end, and few words on each page so that the young reader can focus on the all important concerns of top-to-bottom, left-to-right, directionality and the one-to-one match of oral to print.

Illustrations for young children should support the meaning of the text and language patterns, and predictable text structures should make these texts appealing to young readers.

Most important of all, the content of the story should relate to the children's interests and experiences as the teacher knows them. The words should include lots of monosyllabic ones and lots of rhyming ones.

Only after all these considerations have been addressed can the teacher select "just right" books from an already leveled bin or list.

In a similar fashion, when the teacher is selecting books for transitional and fluent readers, the following ideas need to be taken into account:

- **Book Length**—the book should take at least two sittings to read, so children can get used to reading longer books.
- **Character Complexity and Plot Intricacy**—the fluent and transitional reader needs to deal with more complex characters and more intricate plotting.

Look for books that set the stage for plot development with a preliminary introduction. Age appropriateness of the concepts, plot and themes is important so that the child will sustain interest in the book.

Look for book features such as a table of contents, index, and glossary that are readily accessible to the children and will help them to navigate through the book.

Series books are wonderful to introduce at this point in the children's development.

Awareness of Text Leveling

The classroom library in the context of the balanced literacy approach to reading instruction is focused on leveled book pots. These are books which have been leveled with the support of Fountas and Pinnell's Guided Reading: *Good First Teaching for All Children* and *Matching Books to Readers: Using Leveled Reading in Guided Reading,* K-3.

The books that are leveled according to the designations in these reference books need to be stored in pots with their front covers facing out. This makes them much easier for the children to identify. In that way, the children can go through the appropriate levels and find those books that they are particularly interested in which are also at the right level for them to read. These are those books that the children can read with the right degree of reading accuracy. When young children can see the cover of a book, they are more likely to flip through the book until they can independently identify an appealing book. Then, they will read a little bit of the book to see if it's "just right."

"Just right" leveled books, which children can read on their own, need to be available for them to read during independent reading. The goal is for the more fluent readers to select books on their own. Ultimately, the use of leveled books helps the children, in addition to the teacher; decide which books are "good" or "just right" for them.

Leveled books are leveled by means of blue, yellow, red, and green dot stickers at their right upper corners that parallel emergent, early, transitional, and fluent reading stages. They are then kept in book pots with other "blue," red," "yellow" and "green" books. Other lists and resources other than Fountas and Pinnell that can be used to match children with "just right" books include the Reading Recovery level list. Ultimately, the teacher has to individualize whatever leveling is used in the library to address the individual learners' needs.

Awareness of the Challenges and Supports in a Text

Illustrations can be key supports for emergent and early readers. Teachers should not only use wordless stories (books which tell their narratives through pictures alone), but can also make targeted use of Big Books for read-alouds so that young children become habituated in the use of illustrations as an important component for constructing meaning. The teacher should model how to reference an illustration for help in identifying a word in the text that the child does not recognize.

Of course, children can also go on a picture walk with the teacher as part of a mini-lesson or guided reading and anticipate the story (narrative) using the pictures alone to construct meaning.

Decodability–use literature that contains examples of letter-sound correspondences you wish to teach. First, read the literature with the children, or read it aloud to them. Then take a specific example from the text and have the children reread it as the teacher points out the letter-sound correspondence to the children. Then ask the children to go through the now familiar literature to find other letter-sound correspondences.

Once the children have correctly made the text-sound correspondence, have them share other similar correspondences they find in other works of literature. The opportunity may also be used for repeated readings of various literature works, which will enhance the children's ownership of their letter-sound correspondence ability and their pleasure in oral reading.

Cooper (2004) suggests that children can be told to become word detectives so that they can independently and fluently decode on their own. The child should learn the following word detective routines so that he/she can function as an independent fluent reader who can decode words on his/her own. First, the child should read on to the end of the sentence. Then the child should search for word parts that he or she knows. The child should also try to decode the word from the letter sounds. As a last resort, the child should ask someone for help or go to look up the word in the dictionary.

Skill 5.4   Identify effective methods for locating, evaluating and using literature to promote the literacy development of readers of all abilities and age

Evaluating and using literature is significantly different in elementary and middle/high schools. See previous skills for strategies for using literature in the elementary grades.

The social changes of post-World War II significantly affected adolescent literature. The Civil Rights movement, feminism, the protest of the Vietnam Conflict, and issues surrounding homelessness, neglect, teen pregnancy, drugs and violence has bred a new vein of contemporary fiction that helps adolescents understand and cope with the world they live in.

Popular books for preadolescents deal more with establishing relationships with members of the opposite sex (*Sweet Valley High* series) and learning to cope with their changing bodies, personalities, or life situations, as in Judy Blume's *Are You There, God? It's Me, Margaret.* Adolescents are still interested in the fantasy and science fiction genres, as well as popular juvenile fiction. Middle school students still read the *Little House on the Prairie* series and the mysteries of the Hardy boys and Nancy Drew. Teens value the works of Emily and Charlotte Bronte, Willa Cather, Jack London, William Shakespeare and Mark Twain as much as those of Piers Anthony, S.E. Hinton, Madeleine L'Engle, Stephen King and J.R.R. Tolkein because they're fun to read, whatever their underlying worth may be.

Older adolescents enjoy the writers in these genres.
1. Fantasy–Piers Anthony, Ursula LeGuin, Ann McCaffrey
2. Horror–V.C. Andrews and Stephen King
3. Juvenile fiction–Judy Blume, Robert Cormier, Rosa Guy, Virginia Hamilton, S.E. Hinton, M.E. Kerr, Harry Mazer, Norma Fox Mazer, Richard Newton Peck, Cynthia Voight and Paul Zindel.
4. Science fiction–Isaac Asimov, Ray Bradbury, Arthur C. Clarke, Frank Herbert, Larry Niven and H.G. Wells

These classic and contemporary works combine the characteristics of multiple theories. Functioning at the concrete operations stage (Piaget), being of the "good person" orientation (Kohlberg), still highly dependent on external rewards (Bandura) and exhibiting all five needs previously discussed from Maslow's hierarchy, eleven- to twelve-year-olds should appreciate the following titles, which are grouped by reading level. These titles are also cited for interest at that grade level and do not reflect high-interest titles for older readers who do not read at grade level. Some high interest titles will be cited later.

Reading level 6.0 to 6.9
- *Lilies of the Field* by William Barrett
- *Other Bells for Us to Ring* by Robert Cormier
- *Danny, Champion of the World & Charlie and the Chocolate Factory* by Roald Dahl
- *Pippi Longstocking* by Astrid Lindgren
- *Three Lives to Live* by Anne Lindbergh
- *Rabble Starkey* by Lois Lowry
- *The Year of the Gopher & Reluctantly Alice* by Phyllis Naylor
- *Arly* by Robert Newton Peck
- *The Witch of Blackbird Pond* by Elizabeth Speare
- *The Boy Who Reversed Himself* by William Sleator

For Seventh and Eighth Graders

Most seventh- and eighth-grade students, according to learning theory, are still functioning cognitively, psychologically, and morally as sixth graders. As these are not inflexible standards, there are some twelve- and thirteen-year-olds who are much more mature socially, intellectually and physically than the younger children who share the same school. They are becoming concerned with establishing individual and peer group identities, which presents conflicts with breaking from authority and the rigidity of rules. Some at this age are still tied firmly to the family and its expectations, while others identify more with those their own age or older. Enrichment reading for this group must help them cope with life's rapid changes or provide escape, and thus must be either realistic or fantastic, depending on the child's needs. Adventures and mysteries (the *Hardy Boys* and *Nancy Drew* series) are still popular today. These preteens also become more interested in biographies of contemporary figures rather than legendary figures of the past.

Reading level 7.0 to 7.9

- *Sounder* by William Armstrong
- *National Velvet* by Enid Bagnold
- *Peter Pan* by James Barrie
- *White Fang* & *Call of the Wild* by Jack London
- *Taking Care of Terrific* by Lois Lowry
- The *Dragonsinger* series by Anne McCaffrey
- *Anne of Green Gables* & sequels by L.M. Montgomery
- *The Pearl* by John Steinbeck
- *The Hobbit* by J.R.R. Tolkein
- *The Pigman* by Paul Zindel

Reading level 8.0 to 8.9

- *I Am the Cheese* by Robert Cormier
- *The Member of the Wedding* by Carson McCullers
- *Rascal* by Sterling North
- *The Adventures of Tom Sawyer* by Mark Twain
- *My Darling, My Hamburger* by Paul Zindel

For Ninth Graders

Depending upon the school environment, a ninth grader may be top dog in a junior high school or underdog in a high school. His peer associations motivate much of his social development, and thus his reading interests. He is technically an adolescent operating at the early stages of formal operations in cognitive development. His perception of his own identity is becoming well defined and he is fully aware of the ethics required by society. He is more receptive to the challenges of classic literature but still enjoys popular teen novels.

Reading level 9.0 to 9.9

- *Bury My Heart at Wounded Knee* by Dee Brown
- *Robinson Crusoe* by Daniel Defoe
- *David Copperfield* by Charles Dickens
- *I Never Promised You a Rose Garden* by Joanne Greenberg
- *Captains Courageous* by Rudyard Kipling
- *Kaffir Boy* by Mark Mathabane
- *Mutiny on the Bounty* by Charles Nordhoff
- *Frankenstein* by Mary Shelley
- *Up From Slavery* by Booker T. Washington

For Tenth-Twelfth Graders

All high school sophomores, juniors and seniors can handle most other literature, except for a few of the very most difficult titles, such as *Moby Dick* or *Vanity Fair*. However, since many high school students do not progress to the eleventh or twelfth grade reading level, they will still have their favorites among authors whose writings they can more easily understand. Many will struggle with assigned novels but still read high interest books for pleasure. A few high interest titles are listed below without reading level designations, though most are 6.0 to 7.9.

- *Squashed* by Joan Bauer
- *When the Legends Die* by Hal Borland
- *Remember Me to Herald Square* by Paula Danzinger
- *Stranger with My Face* by Lois Duncan
- *The Planet of Junior Brown* by Virginia Hamilton
- *The Outsiders* by S.E. Hintion
- *The Great Gilly Hopkins* by Katherine Paterson

Teachers of students at all levels must be familiar with the materials offered by the libraries in their own schools. Only then can they guide their students into appropriate selections for their social age and reading level development.

Skill 5.5   Identify appropriate reading resources, materials and technologies that can be used to support reading and writing instruction

If we have learned anything in education over the last few decades, it is that student's do not all learn in the same way. Furthermore, we have learned that a steady diet of lecture and textbook reading is an extremely ineffective method of instruction. While students definitely should be exposed to lectures and textbooks, they will greatly benefit from the creativity and ingenuity of teachers who find outside resources to assist in the presentation of new knowledge.

Let's first discuss some possibilities: textual and media references, hands-on materials, and technology. Lately, some people have referred to the concept of "multiple texts" as a method of bringing into the classroom multiple types of texts. For example, a social studies teacher might ask students to read an historical novel to complement a unit of study.

In addition to texts, appropriately selected video or audio recordings may be useful. For example, a science teacher may wish to show a short clip of a video that demonstrates how to conduct a particular experiment before students do it on their own. Or, a Language Arts teacher may bring in an audio recording of a book to present a uniquely dramatized reading of the book.

Hands-on materials are very important to student learning. For example, math teachers may introduce geometric principles with quilt blocks. The very idea of a science experiment is that hands-on materials and activities more quickly convey scientific ideas to students than do lectures and textbooks.

Finally, technologies, such as personal computers, are very important for student learning. First, it is extremely important that students learn new technologies so that they can easily adapt to the myriad of uses found in business and industry. Second, technology can provide knowledge resources that go beyond what a school library, for example, may be able to offer. Students will increasingly need to learn how to search for, evaluate, and utilize appropriate information on the Internet.

Choosing an appropriate reference, text, material, or technology depends on many factors. First, realize that whatever is brought into the class should be done so based on the knowledge that the item will assist students in learning academic standards. There is no reason for any teacher, for example, to show a movie to his or her students if it is not for the explicit purpose of helping students reach specific academic objectives tied to the curriculum. Second, consider the developmental level of the students you are working with. You would not want to introduce complex experiments to second graders; likewise, you would not want to assume that twelfth graders have no knowledge of the Internet.

Differentiation of instruction means that the teacher will vary the content, process, or product (Tomlinson, 1995). When a teacher varies content, it means that she or he will allow students to learn different things. For example, when studying the American Revolution, students in a social studies class might get a choice of whether they can study battles, daily life in the colonies at the time, or politics. When the teacher varies process, it means that he or she will allow students various ways of completing the same type of work. For example, some students in a math class may be very proficient with a type of math activity and do not need to work out the problem by hand; other students may need the extra time in order to come to the correct answer. Finally, when teachers vary the product, their students will turn in different things that all show competency in one area.

For example, in Language Arts, after reading a book, some students might write a book report, others might complete an art project, and others might do a dramatic interpretation of a section of the book. The reasons for differentiating instruction are based on two important differences in children: interest and ability.

Differentiating reading instruction is a bit more complex. Usually, when a teacher wants to ensure that each student in his or her class is getting the most out of the reading instruction, the teacher will need to consider the level at which the student is proficient in reading—as well as the specific areas that each student struggles with. It is first important to use a variety of sources of data to make decisions on differentiation, rather than rely on just one test, for example.

When teachers have proficient readers in their classrooms, they usually feel that these students need less attention and less work. This is wrong. If these students do not get careful instruction and challenging activities to increase their reading abilities even further, they may become disengaged with school. These students benefit greatly from integrating classroom reading with other types of reading, perhaps complementing the whole-class novel with some additional short stories or non-fiction pieces. They also benefit from sustained silent reading, in which they can choose their own books and read independently. Discussion groups and teacher-led discussion activities are also very useful for these students. It is important, however, to ensure that these students do not feel that they have to do extra work than everyone else. Remember, differentiation does not distinguish differences in quantity; it distinguishes differences in type of work.

Average readers may benefit from many of the things that highly proficient readers should do; however, they may need more skill instruction. Most likely, they will not need as much skill instruction as weak readers, but they will benefit highly from having a teacher who knows which skills they are lacking and who teaches them to use those skills in their own reading.

Weak readers need to focus highly on skills. Teachers will want to encourage them to make predictions, connect ideas, outline concepts, evaluate, and summarize. The activities that these students engage in should be developed for the purpose of instilling reading strategies that they can use in their independent reading, as well as to propel them toward higher levels of reading.

While the teaching of writing undoubtedly involves an enormous amount of work on the composition of text, it also involves the general idea of ideas conveyed in the best possible manner. In other words, I could explain the results of a survey in words, but it might be easier to understand in a graph or chart. If that were the case, why would we want to present it in words? The important point is for the information to be conveyed.

So, as students write reports and respond to ideas in writing, they can learn how to incorporate multiple representations of information, including various graphic representations, into written text. While this is seemingly fairly easy to do considering the word processing technology we have available to us, students struggle with knowing how to appropriately and successfully do this. They can learn to do this in three primary ways: explanation, observation/modeling and practice.

First, students need to have clear explanations from teachers on appropriate forms of graphical representations in text, as well as the methods in which to include those representations. They need to see plenty of examples of how it is done.

Second, they need to be able to see teacher-modeled examples where text has been replaced or enhanced by graphical representations. The more examples they see, the clearer the concepts will be to them.

Finally, students need to get a chance to practice incorporating graphical representations in their writing. This, of course, will require technology and plenty of feedback.

Students will most likely appreciate the ability to utilize graphical representations in place of text, but they will soon realize that deciding which type of representation to use and how to actually use it will be very challenging. Generally, graphical representations should be used only if they can convey information better than written text can. This is an important principal that students will need to learn through constant practice.

COMPETENCY 6.0   UNDERSTAND METHODS FOR ASSESSING LITERACY DEVELOPMENT AND MODELS OF READING DIAGNOSIS.

Skill 6.1   Identify effective strategies for assessing phonemic awareness, concepts of print, proficiency with print conventions, word recognition and analysis and vocabulary skills

Assessment skills should be an integral part of teacher training so that teachers are able to monitor student learning using pre- and post-assessments of content areas; analyze assessment data in terms of individualized support for students and instructional practice for teachers and design lesson plans that have measurable outcomes and definitive learning standards. Assessment information should be used to provide performance-based criteria and academic expectations for all students in evaluating whether students have learned the expected skills and content of the subject area.

Teachers can use assessment data to inform and impact instructional practices by making inferences on teaching methods and gathering clues for student performance. By analyzing the various types of assessments, teachers can gather more definitive information on projected student academic performance. Instructional strategies for teachers would provide learning targets for student behavior, cognitive thinking skills and processing skills that can be employed to diversify student learning opportunities.

Assessment for learning is the main focus that teachers should employ. Instead of testing simply to find out what students have learned, teachers need to assess to find out what students need to learn. In this way, assessment drives the instruction. By assessing students' prior knowledge and keeping notes on what they can and cannot do, teachers are better able to help students who need extra instruction and to allow those students that are succeeding to move on to higher order skills and challenges.

Some of the different methods that teachers can employ to assess for learning involve both formative and summative evaluation. Since formative assessment consists of testing, these do play a part. However, teachers can make summative assessment part of their daily routine by using such measures as:

- Anecdotal records
- Portfolios
- Listening to children read
- Oral presentations
- Checklists
- Running records
- Samples of work
- Self-evaluation

Information gathered from all of these sources provides the teacher with the material he/she needs to determine how much help students need to become independent readers and to communicate to parents about how their children are doing.

Skill 6.2 **Identify effective strategies for assessing students' motivation and proficiency with reading fluency, comprehension and self-monitoring**

Tests are essential instructional tools. They can greatly influence students' learning and should not be taken lightly nor be given without due regard for the importance of preparation. Several studies have been carried out which indicate conclusively that students perform better when they understand what type of test they are going to take, and why they are taking the test, before they take the test. If students perceive a test to be important or to have relative significance, they will perform better. In a recent study, students who were informed by their teachers as to how their test scores were to be used and who were also urged by their teachers to put forth their best effort, scored higher on the Differential Aptitudes Test than students who did not receive this coaching.

Motivation to perform well on tests begins with how well the student wants to do on an exam. The intrinsic motivation is an internal drive by the student who aspires to do his/her best in school.

The extrinsic motivation may be as simple as a student wanting to learn a basic mathematical skill to complete a remedial math class or as complex as a student needing to pass a Pre-Calculus class to take an AP (Advanced Placement) Calculus class during Senior year to gain college credit and enter Stanford or Harvard University as an early college admission's applicant.

It is also a recognized fact that students will attain higher test scores if they are familiar with the format of the test. It is important for the students to know whether they will be taking a multiple-choice test or an essay test. Being prepared for a specific test format can enhance test scores. Teachers can help students boost their test performance by providing them with explicit information in regard to the content of the test.

Fluency

Fluency is the ability to read a text quickly and accurately. In silent reading, fluent readers can recognize words automatically, and they fully comprehend what they read. If comprehension is not immediate, these readers can use context clues to grasp the meaning of the sentence or paragraph. When reading aloud, fluent readers display confidence, and they read effortlessly and with expression (prosody). This is in contrast to readers that are not fluent; they read slowly, often one word at a time, so that meaning is lost in an effort to read words with accuracy.

Fluency is an important skill when learning to read because it helps readers to progress from the word recognition stage to one where they can understand what they read. When readers don't have to spend time focusing on reading individual words, they can group words together to form ideas, which leads to comprehension. Not only can they grasp the main idea of the text, but they can also make connections between the text and their prior knowledge and events in their own lives.

Fluency is a skill that readers have to develop over time and with repeated practice and exposure to literature and opportunities to read for various purposes. Early readers read words rather than phrases and sentences, and the act of reading often appears to be laborious rather than enjoyable. In order to become fluent, readers have to decode the letters and words. Eventually, this leads to comprehension of ideas.

Even when readers do have a repertoire of words that they recognize easily, they may not be fluent readers. This is because the expression is missing from the reading. Reading fluently with expression means that the reader must be able to chunk the text into meaningful segments, i.e., phrases and clauses. Fluency changes over time as readers are exposed to more difficult texts. The most fluent readers at one level may read slowly when they are first introduced to a more difficult text because they need time for comprehension.

Some techniques to use when teaching students to read fluently include:
- Repeated reading of the same text
- Oral reading practice using audiotapes
- Provide models of what fluent reading looks and sounds like
- Read to students
- Choral reading
- Partner reading
- Readers' Theatre

Automaticity

Automaticity is not the same as fluency. This is the fast and effortless recognition of words that only comes through repeated practice. Automaticity refers to accurate reading of words. It does not refer to reading with expression or reading with comprehension. It deals with word recognition only. It is necessary for fluency, but it is not the only factor that determines whether or not a student can read fluently.

Skill 6.3   Identify effective strategies for determining students' reading levels (e.g., independent, instructional and frustrational).

When considering both formal and informal assessment data gathered on students, it is important to quantify the information into terms easily recognized by other teachers, administrators and parents. In reading, general practice is to categorize the information into levels of reading. These levels go across both kinds of assessments. They are compromised of a combination of a word accuracy percentage and a comprehension percentage.

Independent—this level is the level at which students can read text totally on their own. When reading books at the independent level, students will be able to decode between 95 and 100% of the words and comprehend the text with 90% accuracy or better. Many bodies of research indicate that about 98% accuracy makes for a good independent reader; however, there is other research that goes as low as 95% accuracy.

Instructional—this is the level at which students should be taught because it provides enough difficulty to increase their reading skills without providing so much that it becomes too cumbersome to finish the selection. Typically, the acceptable range for accuracy is between 85-94%, with 75% or greater comprehension. Some standards rely on the number of errors made instead of the accuracy percentage, with no more than one error out of twenty words read being the acceptable standard.

Frustrational—books at a student's frustrational level are too difficult for that child and should not be used. The frustrational level is any text with less than 85% word accuracy and/or less than 75% comprehension.

The use of independent, instructional, and frustrational levels allow educators to provide children with texts of different ranges, depending on the skills necessary to be completed. Typically, standardized or formal assessments test to the instructional level. Therefore, if reading a standardized assessment, such as an Iowa Test of Basic Skills, the reported reading level would be the instructional level for that student.

Additionally, some formal and informal test results use alternate methods of reporting information. Some use the grade level and month equivalent, where a 3.2 reading level would indicate the child is reading at the third grade level second month or typically October. Still, others use their own leveling system. The Developing Readers Assessment (DRA) has its own unique method of coding book levels based on the work of Fountas and Pinnell. Regardless of the levels listed, the work can easily be translated into independent, instructional, and frustrational levels by examining the comprehension and the word reading accuracy portions of the assessment.

Skill 6.4 **Recognize a variety of informal and formal assessments of reading, writing, spelling and oral language and how they determine students' strengths and needs in these areas**

Reading Assessment and Instruction
It is essential that teachers understand the use of data and ongoing reading assessment to adjust instruction to meet students' reading needs.

Assessment is the practice of collecting information about something from children's responses and evaluating is the process of judging the children's responses to determine how well they are achieving particular goals or demonstrating reading skills.

When a teacher asks a child to retell a story, this is a form of assessment. After the child retells the story, the teacher judges how accurate it was and gives it a grade or score and sometimes also makes anecdotal comments about the child in the course of listening to the child's retelling of the story.

Assessment and evaluation have to be intricately connected in the literacy classroom Assessment is necessary because teachers need ways to determine what students are learning and how they are progressing. In addition, assessment can be a tool that also helps students take ownership of their own learning and become partners in their ongoing development as readers and writers. In this day of public accountability, clear, definite, and reliable assessment engenders confidence in public education.

There are two broad categories of assessment:
- **Informal Assessment**–utilizes observations and other non-standardized procedures to compile anecdotal and observation data/evidence of children's progress. Informal assessments include, but are not limited to: checklists, observations, and performance assessments/tasks.
- **Formal Assessment**–is comprised of standardized tests and procedures carried out under specified conditions. Formal assessments include: state tests, standardized achievement tests, NAEP tests and etc.

To be an effective assessment, it should have the following characteristics:

1. It should be an ongoing process, with the teacher making some kind of an informal or formal assessment almost every time the child speaks, listens, reads, writes or views something in the classroom. The assessment should be a natural part of the instruction and not intrusive.

2. The most effective assessment is integrated into ongoing instruction. Throughout the teaching and learning day, the child's written, spoken, and reading contributions to the class or lack thereof, need to and can be continually accessed.

3. Assessment should reflect the actual reading and writing experiences that classroom learning has prepared the child for. The child should be able to show that he or she can read and explain or react to a similar literary or expository work.

4. Assessment needs to be a collaborative and reflective process. Teachers can learn from what the children reveal about their own individual assessments. Children, even as early as grade two, should be supported by their teacher to continually and routinely ask themselves questions to assess their reading (and other skill progress). They might ask: "How have I done in understanding what the author wanted to say?" " What can I do to improve my reading?" and "How can I use what I have read to learn more about this topic?" Teachers need to be informed by their own professional observation AND by children's comments as they assess and customize instruction for children.

5. Quality valid assessment is multidimensional and may include, but not be limited to: samples of writings, student retellings, running records, anecdotal teacher observations, self-evaluations, records of independent reading and etc. From this multidimensional data, the teacher can derive a consistent level of performance and design additional instruction that will enhance the level of student performance.

6. Assessment must take into account children's age and ethnic/cultural patterns of learning.

7. Assess to teach children from their strengths, not their weaknesses. Find out what reading behaviors children demonstrate well, and then design instruction to support those behaviors.

8. Assessment should be part of children's learning process and not done ON them, but rather done WITH them.

It should also be noted that that, for these purposes, the term PERCENTILE is defined as a score on a scale of 100, showing the percentage of a distribution that is equal to it or below it.

The following are examples of key criterion-referenced tests, which measure a child's performance against a standard:

- **Degrees of Reading Power (DRP)**—this test is targeted to assess how well children understand the meaning of written text in real life situations. This Test is designed to measure the process of children's reading, not the products of reading, such as identifying the main idea and author's purpose.
- **CTPIII**—this is a criterion-referenced test that measures verbal and quantitative ability in grades 3-12. It is targeted to help differentiate among the most capable students, i.e., those who rank above the 80th percentile on other standardized tests. This is a test that emphasizes higher order thinking skills and process-related reading comprehension questions.

Terra Nova/Comprehensive Test Of Basic Skills (CTBS)
The following are examples of Norm-Referenced Tests, which fall into this category because test scores are reported as percentile ratings.

Concepts of Validity, Reliability, and Bias in Testing
Validity is how well a test measures what it is supposed to measure. Teacher-made tests are therefore not generally extremely valid, although they may be an appropriate measure for the validity of the concept the teacher wants to assess for his/her own children's achievement.

Reliability is the consistency of the test. This is measured by whether the test will indicate the same score for the child who takes it twice.

Bias in testing occurs when the information within the test or the information required to respond to a multiple choice question or constructed response (essay question on the test) is information that is not available to some test takers who come from a different cultural, ethnic, linguistic or socio-economic background than do the majority of the test takers. Since they have not had the same prior linguistic, social, or cultural experiences that the majority of test takers have had, these test takers are at a disadvantage in taking the test, and no matter what their actual mastery of the material taught by the teacher, cannot address the "biased" questions. Generally, other "non-biased" questions are given to them, and eventually the biased questions are removed from the examination.

To solidify what might be abstract to the reader, on a recent reading test in my school system, the grade four reading comprehension multiple choice had some questions about the well-known fairy tale of the gingerbread boy. These questions were simple and accessible for most of the children in the class. But two children who were recent arrivals from the Dominican Republic had learned English there. They were reading on the grade four levels, but in their Dominican grade school, the story of the gingerbread boy was not a major one. Therefore, a question about this story on the standardized reading test did demonstrate examiner bias and was not fair to these test takers.

Holistic scoring involves assessing a child's ability to construct meaning through writing. It uses a scale called a RUBRIC, which ranges from 0 to 4:

- O—This score would be for a piece that cannot be scored. It does not respond to the topic asked or is illegible.

- 1—This score would be given to a writing that does respond to the topic, but does not cover it accurately.

- 2—This would be for a response that is on the topic, but lacks sufficient details to convey the purpose and to accomplish the writing task requested.

- 3—This score would be given to a paper that, in general, fulfills the purpose of the writing assignment and demonstrates that the reader correctly constructed meaning. The reader showed that he or she understands the writer's purpose and message.

- 4—This response has the most details and best organization and presents a well-expressed reaction to the original writer's piece.

Miscue Analysis

This is a procedure that allows the teacher a look at the reading process. By definition, the miscue is an oral response different from the text being read. Sometimes miscues are also called unexpected responses or errors. By studying a student's miscues from an oral reading sample, the teacher can determine which cues and strategies the student is correctly using or not using in constructing meaning. Of course, the teacher can customize instruction to meet the needs of this particular student.

Informal Reading Inventories (IRI)

These are a series of samples of texts prearranged in stages of increasing difficulty. By listening to children read through these inventories, the teacher can pinpoint their skill level and the additional concepts they need to work on.

Group Versus Individual Reading Assessments

Part of the successful teaching of reading is the organizational strategy of using flexible groups, in contrast to whole class and individual activities. Flexible groups may consist of two, three or more students working together to accomplish a specific purpose.

In evaluating school reform improvements for school communities, educators may implement and assess student academic performance using norm-referenced, criterion-referenced, and performance-based assessments. Effective classroom assessment can provide educators with a wealth of information on student performance and teacher instructional practices. Using student assessment can provide teachers with data in analyzing student academic performance and making inferences on student learning plans that can foster increased academic achievement and success for students.

Assessments

The process of collecting, quantifying, and qualifying student performance data using multiple assessment information on student learning is called assessment. A comprehensive assessment system must include a diversity of assessment tools, such as norm-referenced, criterion-referenced, performance-based or any student-generated alternative assessments that can measure learning outcomes and goals for student achievement and success in school communities.

Norm-referenced Assessments

Norm-referenced tests (NRT) are used to classify students for homogenous groupings based on ability levels or basic skills into a ranking category. In many school communities, NRTs are used to classify students into AP (Advanced Placement), honors, regular or remedial classes, which can significantly impact student future educational opportunities or success. NRTs are also used by national testing companies, such as Iowa Test of Basic Skills (Riverside), Florida Achievement Test (McGraw-Hill), and other major test publishers to test a national sample of students to norm against standard test takers. Stiggins (1994) states, "Norm-referenced tests (NRT) are designed to highlight achievement differences between and among students to produce a dependable rank order of students across a continuum of achievement from high achievers to low achievers."

Educators may select NRTs to focus on students with lower basic skills which could limit the development of curriculum content that needs to provide students with academic learnings that accelerate student skills from basic to higher skill application to address the state assessments and core subject expectations.

NRT rankings range from 1-99, with 25% of students scoring in the lower ranking of 1-25 and 25% of students scoring in the higher ranking of 76-99. Florida uses a variety of NRTs for student assessments that range from Iowa Basic Skills Testing to California Battery Achievement testing to measure student learning in reading and math.

Criterion-referenced Assessments

Criterion-referenced assessments look at specific student learning goals and performance compared to a norm group of student learners. According to Bond (1996), "Educators or policy makers may choose to use a criterion-referenced test (CRT) when they wish to see how well students have learned the knowledge and skills which they are expected to have mastered." Many school districts and state legislation use CRTs to ascertain whether schools are meeting national and state learning standards. The latest national educational mandate of "No Child Left Behind" (NCLB) and Adequate Yearly Progress (AYP) use CRTs to measure student learning, school performance, and school improvement goals as structured accountability expectations in school communities. CRTs are generally used in learning environments to reflect the effectiveness of curriculum implementation and learning outcomes.

Performance-based Assessments

Performance-based assessments are currently being used in a number of state testing programs to measure the learning outcomes of individual students in subject content areas. Washington State uses performance-based assessments for the WASL (Washington Assessment of Student Learning) in reading, writing, math, and science to measure student-learning performance. Attaching a graduation requirement to passing the required state assessment for the class of 2008 has created a high-stakes testing and educational accountability for both students and teachers in meeting the expected skill-based requirements for 10th grade students taking the test.

In today's classrooms, performance-based assessments in core subject areas must have established and specific performance criteria that start with pre-testing in a subject area and maintain daily or weekly testing to gauge student learning goals and objectives. To understand a student's learning is to understand how a student processes information. Effective performance assessments will show the gaps or holes in student learning, which allows for an intense concentration on providing fillers to bridge non-sequential learning gaps. Typical performance assessments include oral and written student work in the form of research papers, oral presentations, class projects, journals, student portfolio collections of work, and community service projects.

Summary

With today's emphasis on student learning accountability, the public and legislature demands for school community accountability for effective teaching and assessment of student learning outcomes will remain a constant mandate of educational accountability. In 1994, thirty-one states used NRTs for student assessments, while thirty-three states used CRTs in assessing student learning outcomes (Bond, 1996). Performance-based assessments are being used exclusively for state testing of high school students in ascertaining student learning outcomes based on individual processing and presentation of academic learning. Before a state, district or school community can determine which type of testing is the most effective, there must be a determination of testing outcome expectation; content learning outcome; and deciding effectiveness of the assessments in meeting the learning goals and objectives of the students.

Skill 6.5   **Demonstrate knowledge of ways to gather and interpret information for diagnosing reading problems and measuring reading progress of individual students**

(See skill 6.4.)

COMPETENCY 7.0 UNDERSTAND PROCESSES FOR IMPLEMENTING READING INSTRUCTION FOR STUDENTS WITH LEARNING DIFFICULTIES RELATED TO LITERACY.

Skill 7.1 **Recognize effective ways to interpret and explain diagnostic information for families, general education teachers and other specialists to use in planning instructional programs**

Teachers need to take the information from assessments and understand how to transfer that into instructional objectives and teachable points. This can be a confusing process. As the reading specialist, it is important that you be able to help teachers, other specialists and parents work through this process. Taking the time to explain the process and how you arrived at specified instructional objectives will help more than one student.

Looking at the assessment information provided, the reading specialist needs to be able to determine which area of reading is impacted and what skills in that area need to be taught. Keeping in mind the five big ideas of reading, comprehension, phonemic awareness, phonics, vocabulary, and fluency, the specialist can begin to categorize the information and better plan appropriate instruction.

Concepts of Validity, Reliability, and Bias in Testing

(See Skill 6.4.)

Skill 7.2 **Recognize a variety of individualized and group instructional interventions or programs for students who have difficulty reading and processes for designing, implementing and evaluating appropriate reading programs for small groups and individuals**

There are many different strategies to help children who are struggling with their reading skill development. A beginning step is to identify the area of difficulty within the area of reading. Universal screening will help to determine which of the big ideas within the area of reading the student may be struggling with at any given time. An example of a universal screening tool is the Dynamic Indicators of Basic Early Literacy Skills (DIBELS). Once the overall area is determined, further assessments may be required. For example, a simple assessment to help determine the exact area of in phonics difficulty is the CORE Phonics Survey, which can be downloaded free. Once the area of deficit has been identified, small group instruction can be developed around these areas to increase specific skills.

When working on specific skills, it is important to utilize texts that specifically support these skills. If phonics is the issue, you would want to use decodable texts. There are numerous publishers who have available a variety of different skills and texts for use within the classroom. If students continue to struggle, it may be necessary to utilize a more specific systematic and explicit program. Some examples of these include: Wilson Reading, Early Intervention Reading, SRA Reading, and Open Court.

Skill 7.3   Identify strategies for planning and modeling the use of comprehension strategies across the content areas

"Reading has a central goal, building meaning, that recurs from one situation to the next. Teachers would be better off to regard their role as journeymen readers working with knowledge and purposeful apprentices rather than purveyors of truth." --P.D. Pearson

Teachers must posses the knowledge of levels of reading comprehension (literal, inferential, and evaluative) and strategies for promoting comprehension of informational/expository texts at all three levels.

There are five key strategies for students' reading of informational/expository texts:

1. Inferencing is an evaluative process that involves the reader making a reasonable judgment based on the information given and that engages children in literally constructing meaning. In order to develop and enhance this key skill in children, a teacher might have a mini-lesson where the teacher demonstrates this key skill by reading an expository book aloud (i.e., one on skyscrapers for young children) and then demonstrates for them the following reading habits: looking for clues, reflecting on what the reader already knows about the topic (activating prior knowledge) and using the clues in the expository text to figure out what the author means/intends.

2. Identifying main ideas in an expository text can be improved when the children have an explicit strategy for identifying important information. They can be included into making this strategy part of their everyday reading style by being focused and "walked through" the following exercises as a part of a series of guided reading sessions. The child should read the passage so that the topic is readily identifiable to him or her. It will be what most of the information is about.

3. Next the child should be asked to be on the lookout for a sentence within the expository passage that summarizes the key information in the paragraph or in the lengthier excerpt. Then the child should read the rest of the passage or excerpt in light of this information and also note which information in the paragraph is not important. The important information the child has identified in the paragraph can be used by the child reader to formulate the author's main idea. The child reader may even want to use some of the author's own language in formulating that idea.

4. Monitoring means self-clarifying: As a reader reads, the reader often realizes that what he or she is reading is not making sense. The reader then has to have a plan for making sensible meaning out of the excerpt. Cooper and other balanced literacy advocates have a stop and think strategy that they use with children. The child reflects, "Does this make sense to me?" When the child concludes that it does not, the child then either: re-reads, reads ahead in the text, looks up unknown words or asks for help from the teacher.

    What is important about monitoring is that some readers ask these questions and try these approaches without ever being explicitly taught them in school by a teacher. However, the key philosophy of the foundations of reading theorists mentioned here is that these strategies need to be explicitly modeled and practiced under the guidance of the teacher by most, if not all, child readers.

5. Summarizing engages the reader in pulling together into a cohesive whole the essential bits of information within a longer passage or excerpt of text. Children can be taught to summarize informational or expository text by following these guidelines. First, they should look at the topic sentence of the paragraph or the text, and delete the trivia. Then they should search for information which has been mentioned more than once and make sure it is included only once in their summary. Next, they should find related ideas or items, and group them under a unifying heading. Then, search for and identify a main idea sentence. Finally, put the summary together using all these guidelines.

Generating questions can motivate and enhance children's comprehension of reading in that they are actively involved in generating their own questions and then answering these questions based on their reading. The following guidelines will help children generate meaningful questions that will trigger constructive reading of expository texts. First, children should preview the text by reading the titles and subheads. Then they should also look at the illustrations and the pictures. Finally, they should read the first paragraph. These first previews should yield an impressive batch of specific questions.

Next, children should get into their Dr. Seuss mode, and ask themselves a "THINK" question. For younger children, having a "THINK" silly hat in the classroom might be effective as well so that the children could actually go over and put it on. Make certain that the children write down the question. Then, have them read to find important information to answer their "Think" questions. Ask that they write down the answer they found and copy the sentence or sentences where they found the answer. Also, have them consider whether, in light of their further reading through the text, their original questions were good ones or not.

Ask them to be prepared to explain why their original questions were good ones or not. Once the children have answered their original "think" questions, have them generate additional ones, and then find their answers and judge whether these questions were "good" ones in light of the text.

Strategies for identifying point of view, distinguishing facts from opinions and detecting faulty reasoning in informational/expository texts:
Expository texts are full of information that may or may not be factual and which may reflect the bias of the editor or author. Children need to learn that expository texts are organized around main ideas. They are usually found in newspapers, magazines, content textbooks, and informational reference books (i.e., an atlas, almanac, yearbook, or encyclopedia).

The five types of expository texts to which the children should be introduced to through modeled reading and a teacher-facilitated walk through are:

Description process—this usually describes a particular topic or provides the identifying characteristics of a topic. It can be depended upon to be factual. Within this type of text, the child reader has to use all of his or her basic reading strategies because these types of expository texts do not have explicit clue words.

Causation or Cause-Effect text—this is one where faulty reasoning may come into play, and the child reader has to use the inferential and self-questioning skills already mentioned to help assess whether the stated cause-effect relationship is a valid and correct one. This text appears in content area textbooks, newspapers, magazines, advertisements, and on some content area and general information web sites. Clue words, which the reader must note and then decide whether or not the evidence available or presented in the excerpt is sufficient, are: therefore, the reasons for, as a result of, because, in consequence of, and since.

Comparison Text–this is an expository text that is centered on the reader's noting the contrasts and similarities between two or more objects and ideas. Many social studies, art and science textbooks and non-fiction books include this contrast. Sometimes newspaper columnists use it as well in their editorial commentary.

Again, strategies for supporting children in being able to first comprehend the comparison and contrast intended by the author. Then be able to decide if this comparison is correctly taken, lies in focusing them on the use of key clue words and phrases. Among these are: like, unlike, resemble, different, different from, similar to, in contrast with, in comparison to, and in a different vein. It is important that as children examine texts that are talking about illustrated or photographed entities, they can also review the graphic representations for clues to support or contradict the text.

Collection Text–this is an expository text that presents ideas in a group. The writer's goal is to present a set of related points or ideas. Another name for this structure of expository writing is a listing or a sequence. The author frequently uses clue words, such as first, second, third, finally and next to alert the reader to the sequence. Based on how well the writer structures the sequence of points or ideas, the reader should be able to make connections. It is important that the writer make clear in the expository text how the items are related and why they follow in that given sequence.

Simple collection texts that can be literally modeled for young children include recipe making. A class of first graders, beginning readers and writers, were literally spellbound by the author's presentation of a widely-known copyrighted collection text. The children were thrilled as the author followed the sequences of this collection text and finally took turns stirring it until it was creamy and smooth. After it had cooled, they each had a taste using their plastic spoons. Can you guess what it was? No? What gourmet children's delight would have first graders begging for a taste? Can't guess? Cream Farina from a commercial cereal box that had cooking directions on it (i.e., known as a collection text).

You can bet that the children had constructed meaning from this five-minute class demonstration and that they would pay close attention to collection texts on other food and product instruction boxes now because this text had come to be an authentic part of their lives.

Response structure—this is an expository text that presents a question or response followed by an answer or a solution. Of course, entire mathematics textbooks, and some science and social studies textbooks, are filled with these types of questions. Again, it is important here to walk the child reader through the excerpt and to sensitize the child to the clue words that signal this type of structure. These words include, but are not limited to: the problem is, the questions is, you need to solve for, one probable solution would be, an intervention could be, the concerns is, and another way to solve this would be.

Newspapers provide wonderful features that can be used by the teacher as read-alouds to introduce children in grades 3-6 to point-of-view distinctions, specifically, editorials, editorial cartoons and key sports editorial cartoons (i.e., Bill Gallo of the New York Daily News). Children can also come to understand the distinction between fact and fiction when they examine a newspaper advertisement or a supermarket circular for a product they commonly use, eat, drink, or wear and that includes exaggerated claims about what the product can actually do for or with the individual in question.

Finally, the fact versus opinion distinction can be nicely explored if a teacher takes the children online to look at some star web sites and walks them through some exaggerated claims made about their particular movie star favorites. It is very important at some point, if the children have access to the internet, that the teacher show them how to examine web sites, look at who developed a particular web site, and consider how credible or trustworthy the developers of the site are.

Use of reading strategies for different texts—as children progress to the older grades (3-6), it is important for the teacher to model for them that in research on a social studies or science exploration, it may not be necessary to read every single word of a given expository information text. For instance, if the child is trying to find out about hieroglyphics, he or she might only read through those sections of a book on Egyptian or Sumerian civilization that dealt with picture writing. The teacher, assisted by a child, should model how to go through the table of contents and the index of the book to identify only those pages that deal with picture writing. In addition, other children should come to the front of the room or to the center of the area where the reading group is meeting. They should then, with the support of the teacher, skim through the book for illustrations or diagrams of picture writing, which is the focus of their need.

Children can practice the skills of skimming texts and scanning for particular topics that connect with their grade social studies, science and mathematics content area interests.

Certainly, children need to understand and to be comfortable with the fact that not every single expository text is meant to be read thoroughly and completely.

Use of Comprehension Skills Before, After and During Reading.

Cooper (2004) advocates that the child ask himself or herself what a text is about before he or she reads it, and even as he or she is in the process of reading the text, and that he or she notes what he or she thinks the text is going to be about. While the child is reading the text, Cooper (2004) feels that the child should be continually questioning himself or herself as to whether the text confirmed the child's predictions. Of course, after completing the text, the child can then review the predictions and verify whether they were correct.

Again, within the framework set by Cooper in *Literacy: Helping Children Construct Meaning*, the child reader looks over the expository text subheads, illustrations, captions, and indices to get an idea about the book. Then the child, still before reading the text, decides that perhaps he or she can find the answer to this question.

During the reading, the child is asking himself or herself, "Am I finding the answer to my question?"

After the reading, the child notes: "I have found the answer to my question. This book or electronic text is an excellent source of information for me about my question." (Or perhaps, "No, I have not found the answer to my question. This book or electronic text is not a good source of information for me about my question. I will have to look for other resources.").

Ability to Apply Reading Skills for Various Purposes.

What is really intriguing about the use of newspapers as a model and an authentic platform for introducing and inculcating children into recognizing and using expository text structures, features, and references, is that the children can demonstrate their mastery of these structures by putting out their own newspapers detailing their school universe by using some of these text structures.

They can also create their own timelines for projects or research papers that they have done in class by using newspaper models.

Application of Comprehension Strategies for Electronic Texts

If the class gets newspapers in the classroom as part of an ongoing Newspapers in Education (NIE) program, it is natural and easy for the teacher to take the time to show children how their same news is covered online. All of the newspapers have e-news. Children can first do a K-W-L on what they know or think they know about e-news and then actually review their specific daily newspaper's site.

With the support of the teacher or an older peer, they can examine the resource and perhaps note the following differences in electronic text:

- Use of moving pictures and video to document events.
- Use of sound clips in addition to written text.
- Use of music/sound effects not in printed text.
- Links to other web resources and to other archived articles.

Of course, this can lead to much rich discussion and to further detailed web versus print news resource analysis. For children in grades 5 and 6, this might even include a research investigation of a particular news story or event, including broadcast media coverage.

Any content area can be taught through reading; because of this, it is important to make books and reading an integral part of all learning. Teaching students to access information through books and technology allows them to realize the true benefits of life-long learning.

Skill 7.4 Demonstrate knowledge of strategies for teaching reading skills applicable to real-life situations

As previously discussed in Skill 7.3, it is important to apply reading skills to real-life situations. Students who understand the applications of the newspaper, technology and other real-life situations are able to make the final connection to life-long learning. Specific strategies for the implementation of authentic reading are discussed in depth in Skill 7.3.

Skill 7.5 Demonstrate knowledge of the scope and sequence and the design of lesson plans for reading instruction at all developmental levels

Though, within any district, teachers will be required to follow a specific reading curriculum to ensure all students are making the appropriate steps toward achieving the state and federal standards, there is a general progression of skills the teacher should keep in mind.

Pre-K- Kindergarten—students at the ages of four through six generally will be focusing on building their phonemic awareness skills. The majority of emphasis on instruction during this time should be devoted to developing the phonemic awareness of students. That is not to say, phonics, vocabulary and all of the other areas of reading should not be taught, because they should; however, developmentally, it is important to all future reading that students have reached proficient levels of phonemic awareness.

First and Second Grade—the shift occurs here from phonemic awareness to phonics. Students are tying the oral sounds to the written letters and applying both decoding and encoding together to become readers and writers. Sight vocabulary is important at this time as well, as students need to be able to read words quickly and efficiently.

Third, Fourth and Fifth Grades—third grade is a transitional year for beginning readers. It is here that the first shift from learning to read to reading to learn occurs. Phonics skills become solidified and a greater emphasis is placed on other skills in both reading and writing. Comprehension also begins to take the forefront.

Middle School—in middle school, students are beginning to analyze literature and expand their selections of reading. It is also during this time that content area reading expands and becomes as much a part of the day-to-day instruction as the reading of literature itself. Writing expands as a method for responding, along with discussions about the text. More figurative texts are read, with much less literal interpretations possible.

High School—high school reading is very much centered on learning from reading. It is expanded to almost all content areas as the central method for delivering information to the students. In English classes, classics and very interpretative literature are read and discussed. Students develop their thinking skills through the process of trying to understand texts presented. Classroom discussions are vibrant and filled with subjective examples of the underlying reasons things are happening within stories. Preparing students to be thinkers and evaluators outside of the school setting is the most important learning that occurs in high schools.

Skill 7.6 **Identify effective ways to adjust reading instruction to meet the needs of diverse learners (e.g., gifted students, students for whom English is a second language, students with disabilities and students who speak nonstandard dialects)**

Students who are gifted require significantly different types of reading skills than struggling or even average readers. Breaking the code generally comes quite easily to the gifted. They are usually reading several grade levels above their age-prescribed grade level.

Curriculum compacting generally is encouraged throughout the education of the gifted. In this way, the student who requires many fewer repetitions than the average student to master skills can move forward in their learning without having to wait for the children who require more time to reach proficiency. This strategy allows the gifted students to be exposed to and master the same required curriculum as all other students, simply at a different pace.

Comprehension is often the focus for literacy instruction for the students who are also gifted. Literature circles is a strategy where the students themselves are taught to build a discussion and dialogue about the book read. There are generally roles assigned within the group of students who will be discussing a piece of literature. The teacher takes a backseat and perhaps provides periodic questions for discussion if the conversation lags. Otherwise, the topics, questions, and discussion are generated from the students. They generally discuss higher-level questions and not simple recall. Additionally, often times the questions have no solid right or wrong answer; instead, they are designed to promote conversation.

Content area reading is another way to encourage and develop literacy skills in the gifted. Often times, there are numerous topics of which the students are very curious about and would like to learn more and explore. Setting up independent learning projects revolving around these self-selected topics, and providing appropriate reading materials, encourages the students to learn more and more about the topics. Periodic meetings and conversations with the teacher ensure adequate comprehension and provide the necessary accountability.

There are identified students who are gifted for whom reading is not enjoyable. There are also students who are gifted but also have a learning disability. It is important to keep these things in mind as well. These students would benefit from similar incentive and strategies that work for other students who may be struggling with reading. However, remember that these particular students may find it even more of a frustrating experience than other struggling readers due to their higher level of acquiring and processing information.

When considering students for whom English is not the primary language, it is critical to understand the natural development of second language acquisition before applying the general knowledge of reading assessments to this subgroup of students.

In general, second language students can take up to seven years to become proficient in the second language. This factors in the acculturation process with speaking, listening, reading and writing. Students who are fluent and able to read in their primary language before starting the second language are more likely to become fluent in the second language than those who are not fluent in the primary language.

This group of students attempting to learn in a second language generally tends to lag behind, in vocabulary particularly. The connection between words and their meanings is essential to understand what is being read. Students who can make the transition easily between the two languages have the advantage of seeing or hearing a word, translating it in their minds to the same or a similar word in their native languages, and then making the connection and being able to access that information to help them understand the text. Though this is a slow and labor-intensive process, in the end the students are able to understand.

However, it is the students who are unable to complete these numerous steps who will require additional support, particularly in vocabulary development. Helping to build background knowledge is critical when introducing texts to these students through as concrete a process as is possible. The more concrete examples a teacher can provide the better for the students.

In looking at the other areas of reading, phonics and phonemic awareness skills can also pose problems. Students will sometimes substitute the sounds from their native languages in the middle of the process or at other times. Additionally, they may have no connection within their native language because there may be no letters/combinations that make those sounds.

In the end, good reading assessment and instruction is essential when working with students acquiring a second language. However, it must be married well with the body of research on how one learns a second language. Remembering that oral language will develop first (receptive before expressive), and after oral language reaches a conversational level, one can begin the reading instruction.

Along with students for whom English is not the primary language, there will sometimes be specific students who have dialect issues, which makes applying phonics difficult. It is important for all personnel involved in the literacy education of these students to understand the various dialects from within our country. While it is appropriate to teach Standard English pronunciation and decoding skills, it is also critical to accept these differences in application.

Skill 7.7   **Identify processes for developing instructional plans to address the unique needs of students with severe learning difficulties related to literacy**

When students have severe learning difficulties, it is sometimes necessary to think outside of the box when developing their instructional plans. In the development of the IEP, it may be necessary to know the specific strengths of the student through more nontraditional methods of teaching.

It is important to have data and supportive documentation showing why the steps you are taking are necessary. For example, if you have tried a number of technology based programs, and one in particular has shown tremendous benefit to a particular student, it would be important to note this when developing the instructional plan for this student. Other academic areas may be impacted so that the student receives the necessary access to the program necessary to make the desired progress. All of this needs to be clearly stated and pointed out in the IEP, along with appropriate documentation.

Skill 7.8   **Demonstrate knowledge of ways to incorporate the Illinois Learning Standards in areas of reading in the development of instruction and Individualized Education Programs (IEPs)**

Incorporating the Illinois Learning Standards into any educational program in Illinois is essential. The IEP goals and objectives should be based ultimately on these standards. They may be outside of grade level or age level, but the goals and objectives need to directly relate to the Illinois Learning Standards for the instructional area you are teaching.

It is essential to use the school system's course of study and the student's IEP to prepare and organize materials to implement daily lesson plans. IEPs have to demonstrate that the student is working on goals as close to their general education peers as possible. Therefore, the school system's course of study, including IL State Standards, curriculum and other pertinent materials, should be a document used to create the annual goals of the IEP. The materials gathered should be adapted to fit the needs of each student, or specially-designed materials should be purchased.

The IEP must also include any assistive technology that may be needed for the student to be successful. The teacher must gather the necessary technology before planning a lesson.

A complete listing of the Illinois Learning Standards can be found at http://www.isbe.state.il.us/ils/. This site also has references for aligning classroom lesson plans specifically with the IL Learning Standards. It is an invaluable site and should be reviewed completely.

COMPETENCY 8.0   UNDERSTAND FUNDAMENTAL CONCEPTS RELATED TO NUMBERS, NUMBER SENSE, AND NUMERATION.

Skill 8.1   Recognize ways to promote the development of number sense in children and factors that can affect the development of number sense.

Seriation

The ability to seriate underlies our entire number system. Seriation, or ordering, is demonstrated by a young child when he successfully places a series of rings of graduated sizes on a cone. More complex seriation tasks involve lining up objects of graduated height or diameter in ascending order. Eventually, the child is able to seriate on the basis of number in a series of sets.

1. **Linear**—can the child:
   a. State the basis for linear serial groupings based on increasing size?
   b. Arrange objects in order of increasingly intense color?
   c. Select an item missing in a serial grouping?

2. **Unit**—can the child:
   a. State relationships between sets of 1, 2, 3, 4 and so on?
   b. Manually sequence objects based on units in each?
   c. Count to 10 or higher, and tell which numeral is more?

3. **Temporal**—can the child:
   a. State what he did first, last, and so on, in a simple task?
   b. Follow directions, such as, "First put the block on top of the box. Then, place a penny beside the block"?
   c. Tell you what happens after breakfast, before dinner, or in another time period?

4. **One-to-one Correspondence**—can the child:
   a. State the number of chairs that will be needed for a group of three children?
   b. Distribute something like paper and pencils to each student in the group?
   c. Pair objects like shoes and gloves with their owners?

5. **Spatial relations**—can the child:
   a. State whether an object is over, under, beside, behind, or in front of another object?
   b. Match geometric objects with the openings in which they fit?
   c. Demonstrate an understanding between right and left?

Teaching Strategies Appropriate to the Development of Number Concepts
Numbers appear in many daily situations. Children see numbers on clock faces, on telephone dials or buttons, on mailboxes, on car license plates, on price tags of toys, and on food items. How do children grow in their understanding and use of numbers? Early readiness skills involve classifying, comparing, and ordering numbers, which in essence provide some primitive practice in quantification. Stages of concept formation progress as children mature, develop and experience situations involving numbers.

1. **One-to-one Matching**–children may be asked to match the items in two groups, one-by-one and to describe what they find. One group may be identified as having more or less than another.

2. **Rote Counting**–many young children can count from one to ten or higher using rote memory. They can name the numbers in correct sequence, but may not really understand what the numbers mean. For example, they may be able to sing number songs, but cannot pick up five blocks upon request.

3. **Selection of Correct Number of Objects**–Jean Piaget describes three phases through which children pass in mastering this concept. In the first, a child believes the number changes when the design or number of objects is rearranged. A child in the second phase understands conservation, in the sense that the number is the same no matter how different the set may appear. Children in the final stage can reverse their thinking and understand that the number does not change when objects are returned to their original positions. They can show one-to-one matching of rows of objects. Counting has become meaningful.

4. **Ordinality and Cardinality**–*ordinality* refers to the relative position or order of an object within a set in relation to the other objects, like first, second and etc. *Cardinality* answers the question of "How many?" in reference to the total number of objects is a group. When counting, children use numbers cardinally as they say "one" for the first object, "two" for the second, and so on. It helps them to move the objects as they are counted. Thus, when the counting is complete, and children can tell that there are four balls in all, they can use the ordinal for any number of the group. The number "4"—a cardinal—is associated with all four objects; the last is the 4th—an ordinal.

5. **Sequencing Numbers to Ten**–prior work in comparing and ordering quantities is gradually extended. Children learn that five, which is more than three, comes after three in counting sequence.

6. **Zero**–developmental work with zero occurs within the 1 to 10 sequence rather than first. The meaning of zero as "none at all" is easier for children to understand when they can use it in relations to known quantities. For example, "There were two cookies on the plate. My dad and I each had one. Now they are all gone."

7. **Symbols**—children learn to recognize and write numerals in a cognitive manner. The concepts of greater than and less than are also understood. Finally, children learn to name and use numerals of symbols for comparison, even when the objects are no longer present.

8. **Sight Groups**—children learn to recognize, without counting, the number of objects in groups having four or less items. Eventually, children will learn to sight sub-groups with larger numbers of objects.

9. **Writing numerals**—after children have learned to recognize a numeral and associate it with the correct number of objects, writing is begun. However, even when the focus is on writing, continued reference to quantities named should be made.

10. **Sequencing Tasks**—earlier work, in which children used one-to-one matching to tell whether a group has more, less, or as many objects as another, is extended. Children come to recognize that when a number means more, it comes after another in the process of counting. Conversely, when a number means less, it comes before another in counting.

The stages just described serve as precursors in the development of number concepts. The conceptual understanding of number concepts further extends into mathematical operations, place value, re-groupings, and decimals later.

Skill 8.2   **Apply knowledge of the properties of whole numbers and the whole number system and concepts of the number and numeration systems to compare, order and round numbers**

Instruction for Whole Numbers: Addition, Subtraction, Multiplication and Division

1. **Phase 1—Conceptualization**
   a. Relate arithmetic operations to physical operations.
   b. Develop a process for finding answers using concrete objects or pictures of objects.

2. **Phase 2—Fact Mastery**
   a. Easy facts
      1. Figure them out using already developed processes.
      2. Organize them in different ways to see relationships.
      3. Memorize them.

    b. Develop more efficient techniques for remembering facts that:
       1. Are mental processes.
       2. Use easier facts already memorized.
    c. Harder facts
       1. Figure them out using new efficient processes.
       2. Organize them.

3. **Phase 3–Algorithm Learning**
    a. De-emphasize superficial rules.
    b. Stress big ideas, and relate them to concrete models.
    c. Develop computational expertise apart from models.

The conceptualization phase should include (1) interaction with concrete, tangible materials; (2) use of pictures or dots, number lines, representation manipulatives, such as semi concrete representations; and last, (3) work on a symbolic or abstract level (Henley, Ramsey, & Algozzine, 1993: Morsink, 1984). Too often, teachers use the pictures in match texts as their sole means of offering a meaningful foundation to a newly-introduced concept, rather than providing concrete, manipulative aids. Understanding is better assured whenever a relationship between manipulative, pictures, and the abstract concept is fostered. Many things that children do are naturally related to numbers. Activities considered pre-addition or pre-subtraction in math include: (1) basic number meanings, (2) visual and meaningful recognition of numerals, and (3) counting skills. Children learn that = + = means put together and that * - * means take away as they manipulate objects within groups. When children are making final steps toward fact mastery, instruction usually moves into writing addition and subtraction algorithms. They are taught to use a written computational procedure in order to obtain an answer. Clustering facts that use the same strategy or relationships aids efforts toward understanding cognitive processes.
Ideas prevail when teaching subtraction: (1) subtract like units, and (2) if the value is insufficient within a given place unit, make a trade (regroup or borrow). The concept of multiplication is closely related to the concept of addition. In fact, multiplication is initially taught as repeated addition. Two or more sets are combined to form a new set; thus, multiplication can be conceptualized as the union of sets, as in addition. However, in multiplication, each of the groups joined must have the same number of objects. The symbol "x" needs to connote an understanding of equal units. For example, 2 x 3 should be conceptualized as two groups of three objects, or three objects combined two times. Like multiplication, division is a process that involves groups of equal size. In multiplication, the equal-sized groups are joined. Since division is the inverse operation of multiplication, division can be related the act of separating a group into parts of equal size. The symbol "-"conveys this process.

Skill 8.3   Demonstrate understanding of the order of operations

The Order of Operations is to be followed when evaluating algebraic expressions. Follow these steps in order:

1. Simplify inside grouping characters, such as parentheses, brackets, square root, fraction bar and etc.
2. Multiply out expressions with exponents.
3. Do multiplication or division, from left to right.
4. Do addition or subtraction, from left to right.

Example: $2 - 4 \times 2^3 - 2(4 - 2 \times 3)$

$$= 2 - 4 \times 2^3 - 2(4 - 6) = 2 - 4 \times 2^3 - 2(^-2)$$

$$= 2 - 4 \times 2^3 + 4 = 2 - 4 \times 8 + 4$$

$$= 2 - 32 + 4 = 6 - 32 = ^- 26$$

Skill 8.4   Apply knowledge of the concepts and skills related to using integers, fractions, decimals, ratios and percents to solve problems

Operating with Percents

Example: 5 is what percent of 20?

This is the same as converting $\dfrac{5}{20}$ to % form.

$$\frac{5}{20} \times \frac{100}{1} = \frac{5}{1} \times \frac{5}{1} = 25\%$$

Example: There are 64 dogs in the kennel. 48 are collies. What percent are collies?

Restate the problem.   48 is what percent of 64?
Write an equation. $48 = n \times 64$
Solve. $\frac{48}{64} = n$

$n = \frac{3}{4}$ = 75%

75% of the dogs are collies.

Example: The auditorium was filled to 90% capacity. There were 558 seats occupied. What is the capacity of the auditorium?

Restate the problem.	90% of what number is 558?
Write an equation.	$0.9n = 558$
Solve.	$n = \frac{558}{.9}$
	$n = 620$

The capacity of the auditorium is 620 people.

Example: A pair of shoes costs $42.00. Sales tax is 6%. What is the total cost of the shoes?

Restate the problem.	What is 6% of 42?
Write an equation.	$n = 0.06 \times 42$
Solve.	$n = 2.52$

Add the sales tax to the cost. $42.00 + $2.52 = $44.52

The total cost of the shoes, including sales tax, is $44.52.

Addition and Subtraction of Fractions

Key Points

1. You need a common denominator in order to add and subtract reduced and improper fractions.

   Example: $\dfrac{1}{3}+\dfrac{7}{3}=\dfrac{1+7}{3}=\dfrac{8}{3}=2\dfrac{2}{3}$

   Example: $\dfrac{4}{12}+\dfrac{6}{12}-\dfrac{3}{12}=\dfrac{4+6-3}{12}=\dfrac{7}{12}$

2. Adding an integer and a fraction of the <u>same</u> sign results directly in a mixed fraction.

   Example: $2+\dfrac{2}{3}=2\dfrac{2}{3}$

   Example: $^-2-\dfrac{3}{4}=^-2\dfrac{3}{4}$

Converting Decimals, Factions and Percents

A **decimal** can be converted to a **percent** by multiplying by 100 or merely moving the decimal point two places to the right. A **percent** can be converted to a **decimal** by dividing by 100 or moving the decimal point two places to the left.

Examples: $0.375 = 37.5\%$
$0.7 = 70\%$
$0.04 = 4\%$
$3.15 = 315\%$
$84\% = 0.84$
$3\% = 0.03$
$60\% = 0.6$
$110\% = 1.1$
$\frac{1}{2}\% = 0.5\% = 0.005$

A **percent** can be converted to a **fraction** by placing it over 100 and reducing to simplest terms.

Example: Convert 0.056 to a fraction.

Multiply 0.056 by $\dfrac{1000}{1000}$ to get rid of the decimal point:

$$0.056 \times \frac{1000}{1000} = \frac{56}{1000} = \frac{7}{125}$$

Example: Find 23% of 1000.

$$= \frac{23}{100} \times \frac{1000}{1} = 23 \times 10 = 230$$

Example: Convert 6.25% to a decimal and to a fraction.

$$6.25\% = 0.0625 = 0.0625 \times \frac{10000}{10000} = \frac{625}{10000} = \frac{1}{16}$$

An example of a type of problem involving fractions is the conversion of recipes. For example, if a recipe serves 8 people, and we want to make enough to serve only 4, we must determine how much of each ingredient to use. The conversion factor, the number we multiply each ingredient by, is:

$$\text{Conversion Factor} = \frac{\text{Number of Servings Needed}}{\text{Number of Servings in Recipe}}$$

Example: Consider the following recipe.

3 cups flour
½ tsp. baking powder
2/3 cups butter
2 cups sugar
2 eggs

If the above recipe serves 8, how much of each ingredient do we need to serve only 4 people?

First, determine the conversion factor.

$$\text{Conversion Factor} = \frac{4}{8} = \frac{1}{2}$$

Next, multiply each ingredient by the conversion factor.

3 x ½ =   1 ½ cups flour
½ x ½ =   ¼ tsp. baking powder
2/3 x ½ = 2/6 =   1/3 cups butter
2 x ½ =   1 cup sugar
2 x ½ =   1 egg

COMPETENCY 9.0   UNDERSTAND FUNDAMENTAL CONCEPTS RELATED TO ALGEBRA AND GEOMETRY.

Skill 9.1   Recognize patterns in numbers, shapes and data

Example:
Given two terms of an arithmetic sequence, find a_1 and d.

$a_4 = 21$ $a_6 = 32$

$a_n = a + (n-1)d$ $a_4 = 21, n = 4$

$21 = a_1 + (4-1)d$ $a_6 = 32, n = 6$

$32 = a_1 + (6-1)d$

$21 = a_1 + 3d$ Solve the system of equations.

$32 = a_1 + 5d$

$21 = a_1 + 3d$

$\underline{-32 = -a_1 - 5d}$ Multiply by -1.

$-11 = -2d$ Add the equations.

$5.5 = d$

$21 = a_1 + 3(5.5)$ Substitute d = 5.5 into one of the equations.

$21 = a_1 + 16.5$

$a_1 = 4.5$

The sequence begins with 4.5 and has a common difference of 5.5 between numbers.

Geometric Sequences
When using geometric sequences, consecutive numbers are compared to find the common ratio.

$$r = \frac{a_{n+1}}{a_n}$$

where r = common ratio
a = the nth term

The ratio is then used in the geometric sequence formula:
$$a_n = a_1 r^{n-1}$$

Example:
Find the 8th term of the geometric sequence 2, 8, 32, 128 ...

$r = \dfrac{a_{n+1}}{a_n}$ Use common ratio formula to find ratio.

$r = \dfrac{8}{2}$ Substitute $a_n = 2$ $a_{n+1} = 8$.

$r = 4$

$a_n = a_1 \bullet r^{n-1}$ Use $r = 4$ to solve for the 8th term.

$a_n = 2 \bullet 4^{8-1}$

$a_n = 32{,}768$

Skill 9.2   **Demonstrate knowledge of how to use variables, expressions, equations and inequalities to describe patterns and express relationships algebraically**

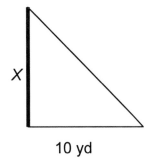
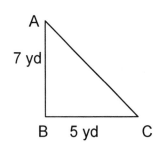

The problem can be determined by setting up the proportion below and solving for X.

$$\frac{X}{10 \text{ yd}} = \frac{7 \text{yd}}{5 \text{yd}}$$

After cross-multiplying, the equation can be written as 5X = 70; X equals 14 yards. Without actually measuring the distance with a measuring tape or other tool, the distance between the points is determined.

Example:
A family wants to enclose 3 sides of a rectangular garden with 200 feet of fence. In order to have the maximum area possible, find the dimensions of the garden. Assume that the fourth side of the garden is already bordered by a wall or a fence.

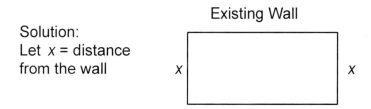

Solution:
Let x = distance
from the wall

Then, $2x$ feet of fence is used for these 2 sides. The remaining side of the garden would use the rest of the 200 feet of fence, that is, $200-2x$ feet of fence. Therefore, the width of the garden is x feet and the length is $200-2x$ ft. The area, called y, would equal length times width:

$$y = x(200 - 2x) = 200x - 2x^2$$

In this equation, a = $^-2$, b = 200, c = 0. The maximum area of this garden would occur at the vertex, where $x = {}^-b/2a$. Substituting for a and b in this equation, this equation becomes $x = {}^-200/(2 \times {}^-2) = {}^-200/({}^-4) = 50$ feet. If x = 50 ft, then $200-2x$ equals the other 100 feet. The maximum area occurs when the length is 100 feet and each of the widths is 50 feet. The maximum area = $100 \times 50 = 5000$ square feet.

Example:
A family wants to enclose 3 sides of a rectangular garden with 200 feet of fence. In order to have a garden with an area of **at least** 4800 square feet, find the dimensions of the garden. Assume that the fourth side of the garden is already bordered by a wall or a fence.

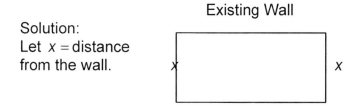

Solution:
Let x = distance
from the wall.

Then, 2x feet of fence is used for these 2 sides. The remaining side of the garden would use the rest of the 200 feet of fence, that is, $200 - 2x$ feet of fence. Therefore, the width of the garden is x feet, and the length is $200 - 2x$ ft. The area, called y, would have to be greater than or equal to the length times the width:

$$y \geq x(200 - 2x) \text{ or } y \geq 200x - 2x^2$$

In this equation, a = $^-2$, b = 200, c = 0. The area, $200x - 2x^2$, needs to be greater than or equal to 4800 sq. ft. So, this problem uses the inequality $4800 \leq 200x - 2x^2$. This becomes $2x^2 - 200x + 4800 \leq 0$. Solving this, we get:

$$2(x^2 - 100x + 2400) \leq 0$$
$$2(x - 60)(x - 40) \leq 0$$

If x = 60 or x = 40, then the area is at least 4800 sq. ft. So, the area will be at least 4800 square feet if the width of the garden is from 40 up to 60 feet. (The length of the rectangle would vary from 120 feet to 80 feet, depending on the width of the garden.)

Graph Relations Involving Quadratics and Estimate Zeros from the Graphs

Quadratic equations can be used to model different real life situations. The graphs of these quadratics can be used to determine information about this real life situation.

Example:
The height of a projectile fired upward at a velocity of v meters per second from an original height of h meters is $y = h + vx - 4.9x^2$. If a rocket is fired from an original height of 250 meters with an original velocity of 4800 meters per second, find the approximate time the rocket would drop to sea level (a height of 0).

Solution:
The equation for this problem is: $y = 250 + 4800x - 4.9x^2$. If the height at sea level is zero, then $y = 0$ so $0 = 250 + 4800x - 4.9x^2$. Solving this for x could be done by using the quadratic formula. In addition, the approximate time in x seconds until the rocket would be at sea level could be estimated by looking at the graph. When the y value of the graph goes from positive to negative, then there is a root (also called solution or x intercept) in that interval.

$$x = \frac{^-4800 \pm \sqrt{4800^2 - 4(^-4.9)(250)}}{2(^-4.9)} \approx 980 \text{ or } ^-0.05 \text{ seconds}$$

Since the time has to be positive, it will be about 980 seconds until the rocket is at sea level.

Skill 9.3 **Recognize types of geometric figures in one, two and three dimensions and their properties**

Characteristics of Common Two- and Three-Dimensional Figures, Such As Triangles, Quadrilaterals and Spheres

A **triangle** is a polygon with three sides.

Triangles can be classified by the types of angles or the lengths of their sides.

Classifying by angles:
An **acute** triangle has exactly three *acute* angles.
A **right** triangle has one *right* angle.
An **obtuse** triangle has one *obtuse* angle.

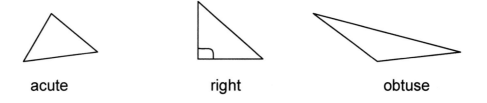

acute   right   obtuse

Classifying by sides:
All *three* sides of an **equilateral** triangle are the same length.
Two sides of an **isosceles** triangle are the same length.
None of the sides of a **scalene** triangle are the same length.

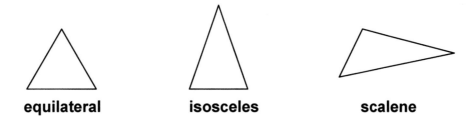

equilateral   **isosceles**   **scalene**

A **polygon** is a simple closed figure composed of line segments. In a **regular polygon**, all sides are the same length, and all angles are the same measure.

The sum of the measures of the **interior angles** of a polygon can be determined using the following formula, where n represents the number of angles in the polygon.

$$\text{Sum of } \angle s = 180(n - 2)$$

The measure of each angle of a regular polygon can be found by dividing the sum of the measures by the number of angles.

$$\text{Measure of } \angle = \frac{180(n-2)}{n}$$

Example:
Find the measure of each angle of a regular octagon.

Since an octagon has eight sides, each angle equals:

$$\frac{180(8-2)}{8} = \frac{180(6)}{8} = 135°$$

The sum of the measures of the **exterior angles** of a polygon, taken one angle at each vertex, equals 360°.

The measure of each exterior angle of a regular polygon can be determined using the following formula, where n represents the number of angles in the polygon.

$$\text{Measure of exterior } \angle \text{ of a regular polygon} = 180 - \frac{180(n-2)}{n}$$

$$\text{or more simply} = \frac{360}{n}$$

Example:
Find the measure of the interior and exterior angles of a regular pentagon.

Since a pentagon has five sides, each exterior angle measures:

$$\frac{360}{5} = 72°$$

Since each exterior angle is supplementary to its interior angle, the interior angle measures 180 - 72 or 108°.

Skill 9.4   **Apply knowledge of the concepts and skills related to angles, perimeter, circumference, volume, symmetry, similarity and congruence to solve problems**

The **perimeter** of any polygon is the sum of the lengths of the sides.
$$P = \text{sum of sides}$$

Since the opposite sides of a rectangle are congruent, the perimeter of a rectangle equals twice the sum of the length and width or:

$$P_{rect} = 2l + 2w \text{ or } 2(l + w)$$

Similarly, since all the sides of a square have the same measure, the perimeter of a square equals four times the length of one side or:
$$P_{square} = 4s$$

The **area** of a polygon is the number of square units covered by the figure.
$$A_{rect} = l \times w$$
$$A_{square} = s^2$$

Example:
Find the perimeter and the area of this rectangle.

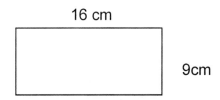

16 cm

9cm

$$P_{rect} = 2l + 2w \qquad\qquad A_{rect} = l \times w$$
$$= 2(16) + 2(9) \qquad\qquad = 16(9)$$
$$= 32 + 18 = 50 \text{ cm} \qquad\qquad = 144 \text{ cm}^2$$

Example:

Find the perimeter and area of this square.

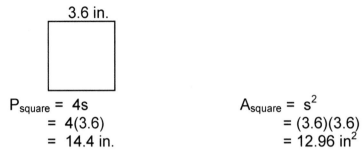

3.6 in.

$$P_{square} = 4s$$
$$= 4(3.6)$$
$$= 14.4 \text{ in.}$$

$$A_{square} = s^2$$
$$= (3.6)(3.6)$$
$$= 12.96 \text{ in}^2$$

In the following formulas, b = the base, and h = the height of an altitude drawn to the base.

$$A_{parallelogram} = bh$$
$$A_{triangle} = \tfrac{1}{2}bh$$
$$A_{trapezoid} = \tfrac{1}{2}h(b_1 + b_2)$$

Example:

Find the area of a parallelogram whose base is 6.5 cm, and the height of the altitude to that base is 3.7 cm.

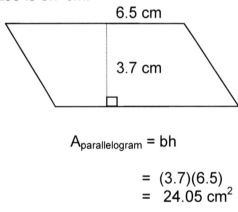

6.5 cm

3.7 cm

$$A_{parallelogram} = bh$$

$$= (3.7)(6.5)$$
$$= 24.05 \text{ cm}^2$$

Example:
Find the area of this triangle.

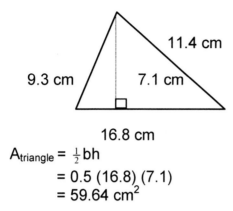

16.8 cm

$A_{triangle} = \frac{1}{2}bh$

$= 0.5\ (16.8)\ (7.1)$

$= 59.64\ cm^2$

Note that the altitude is drawn to the base measuring 16.8 cm. The lengths of the other two sides are unnecessary information.

Example:
Find the area of a right triangle whose sides measure 10 inches, 24 inches and 26 inches.

Since the hypotenuse of a right triangle must be the longest side, the two perpendicular sides must measure 10 and 24 inches.

$A_{triangle} = \frac{1}{2}bh$

$= \frac{1}{2}\ (10)\ (24)$

$= 120\ sq.\ in.$

Example:
Find the area of this trapezoid.

17.5 cm

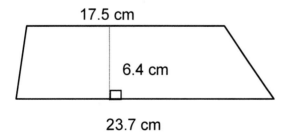

6.4 cm

23.7 cm

The area of a trapezoid equals one-half the sum of the bases times the altitude.

$A_{trapezoid} = \frac{1}{2}h(b_1 + b_2)$

$= 0.5\ (6.4)\ (17.5 + 23.7)$

$= 131.84\ cm^2$

The **lateral** area is the area of the faces, excluding the bases.

The **surface area** is the total area of all the faces, including the bases.

The **volume** is the number of cubic units in a solid. This is the amount of space a figure holds.

Right prism

$V = Bh$ (where B = area of the base of the prism and h = the height of the prism)

Rectangular right prism

$S = 2(lw + hw + lh)$ (where l = length, w = width, and h = height)
$V = lwh$

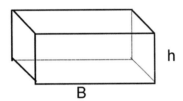

Example:
Find the height of a box whose volume is 120 cubic meters, and the area of the base is 30 square meters.

$$V = Bh$$
$$120 = 30h$$
$$h = 4 \text{ meters}$$

Regular pyramid

$V = 1/3Bh$

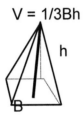

A **transformation** is a change in the position, shape, or size of a geometric figure. **Transformational geometry** is the study of manipulating objects by flipping, twisting, turning, and scaling. **Symmetry** is exact similarity between two parts or halves, as if one were a mirror image of the other.

Example:

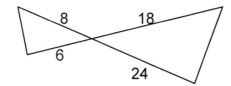

The two triangles are similar since the sides are proportional, and vertical angles are congruent.

Example:
Given two similar quadrilaterals, find the lengths of sides x, y and z.

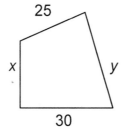 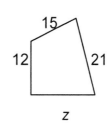

Since corresponding sides are proportional:

$$\frac{15}{25} = \frac{3}{5} \text{ so the scale is } \frac{3}{5}$$

$$\frac{12}{x} = \frac{3}{5} \qquad\qquad \frac{21}{y} = \frac{3}{5} \qquad\qquad \frac{z}{30} = \frac{3}{5}$$

$$3x = 60 \qquad\qquad 3y = 105 \qquad\qquad 5z = 90$$
$$x = 20 \qquad\qquad y = 35 \qquad\qquad z = 18$$

*   *   *

Polygons are similar if and only if there is a one-to-one correspondence between their vertices, such that the corresponding angles are congruent and the lengths of corresponding sides are proportional.

Given the rectangles below, compare the area and perimeter.

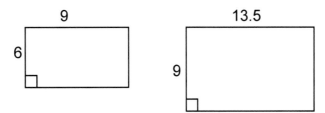

$A = LW$	$A = LW$	1. Write formula.
$A = (6)(9)$	$A = (9)(13.5)$	2. Substitute known values.
$A = 54$ sq. units	$A = 121.5$ sq. units	3. Compute.
$P = 2(L + W)$	$P = 2(L + W)$	1. Write formula.
$P = 2(6 + 9)$	$P = 2(9 + 13.5)$	2. Substitute known
values.		
$P = 30$ units	$P = 45$ units	3. Compute.

Notice that the areas relate to each other in the following manner:

Ratio of sides: $9/13.5 = 2/3$

Multiply the first area by the square of the reciprocal $(3/2)^2$ to get the second area.

$54 \times (3/2)^2 = 121.5$

The perimeters relate to each other in the following manner:

Ratio of sides: $9/13.5 = 2/3$

Multiply the perimeter of the first by the reciprocal of the ratio to get the perimeter of the second.

$30 \times 3/2 = 45$

COMPETENCY 10.0 UNDERSTAND FUNDAMENTAL CONCEPTS RELATED TO MEASUREMENT, STATISTICS, AND PROBABILITY.

Skill 10.1   Recognize appropriate measurement instruments, units and procedures for various measurement problems involving length, area, time, temperature and weight/mass

It is necessary to be familiar with the metric and customary system in order to estimate measurements.

Some common equivalents include:

ITEM	APPROXIMATELY EQUAL TO	
	METRIC	IMPERIAL
large paper clip	1 gram	1 ounce
1 quart	1 liter	
average-sized man	75 kilograms	170 pounds
1 yard	1 meter	
math textbook	1 kilogram	2 pounds
1 mile	1 kilometer	
1 foot	30 centimeters	
thickness of a dime	1 millimeter	0.1 inches

Estimate the measurement of the following items:

The length of an adult cow = _____ meters
The thickness of a compact disc = _____ millimeters
Your height = _____ meters
length of your nose = _____ centimeters
weight of your math textbook = _____ kilograms
weight of an automobile = _____ kilograms
weight of an aspirin = _____ grams

Skill 10.2   Apply knowledge of procedures for estimating and comparing measurements with the customary and metric systems and for using measurements to describe and compare phenomena

Identify relationships between different measures within the metric or customary systems of measurements and estimate an equivalent measurement across the two systems:

The units of **length** in the customary system are inches, feet, yards, and miles.

> 12 inches (in.) = 1 foot (ft.)
> 36 in. = 1 yard (yd.)
> 3 ft. = 1 yd.
> 5280 ft. = 1 mile (mi.)
> 760 yd. = 1 mi.

To change from a **larger unit to a smaller unit, multiply**.

To change from a **smaller unit to a larger unit, divide**.

Example:

4 mi. = _____ yd.
Since 1760 yd. = 1 mile, multiply $4 \times 1760 = 7040$ yd.

Example:

21 in. = _____ ft.
$21 \div 12 = 1\frac{3}{4}$ ft.

The units of **weight** are ounces, pounds and tons.

> 16 ounces (oz.) = 1 pound (lb.)
> 2,000 lb. = 1 ton (T.)

Example:

$2\frac{3}{4}$ T. = _____ lb.
$2\frac{3}{4} \times 2,000 = 5,500$ lb.

The units of **capacity** are fluid ounces, cups, pints, quarts and gallons.

> 8 fluid ounces (fl. oz.) = 1 cup (c.)
> 2 c. = 1 pint (pt.)
> 4 c. = 1 quart (qt.)
> 2 pt. = 1 qt.
> 4 qt. = 1 gallon (gal.)

Example1:

$$3 \text{ gal.} = \underline{\hspace{1cm}} \text{ qt.}$$
$$3 \times 4 = 12 \text{ qt.}$$

Example:

$$1\tfrac{1}{4} \text{ cups} = \underline{\hspace{1cm}} \text{ oz.}$$
$$1\tfrac{1}{4} \times 8 = 10 \text{ oz.}$$

Example:

$$7 \text{ c.} = \underline{\hspace{1cm}} \text{ pt.}$$
$$7 \div 2 = 3\tfrac{1}{2} \text{ pt.}$$

Square units can be derived with knowledge of basic units of length by squaring the equivalent measurements.

1 square foot (sq. ft.) = 144 sq. in.
1 sq. yd. = 9 sq. ft.
1 sq. yd. = 1296 sq. in.

Example:

$$14 \text{ sq. yd.} = \underline{\hspace{1cm}} \text{ sq. ft.}$$
$$14 \times 9 = 126 \text{ sq. ft.}$$

Metric Units

The metric system is based on multiples of <u>ten</u>. Conversions are made by simply moving the decimal point to the left or right.

kilo-	1000	thousands
hecto-	100	hundreds
deca-	10	tens
nit		
deci-	.1	tenths
centi-	.01	hundredths
milli-	.001	thousandths

The basic unit for **length** is the meter. One meter is approximately one yard.

The basic unit for **weight** or mass is the gram.   A paper clip weighs about one gram.

The basic unit for **volume** is the liter. One liter is approximately a quart.

These are the most commonly used units:

1 m = 100 cm	1000 mL= 1 L	1000 mg = 1 g
1 m = 1000 mm	1 kL = 1000 L	1 kg = 1000 g
1 cm = 10 mm		
1000 m = 1 km		

The prefixes are commonly listed from left to right for ease in conversion.

K H D U D C M

Example: 63 km = _____ m
Since there are 3 steps from <u>K</u>ilo to <u>U</u>nit, move the decimal point 3 places to the right.

63 km = 63,000 m

Example: 14 mL = _____ L
Since there are 3 steps from <u>M</u>illi to <u>U</u>nit, move the decimal point 3 places to the left.

14 mL = 0.014 L

Example: 56.4 cm = _____ mm
56.4 cm = 564 mm

Example: 9.1 m = _____ km
9.1 m = 0.0091 km

Example 5:   75 kg = _____ m
75 kg = 75,000,000 m

Skill 10.3   **Apply knowledge of basic concepts and principles of statistics and probability (e.g., mean, median, mode and range).**

Mean, median and mode are three measures of central tendency. The **mean** is the average of the data items. The **median** is found by putting the data items in order from smallest to largest and then selecting the item in the middle (or the average of the two items in the middle). The **mode** is the most frequently occurring item.

Range is a measure of variability. It is found by subtracting the smallest value from the largest value.

Sample problem:

Find the mean, median, mode and range of the test scores listed below:

85	77	65
92	90	54
88	85	70
75	80	69
85	88	60
72	74	95

Mean (X) = sum of all scores ÷ number of scores
= 78

Median = put numbers in order from smallest to largest. Pick the middle number.
54, 60, 65, 69, 70, 72, 74, 75, 77, 80, 85, 85, 85, 88, 88, 90, 92, 95
                                    -- --
                              both in middle
Therefore, the median is average of two numbers in the middle or
=78.5

Mode = most frequent number
= 85

Range = largest number minus the smallest number
= 95 − 54 = 41

Skill 10.4   Identify various methods (e.g., surveys, tables and graphs) of systematically collecting, organizing, describing and analyzing data.

To make a **bar graph** or a **pictograph**, determine the scale to be used for the graph. Then determine the length of each bar on the graph or determine the number of pictures needed to represent each item of information. Be sure to include an explanation of the scale in the legend.

Example: A class had the following grades:
4 A's, 9 B's, 8 C's, 1 D, 3 F's.
Graph these on a bar graph and a pictograph.

Pictograph

Grade	Number of Students
A	☺☺☺☺
B	☺☺☺☺☺☺☺☺☺
C	☺☺☺☺☺☺☺☺
D	☺
F	☺☺☺

Bar graph

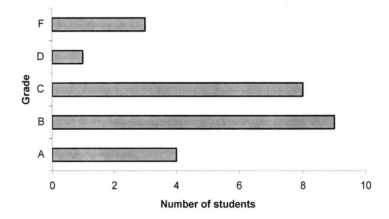

To make a **line graph**, determine appropriate scales for both the vertical and horizontal axes (based on the information to be graphed). Describe what each axis represents and mark the scale periodically on each axis. Graph the individual points of the graph and connect the points on the graph from left to right.

Example: Graph the following information using a line graph.

The number of National Merit finalists/school year

	90-91	91-92	92-93	93-94	94-95	95-96
Central	3	5	1	4	6	8
Wilson	4	2	3	2	3	2

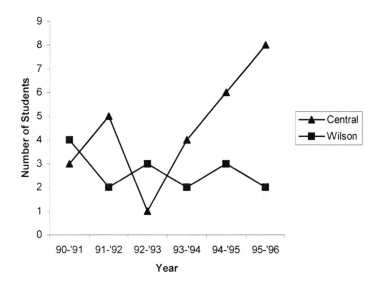

To make a **circle graph**, total all the information that is to be included on the graph. Determine the central angle to be used for each sector of the graph using the following formula:

$$\frac{\text{information}}{\text{total information}} \times 360^\circ = \text{degrees in central} \sphericalangle$$

Lay out the central angles to these sizes, label each section and include its percent.

Example: Graph this information on a circle graph:

Monthly expenses:

Rent, $400
Food, $150
Utilities, $75
Clothes, $75
Church, $100
Misc., $200

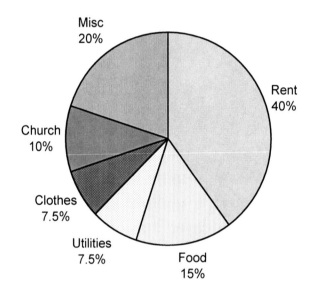

Scatter plots compare two characteristics of the same group of things or people and usually consist of a large body of data. They show how much one variable is affected by another. The relationship between the two variables is their **correlation**. The closer the data points come to making a straight line when plotted, the closer the correlation.

Stem and leaf plots are visually similar to line plots. The **stems** are the digits in the greatest place value of the data values, and the **leaves** are the digits in the next greatest place values. Stem and leaf plots are best suited for small sets of data and are especially useful for comparing two sets of data. The following is an example using test scores:

4	9
5	4 9
6	1 2 3 4 6 7 8 8
7	0 3 4 6 6 6 7 7 7 8 8 8 8
8	3 5 5 7 8
9	0 0 3 4 5
10	0 0

Histograms are used to summarize information from large sets of data that can be naturally grouped into intervals. The vertical axis indicates **frequency** (the number of times any particular data value occurs), and the horizontal axis indicates data values or ranges of data values. The number of data values in any interval is the **frequency of the interval**.

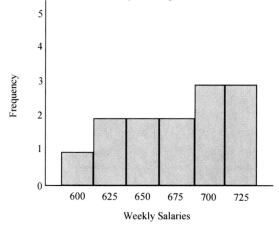

Skill 10.5   Apply knowledge of how to interpret graphic and nongraphic representations of statistical data (e.g., frequency distributions, percentiles)

Percentiles divide data into 100 equal parts. A person whose score falls in the 65th percentile has outperformed 65 percent of all those who took the test. This does not mean that the score was 65 percent out of 100 nor does it mean that 65 percent of the questions answered were correct. It means that the grade was higher than 65 percent of all those who took the test.

Stanine "standard nine" scores combine the understandability of percentages with the properties of the normal curve of probability. Stanines divide the bell curve into nine sections, the largest of which stretches from the 40th to the 60th percentile and is the "Fifth Stanine" (the average of taking into account error possibilities).

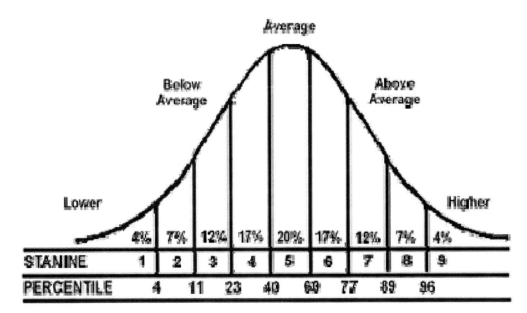

Quartiles divide the data into 4 parts. First find the median of the data set (Q2), then find the median of the upper (Q3) and lower (Q1) halves of the data set. If there are an odd number of values in the data set, include the median value in both halves when finding quartile values. For example, given the data set: {1, 4, 9, 16, 25, 36, 49, 64, 81} first find the median value, which is 25 this is the second quartile. Since there are an odd number of values in the data set (9), we include the median in both halves.

To find the quartile values, we much find the medians of: {1, 4, 9, 16, 25} and {25, 36, 49, 64, 81}. Since each of these subsets had an odd number of elements (5), we use the middle value. Thus the first quartile value is 9 and the third quartile value is 49. If the data set had an even number of elements, average the middle two values. The quartile values are always either one of the data points, or exactly half way between two data points.

Example: Given the following set of data, find the percentile of the score 104.
70, 72, 82, 83, 84, 87, 100, 104, 108, 109, 110, 115

Find the percentage of scores below 104.

7/12 of the scores are less than 104. This is 58.333%; therefore, the score of 104 is in the 58th percentile.

Example: Find the first, second and third quartile for the data listed.
6, 7, 8, 9, 10, 12, 13, 14, 15, 16, 18, 23, 24, 25, 27, 29, 30, 33, 34, 37

Quartile 1: The 1st Quartile is the median of the lower half of the data set, which is 11.

Quartile 2: The median of the data set is the 2nd Quartile, which is 17.

Quartile 3: The 3rd Quartile is the median of the upper half of the data set, which is 28.

COMPETENCY 11.0 UNDERSTAND WAYS OF COMMUNICATING AND CONNECTING MATHEMATICAL CONCEPTS, PROCEDURES, AND REASONING PROCESSES.

Skill 11.1 **Apply appropriate mathematical terminology in a variety of situations, including translation into everyday language**

(See Math Competency 10.0 and Skill 11.3.)

Skill 11.2 **Identify ways to select and use a wide range of manipulatives, instructional resources and technologies that support the learning of mathematics**

Represent a Problem in Alternate Ways, Such As Words, Symbols, Concrete Models and Diagrams to Gain Greater Insight:

For Example: Manipulatives

Example:
Use tiles to demonstrate both geometric ideas and number theory.

Give each group of students 12 tiles, and instruct them to build rectangles. Students draw their rectangles on paper.

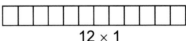
12 × 1

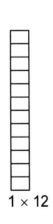
1 × 12

3 × 4

4 × 3

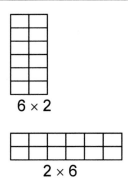

6×2

2×6

Skill 11.3   Apply knowledge of strategies (e.g., estimation, mental mathematics, technologies) used to analyze mathematical ideas, solve problems, and investigate real-world situations

Estimation and approximation may be used to check the reasonableness of answers.

Example:
Estimate the answer.

$$\frac{58 \times 810}{1989}$$

58 becomes 60, 810 becomes 800, and 1989 becomes 2000.

$$\frac{60 \times 800}{2000} = 24$$

Word Problems:
An estimate may sometimes be all that is needed to solve a problem.

Example:
Janet goes into a store to purchase a CD on sale for $13.95. While shopping, she sees two pairs of shoes, prices $19.95 and $14.50. She only has $50. Can she purchase everything?

Solve by rounding:

$19.95 → $20.00
$14.50 → $15.00
$13.95 → $14.00
$49.00 (Yes, she can purchase the CD and the shoes.)

Demonstrate that a solution is correct:

Error Analysis

A simple method for analyzing student errors is to ask how the answer was obtained. The teacher can then determine if a common error pattern has resulted in the wrong answer. There is a value to having the students explain how they arrived at the correct, as well as the incorrect, answers.

Many errors are due to simple **carelessness**. Students need to be encouraged to work slowly and carefully. They should check their calculations by redoing the problem on another paper, not merely looking at the work. Addition and subtraction problems need to be written neatly so that the numbers line up. Students need to be careful regrouping in subtraction. Students must write clearly and legibly, including erasing fully. Use estimation to ensure that answers make sense.

Many students' computational skills exceed their **reading** levels. Although they can understand basic operations, they fail to grasp the concept or completely understand the question. Students must read directions slowly.

Fractions are often a source of many errors. Students need to be reminded to use common denominators when adding and subtracting and to always express answers in simplest terms. Again, it is helpful to check by estimating.

The most common error that is made when working with **decimals** is failure to line up the decimal points when adding or subtracting or not moving the decimal point when multiplying or dividing. Students also need to be reminded to add zeroes when necessary. Reading aloud may also be beneficial. Estimation, as always, is especially important.

Students need to know that it is okay to make mistakes. The teacher must keep a positive attitude, so students do not feel defeated or frustrated.

Recognition and understanding of the relationships between concepts and topics is of great value in mathematical problem solving and the explanation of more complex processes.

For instance, multiplication is simply repeated addition. This relationship explains the concept of variable addition. We can show that the expression $4x + 3x = 7x$ is true by rewriting 4 times x and 3 times x as repeated addition, yielding the expression $(x + x + x + x) + (x + x + x)$. Thus, because of the relationship between multiplication and addition, variable addition is accomplished by coefficient addition.

Applying Strategies for Promoting Students' Use of Critical-Thinking and Problem-Solving Skills in Mathematics

Problem Solving

The skills of analysis and interpretation are necessary for problem solving. Students with learning disabilities find problem solving difficult, with the result that they avoid problem-solving activities. Skills necessary for problem solving include:

1) *Identify the main idea*: What is the problem about?

2) *State the main question of the problem*: What is the problem asking for?

3) *Identify important facts*: What information is necessary to solve the problem?

4) *Choose a strategy and an operation*: How will the student solve the problem and with what operation?

5) *Solve the problem*: Perform the computation

6) *Check accuracy of the computation, and compare the answer to the main question*: Does it sound reasonable?

7) *If solution is correct*: Repeat the steps.

Identify Effective Teaching Methods for Developing the Use of Math Skills in Problem Solving

One of the main reasons for studying mathematics is to acquire the ability to perform problem-solving skills. Problem solving is the process of applying previously acquired knowledge to new and novel situations. Mathematical problem solving is generally thought of as solving word problems; however, there are more skills involved in problem solving than merely reading word problems, deciding on correct conceptual procedures, and performing the computations. Problem-solving skills involve posing questions; analyzing situations; hypothesizing, translating and illustrating results; drawing diagrams; and using trial and error. When solving mathematical problems, students need to be able to apply logic, and thus, determine which facts are relevant.

Problem solving has proven to be the primary area of mathematical difficulty for students. The following methods for developing problem-solving skills have been recommended.

1. Allot time for the development of successful problem-solving skills. It is complex process and needs to be taught in a systematic way.

2. Be sure prerequisite skills have been adequately developed. The ability to perform the operations of addition, subtraction, multiplication and division are necessary sub-skills.

3. Use error analysis to diagnose areas of difficulty. One error in procedure or choice of mathematical operation, once corrected, will eliminate subsequent mistakes, following the initial error, like the domino effect. Look for patterns of similar mistakes to prevent a series of identical errors. Instruct children on the usage of error analysis to perform self-appraisal of their own work.

4. Teach students appropriate terminology. Many words have a different meaning when used in a mathematical context than in every day life. For example, "set" in mathematics refers to a grouping of objects, but it may also be used as a verb, such as in "set the table." Other words that should be defined include "order," "base," "power" and "root."

5. Have students estimate answers. Teach them how to check their computed answer to determine how reasonable it is. For example, Teddy is asked how many hours he spent doing his homework. If he worked on it two hours before dinner and one hour after dinner, and his answer came out to be 21, Teddy should be able to conclude that 21 hours is the greater part of a day, and is far too large to be reasonable.

6. Remember that development of math readiness skills enables students to acquire prerequisite concepts and to build cognitive structures. These prerequisite skills appear to be related to problem-solving performance.

Skill 11.4   Apply knowledge of approaches for interpreting and communicating mathematical information, reasoning, concepts, applications and procedures

A valid argument is a statement made about a pattern or relationship between elements, thought to be true, which is subsequently justified through repeated examples and logical reasoning. Another term for a valid argument is a proof.

For example, the statement that the sum of two odd numbers is always even could be tested through actual examples:

Two Odd Numbers	Sum	Validity of Statement
1+1	2 (even)	Valid
1+3	4 (even)	Valid
61+29	90 (even)	Valid
135+47	182 (even)	Valid
253+17	270 (even)	Valid
1,945+2,007	3,952 (even)	Valid
6,321+7,851	14,172 (even)	Valid

Adding two odd numbers always results in a sum that is even. It is a valid argument based on the justifications in the table above.

Here is another example. The statement that a fraction of a fraction can be determined by multiplying the numerator by the numerator and the denominator by the denominator can be proven through logical reasoning. For example, one-half of one-quarter of a candy bar can be found by multiplying ½ * ¼. The answer would be one-eighth. The validity of this argument can be demonstrated as valid with a model:

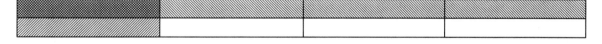

The entire rectangle represents one whole candy bar. The top half section of the model is shaded in one direction to demonstrate how much of the candy bar remains from the whole candy bar. The left quarter, shaded in a different direction, demonstrates that one-quarter of the candy bar has been given to a friend. Since the whole candy bar is not available to give out, the area that is double-shaded is the fractional part of the ½ candy bar that has been actually given away. That fractional part is one-eighth of the whole candy bar, as shown in both the sketch and the algorithm.

Suppose that these statements were given to you and you were asked to try to reach a conclusion. The statements are:

> All rectangles are parallelograms.
> Quadrilateral ABCD is not a parallelogram.

> In "if-then" form, the first statement would be:
> If a figure is a rectangle, then it is also a parallelogram.

Note that the second statement is the negation of the conclusion of statement one. Remember also that the contrapositive is logically equivalent to a given conditional. That is, **"If ~ q, then ~ p."** Since "ABCD is NOT a parallelogram" is like saying **"If ~ q,"** then you can come to the conclusion **"then ~ p."** Therefore, the conclusion is ABCD is not a rectangle. Looking at the Venn diagram below, if all rectangles are parallelograms, then rectangles are included as part of the parallelograms. Since quadrilateral ABCD is not a parallelogram, that it is excluded from anywhere inside the parallelogram box. This allows you to conclude that ABCD cannot be a rectangle either.

PARALLELOGRAMS

quadrilateral
ABCD rectangles

Elapsed time problems are usually one of two types. One type of problem is the elapsed time between 2 times given in hours, minutes and seconds. The other common type of problem is between 2 times given in months and years.

For any time of day past noon, change it into military time by adding 12 hours. For instance, 1:15 p.m. would be 13:15. Remember that when you borrow a minute or an hour in a subtraction problem, you have borrowed 60 more seconds or minutes.

Example:
Find the time from 11:34:22 a.m. until 3:28:40 p.m.

> First change 3:28:40 p.m. to   15:28:40 p.m.
> Now subtract   - 11:34:22 a.m.
>   :18

Borrow an hour, and add 60 more minutes. Then, subtract.

> 14:88:40 p.m.
> - 11:34:22 a.m.
>   3:54:18 ↔ 3 hours, 54 minutes, 18 seconds

Example:

John lived in Arizona from September 91 until March 95. How long is that?

		year	month
March 95	=	95	03
September 91	= -	91	09

Borrow a year, change it into 12 more months, and subtract.

		year	month
March 95	=	94	15
September 91	= -	91	09
		3 yr	6 months

Example:

A race took the winner 1 hr. 58 min. 12 sec. on the first half of the race and 2 hr. 9 min. 57 sec. on the second half of the race. How much time did the entire race take?

```
    1 hr. 58 min. 12 sec.
  + 2 hr.  9 min. 57 sec.    Add these numbers
    3 hr. 67 min. 69 sec.
  + 1 min -60 sec.           Change 60 seconds to 1 min.
    3 hr. 68 min.  9 sec.
  + 1 hr.-60 min.    .       Change 60 minutes to 1 hr.
    4 hr.  8 min.  9 sec. ←final answer
```

COMPETENCY 12.0 UNDERSTAND CONCEPTS RELATED TO MATHEMATICS INSTRUCTION THAT SUPPORT THE LEARNING OF STUDENTS WITH DISABILITIES.

Skill 12.1 Recognize methods for evaluating general curricula and determining the scope and sequence of the academic content area of mathematics

Evaluating general curriculum scope and sequence for any content area is through the same general process. This general process was outlined and explained in detail in the reading areas of this manual. The same overall process applies to math as well.

Skill 12.2 Identify ways to incorporate the Illinois Learning Standards in the area of mathematics in the development of instruction and Individualized Education Programs (IEPs)

(See Skill 7.8.)

Skill 12.3 Apply knowledge of how to develop appropriate lesson plans that incorporate curriculum and instructional strategies with individualized education goals and benchmarks

Evaluating, Selecting and Adapting Instructional Strategies, Materials and Resources to Individualize Instruction and to Facilitate Student Achievement in Mathematics

Etiologies of the learning challenges some students face can be diverse, as can their outcomes. Teachers of students with special needs are skilled at assessing, observing, implementing, reassessing and making changes to the educational environment, tools, and approaches they are using with students.

To accomplish this with math instruction, teachers must begin by identifying the nature of math as a curricular area, using that information to task-analyze the concepts, skills and strategies they want to teach. Then teachers focus on each student's observed and documented strengths and challenges, as well as the relevant information from his/her formal assessments and individualized education plan (IEP). Such analysis may constitute an initial assessment.

In the NCTM journal article, *Planning Strategies for Students with Special Needs* (*Teaching Children Mathematics*, 2004), Brodesky et al. suggest that the next step in deciding on strategies, materials and resources would be to identify the "barriers" that students' documented and observed challenges will present as they work to meet the goals and objectives of the math curriculum and their IEPs. Data-based assessments are an alternative or adjunct to such observational and record review. This information can help direct teachers' thinking about proactive solutions, including the selection and/or adaptation of the best strategies, materials and resources.

Once teachers have developed a clear picture of the goals and needs of their math students with learning differences, they can seek resources for best practices, including school district-based support, the federal and state departments of education, teacher training programs and education literature. Ultimately, skilled teachers will layer creativity and keen observation with their professional skills to decide how best to individualize instruction and to facilitate student achievement. Examples include:

- Varying learning modalities (visual, kinesthetic, tactile and aural)
- Integrating technology (calculators, computers and game consoles)
- Providing tools and manipulatives (Cuisinart rods, beans and protractors)
- Developing a range of engaging activities (games, music and storytelling)
- Using real world problem solving (fundraising, school-wide projects, shopping, cooking and budgeting)
- Adopting a cross-curricular approach (studying historical events strongly influenced by math and music theory)
- Developing basic skills (guided practice, pencil-and-paper computation, journaling and discussing problem-solving strategies)
- Adaptations (extended wait time, recorded lessons, concept videos, ergonomic work areas and mixed-ability learning groups)

Skill 12.4   Demonstrate knowledge of ways to use resources and materials that are developmentally and functionally valid based on a student's needs

(See skill 12.3.)

Skill 12.5   Recognize ways to apply principles of instruction for generalized math skills to teaching domestic, community, school, recreational or vocational skills that require mathematics

Demonstrating Familiarity with Techniques for Encouraging Students' Application of Mathematics Skills in a Variety of Contexts, Including Practical Daily Living Situations

In a paper published by the ERIC Clearinghouse on Disabilities and Gifted Education, Author Cynthia Warger writes, "...for students with disabilities to do better in math, math must be meaningful for them. Both knowing and doing mathematics must be emphasized to enhance the quality of mathematics instruction and learning for students with disabilities." (Warger, 2002)

Real-world applications of mathematics abound and offer highly-motivating opportunities for computational practice and the development of number sense and mathematical reasoning that can give students confidence in their mathematical abilities. Finding the mathematical connections in outdoor games, planning for the purchase of lunch, comparing heights among classmates, calculating the time until recess, and figuring out which sports team is headed for the playoffs are just a few examples.

Skill 12.6   Apply knowledge of ways to plan and to implement systematic instructional programs to teach individualized priority math skills

The Special Connections Project at the University of Kansas suggests a number of strategies in a paper called *Creating Authentic Mathematics Learning Contexts*:

1   Begin where the students are. Their ages, interests and experiences are excellent clues to the kinds of contexts that will offer the most compelling learning opportunities, whether school-, family- or community-related.

2   Document interests. Comparing and contrasting them can help identify patterns and differences and assist with lesson and activity planning. Documenting and reviewing this information (student name, hobbies, interests, family activities and etc.) could be an activity you share with your students.

3   Model the desired concept, skill or strategy explicitly and within the real-world context. Observing your problem-solving approach and its outcome helps ground students in the math and begins to strengthen associations between mathematics concepts and real-life situations.

4   Reinforce the associations by demonstrating the relevance of the concept, skill or strategy being taught to the "authentic context."

5   Offer opportunities for guided, supported practice of the concept, skill or strategy; this includes feedback, redirection, remodeling, if needed, and acknowledgement of progress and successes.

COMPETENCY 13.0 UNDERSTAND FUNDAMENTAL CONCEPTS AND PRINCIPLES RELATED TO LIFE AND ENVIRONMENTAL SCIENCE.

Skill 13.1   Recognize basic processes and concepts related to cells and the characteristics, needs and organization of living things

The structure of the cell is often related to the cell's function. Root hair cells differ from flower stamens or leaf epidermal cells. They all have different functions.

Animal Cells—begin a discussion of the nucleus as a round body inside the cell. It controls the cell's activities. The nuclear membrane contains threadlike structures called chromosomes. The genes are units that control cell activities found in the nucleus. The cytoplasm has many structures in it. Vacuoles contain the food for the cell. Other vacuoles contain waste materials. Animal cells differ from plant cells because they have cell membranes.

Plant Cells—have cell walls. A cell wall differs from cell membranes. The cell membrane is very thin and is a part of the cell. The cell wall is thick and is a nonliving part of the cell. Chloroplasts are bundles of chlorophyll.

Members of the five different kingdoms of the classification system of living organisms often differ in their basic life functions. Here we compare and analyze how members of the five kingdoms obtain nutrients, excrete waste, and reproduce.

Bacteria—prokaryotic, single-celled organisms that lack cell nuclei. The different types of bacteria obtain nutrients in a variety of ways. Most bacteria absorb nutrients from the environment through small channels in their cell walls and membranes (chemotrophs), while some perform photosynthesis (phototrophs). Chemo-organotrophs use organic compounds as energy sources, while chemo-lithotrophs can use inorganic chemicals as energy sources. Depending on the type of metabolism and energy source, bacteria release a variety of waste products (e.g., alcohols, acids and carbon dioxide) to the environment through diffusion. All bacteria reproduce through binary fission (asexual reproduction), producing two identical cells. Bacteria reproduce very rapidly, dividing or doubling every twenty minutes in optimal conditions. Asexual reproduction does not allow for genetic variation, but bacteria achieve genetic variety by absorbing DNA from ruptured cells and conjugating or swapping chromosomal or plasmid DNA with other cells.

Animals—multi-cellular, eukaryotic organisms. All animals obtain nutrients by eating food (ingestion). Different types of animals derive nutrients from eating plants, other animals, or both. Animal cells perform respiration that converts food molecules, mainly carbohydrates and fats, into energy. The excretory systems of animals, like animals themselves, vary in complexity. Simple invertebrates eliminate waste through a single tube, while complex vertebrates have a specialized system of organs that process and excrete waste.

Most animals, unlike bacteria, exist in two distinct sexes. Members of the female sex give birth or lay eggs. Some less-developed animals can reproduce asexually. For example, flatworms can divide in two, and some unfertilized insect eggs can develop into viable organisms. Most animals reproduce sexually through various mechanisms. For example, aquatic animals reproduce by external fertilization of eggs, while mammals reproduce by internal fertilization. More developed animals possess specialized reproductive systems and cycles that facilitates reproduction and promotes genetic variation.

Plants—like animals, are multi-cellular, eukaryotic organisms. Plants obtain nutrients from the soil through their root systems and convert sunlight into energy through photosynthesis. Many plants store waste products in vacuoles or organs (e.g., leaves, bark) that are discarded. Some plants also excrete waste through their roots.

More than half of the plant species reproduce by producing seeds from which new plants grow. Depending on the type of plant, flowers or cones produce seeds. Other plants reproduce by spores, tubers, bulbs, buds, and grafts. The flowers of flowering plants contain the reproductive organs. Pollination is the joining of male and female gametes that is often facilitated by movement by wind or animals.

Fungi—are eukaryotic, mostly multi-cellular organisms. All fungi are heterotrophs, obtaining nutrients from other organisms. More specifically, most fungi obtain nutrients by digesting and absorbing nutrients from dead organisms. Fungi secrete enzymes outside of their body to digest organic material and then absorb the nutrients through their cell walls.

Most fungi can reproduce asexually and sexually. Different types of fungi reproduce asexually by mitosis, budding, sporification or fragmentation. Sexual reproduction of fungi is different from sexual reproduction of animals. The two mating types of fungi are plus and minus, not male and female. The fusion of hyphae, the specialized reproductive structure in fungi, between plus and minus types produces and scatters diverse spores.

Protists—eukaryotic, single-celled organisms. Most protists are heterotrophic, obtaining nutrients by ingesting small molecules and cells and digesting them in vacuoles. All protists reproduce asexually by either binary or multiple fission. Like bacteria, protists achieve genetic variation by exchange of DNA through conjugation.

Behavioral Responses to External and Internal Stimuli in a Variety of Organisms

Response to stimuli is one of the key characteristics of any living thing. Any detectable change in the internal or external environment (the stimulus) may trigger a response in an organism. Just like physical characteristics, organisms' responses to stimuli are adaptations that allow them to better survive. While these responses may be more noticeable in animals that can move quickly, all organisms are actually capable of responding to changes.

Single-celled Organisms—these organisms are able to respond to basic stimuli, such as the presence of light, heat, or food. Changes in the environment are typically sensed via cell surface receptors. These organisms may respond to such stimuli by making changes in internal biochemical pathways or initiating reproduction or phagocytosis. Those capable of simple motility, using flagella for instance, may respond by moving toward food or away from heat.

Plants—typically do not possess sensory organs, so individual cells recognize stimuli through a variety of pathways. When many cells respond to stimuli together, a response becomes apparent. Logically then, the responses of plants occur on a rather longer timescale that those of animals. Plants are capable of responding to a few basic stimuli, including light, water, and gravity. Some common examples include the way plants turn and grow toward the sun, the sprouting of seeds when exposed to warmth and moisture, and the growth of roots in the direction of gravity.

Animals—lower members of the animal kingdom have responses similar to those seen in single-celled organisms. However, higher animals have developed complex systems to detect and respond to stimuli. The nervous system, sensory organs (eyes, ears, skin, etc.), and muscle tissue all allow animals to sense and quickly respond to changes in their environment. As in other organisms, many responses to stimuli in animals are involuntary. For example, pupils dilate in response to the reduction of light. Such reactions are typically called reflexes. However, many animals are also capable of voluntary response. In many animal species, voluntary reactions are instinctual. For instance, a zebra's response to a lion is a voluntary one, but, instinctually, it will flee quickly as soon as the lion's presence is sensed. Complex responses, which may or may not be instinctual, are typically termed behavior. An example is the annual migration of birds when seasons change. Even more complex social behavior is seen in animals that live in large groups.

Skill 13.2   Recognize basic structures and functions of the human body in comparison with those of other organisms

(See skill 13.1.)

Skill 13.3   Recognize processes by which energy and nutrients cycle through ecosystems

Trophic levels are based on the feeding relationships that determine energy flow and chemical cycling.

Autotrophs are the primary producers of the ecosystem. **Producers** mainly consist of plants. **Primary consumers** are the next trophic level. The primary consumers are the herbivores that eat plants or algae. **Secondary consumers** are the carnivores that eat the primary consumers. **Tertiary consumers** eat the secondary consumer. These trophic levels may go higher depending on the ecosystem. **Decomposers** are consumers that feed off animal waste and dead organisms. This pathway of food transfer is known as the food chain.

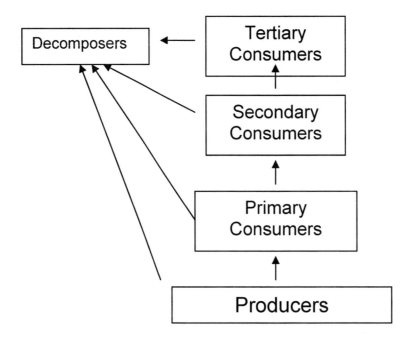

Most food chains are more elaborate, becoming food webs.

Energy is lost as the trophic levels progress from producer to tertiary consumer. The amount of energy that is transferred between trophic levels is called the ecological efficiency. The visual of this energy flow is represented in a **pyramid of productivity**.

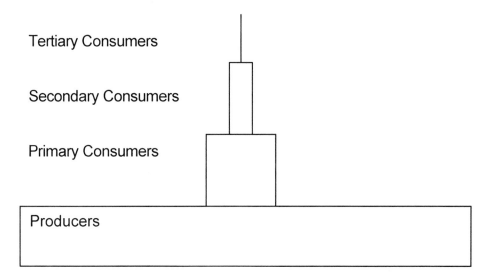

The **biomass pyramid** represents the total dry weight of organisms in each trophic level. A **pyramid of numbers** is a representation of the population size of each trophic level. The producers, being the most populous, are on the bottom of this pyramid, and the tertiary consumers are on the top with the fewest numbers.

Skill 13.4   Analyze how organisms interact with one another and with their environment

There are many interactions that may occur between different species living together. Predation, parasitism, competition, commensalisms and mutualism are the different types of relationships populations have amongst each other.

Predation and **parasitism** result in a benefit for one species and a detriment for the other. Predation is when a predator eats its prey. The common conception of predation is of a carnivore consuming other animals. This is one form of predation. Although not always resulting in the death of the plant, herbivory is a form of predation. Some animals eat enough of a plant to cause death. Parasitism involves a predator that lives on or in their hosts, causing detrimental effects to the host. Insects and viruses, living off and reproducing in their hosts, are examples of parasitism. Many plants and animals have defenses against predators. Some plants have poisonous chemicals that will harm the predator if ingested, and some animals are camouflaged so they are harder to detect.

Competition is when two or more species in a community use the same resources. Competition is usually detrimental to both populations. Competition is often difficult to find in nature because competition between two populations is not continuous. Either the weaker population will no longer exist, or one population will evolve to utilize other available resources.

Symbiosis is when two species live close together. Parasitism, described above, is one example of symbiosis. Another example of symbiosis is commensalisms. **Commensalism** occurs when one species benefits from the other without harmful effects. **Mutualism** is when both species benefit from the other. Species involved in mutualistic relationships must co-evolve to survive. As one species evolves, the other must as well if it is to be successful in life. Grouper and a species of shrimp live in a mutualistic relationship. The shrimp feed off parasites living on the grouper; thus, the shrimp are fed, and the grouper stays healthy. Many microorganisms are in mutualistic relationships.

The Concepts of Niche and Carrying Capacity

The term "Niche" describes the relational position of a species or population in an ecosystem. Niche includes how a population responds to the abundance of its resources and enemies (e.g., by growing when resources are abundant and predators, parasites, and pathogens are scarce).

Niche also indicates the life history of an organism, habitat and place in the food chain. According to the competitive exclusion principle, no two species can occupy the same niche in the same environment for a long time.

The full range of environmental conditions (biological and physical) under which an organism can exist describes its fundamental niche. Because of the pressure from superior competitors, inferior organisms are driven to occupy a niche much narrower than their previous niche. This is known as the 'realized niche'

Examples of Niche:

1. **Oak trees:**
   * Absorb sunlight by photosynthesis.
   * Act as support for creeping plants.
   * Cover their ground with dead leaves in the autumn.
   * Live in forests.
   * Provide shelter for many animals.
   * Serve as a source of food for animals.

If the oak trees were cut down or destroyed by fire or storms, they would no longer be doing their job, and this would have a disastrous effect on all the other organisms living in the same habitat.

2. **Hedgehogs:**

* eEat a variety of insects and other invertebrates which that live underneath the dead
* eEat slugs and protect plants from them.
* thhHavee spines that are a superb environment for fleas and ticks.s
* pPut the nitrogen back into the soil when they urinate.

   leaves and twigs in the garden.

If there were no hedgehogs around, the population of slugs would explode, and the nutrients in the dead leaves and twigs would not be recycled.

A **population** is a group of individuals of one species that live in the same general area. Many factors can affect the population size and its growth rate. Population size can depend on the total amount of life a habitat can support. This is the carrying capacity of the environment. Once the habitat runs out of food, water, shelter, or space, the carrying capacity decreases and then stabilizes.

Limiting factors can affect population growth. As a population increases, the competition for resources is more intense, and the growth rate declines. This is a **density-dependent** growth factor. The carrying capacity can be determined by the density-dependent factor. **Density-independent factors** affect the individuals regardless of population size. The weather and climate are good examples. Too hot or too cold temperatures may kill many individuals from a population that has not reached its carrying capacity.

Human population increased slowly until 1650. Since 1650, the human population has grown almost exponentially, reaching its current population of over 6 billion. Factors that have led to this increased growth rate include improved nutrition, sanitation, and health care. In addition, advances in technology, agriculture, and scientific knowledge have made the use of resources more efficient and increased their availability.

While the Earth's ultimate carrying capacity for humans is uncertain, some factors that may limit growth are the availability of food, water, space, and fossil fuels. There is a finite amount of land on Earth available for food production. In addition, providing clean, potable water for a growing human population is a real concern. Finally, fossil fuels, important energy sources for human technology, are scarce. The inevitable shortage of energy in the Earth's future will require the development of alternative energy sources to maintain or increase human population growth.

Skill 13.5   Demonstrate knowledge of principles of genetics and evolutionary theory to understand how organisms change over time

Charles Darwin proposed a mechanism for his theory of evolution, which he termed natural selection. Natural selection describes the process by which favorable traits accumulate in a population, changing the population's genetic make-up over time. Darwin theorized that all individual organisms, even those of the same species, are different, and those individuals that happen to possess traits favorable for survival would produce more offspring. Thus, in the next generation, the number of individuals with the favorable trait increases, and the process continues. Darwin, in contrast to other evolutionary scientists, did not believe that traits acquired during an organism's lifetime (e.g., increased musculature) or the desires and needs of the organism affected evolution of populations. For example, Darwin argued that the evolution of long trunks in elephants resulted from environmental conditions that favored those elephants that possessed longer trunks. The individual elephants did not stretch their trunks to reach food or water and pass on the new, longer trunks to their offspring.

Jean Baptiste Lamarck proposed an alternative mechanism of evolution. Lamarck believed individual organisms developed traits in response to changing environmental conditions and passed on these new, favorable traits to their offspring. For example, Lamarck argued that the trunks of individual elephants lengthened as a result of stretching for scarce food and water, and elephants pass on the longer trunks to their offspring. Thus, in contrast to Darwin's relatively random natural selection, Lamarck believed the mechanism of evolution followed a predetermined plan and depended on the desires and needs of individual organisms.

Different molecular and environmental processes and conditions drive the evolution of populations. The various mechanisms of evolution either introduce new genetic variation or alter the frequency of existing variation.

Mutations–random changes in nucleotide sequence, are a basic mechanism of evolution. Mutations in DNA result from copying errors during cell division, exposure to radiation and chemicals, and interaction with viruses. Simple point mutations, deletions, or insertions can alter the function or expression of existing genes, but do not contribute greatly to evolution. On the other hand, gene duplication, the duplication of an entire gene, often leads to the creation of new genes that may contribute to the evolution of a species. Because gene duplication results in two copies of the same gene, the extra copy is free to mutate and develop without the selective pressure experienced by mutated single-copy genes. Gene duplication, and subsequent mutation, often leads to the creation of new genes. When new genes resulting from mutations lend the mutated organism a reproductive advantage relative to environmental conditions, natural selection and evolution can occur.

Recombination–is the exchange of DNA between a pair of chromosomes during meiosis. Recombination does not introduce new genes into a population, but does affect the expression of genes and the combination of traits expressed by individuals. Thus, recombination increases the genetic diversity of populations and contributes to evolution by creating new combinations of genes that nature selects for or against.

Isolation–is the separation of members of a species by environmental barriers that the organisms cannot cross. Environmental change, either gradual or sudden, often results in isolation. An example of gradual isolation is the formation of a mountain range or dessert between members of a species. An example of sudden isolation is the separation of species members by a flood or earthquake. Isolation leads to evolution because the separated groups cannot reproduce together, and differences arise. In addition, because the environment of each group is different, the groups adapt and evolve differently. Extended isolation can lead to speciation, the development of new species.

Sexual Reproduction and Selection–contributes to evolution by consolidating genetic mutations and creating new combinations of genes. Genetic recombination during sexual reproduction, as previously discussed, introduces new combinations of traits and patterns of gene expression. Consolidation of favorable mutations through sexual reproduction speeds the processes of evolution and natural selection. On the other hand, consolidation of deleterious mutations creates completely unfit individuals that are readily eliminated from the population.

Genetic Drift–is, along with natural selection, one of the two main mechanisms of evolution. Genetic drift refers to the chance deviation in the frequency of alleles (traits) resulting from the randomness of zygote formation and selection. Because only a small percentage of all possible zygotes become mature adults, parents do not necessarily pass all of their alleles on to their offspring. Genetic drift is particularly important in small populations because chance deviations in allelic frequency can quickly alter the genotypic make-up of the population. In extreme cases, certain alleles may completely disappear from the gene pool. Genetic drift is particularly influential when environmental events and conditions produce small, isolated populations.

Plate Tectonics–is the theory that the Earth's surface consists of large plates. Movement and shifting of the plates dictate the location of continents, formation of mountains and seas, and volcanic and earthquake activity. Such contributions to environmental conditions influence the evolution of species. For example, tectonic activity resulting in mountain formation or continent separation can cause genetic isolation. In addition, the geographic distribution of species is indicative of evolutionary history and related tectonic activity.

Skill 13.6   Apply knowledge of principles and procedures (e.g., safety practices) related to the design and implementation of scientific investigations and processes to develop explanations of natural phenomena related to life and environmental science

Laboratory Safety Procedures
All science labs should contain the following items of **safety equipment**. Those marked with an asterisk are requirements by state laws.

- An ABC fire extinguisher.
- Chemical spill control kit.
- Containers for broken glassware, flammables, corrosives and waste (container should be labeled).
- Emergency exhaust fans providing ventilation to the outside of the building.
- Emergency eye wash station which that can be activated by the foot or forearm.
- Emergency shower providing a continuous flow of water.
- Eye protection for every student and a means of sanitizing equipment.
- Fire blanket which that is visible and accessible.
- Fume hood with a motor which that is spark proof.
- Ground Fault Circuit Interrupters (GCFI) within two feet of water supplies.
- Have permanently attached handles. Cut-off switches must be clearly labeled.

- Master cut-off switches for gas, electric and compressed air. Switches must.
- Protective laboratory aprons made of flame retardant material.
- Signs designating room exits.
- Signs which that will alert potential hazardous conditions.
- Storage cabinets for flammable materials.

Students should wear safety goggles when performing dissections, heating, or while using acids and bases. Hair should always be tied back, and objects should never be placed in the mouth. Food should not be consumed while in the laboratory. Hands should always be washed before and after laboratory experiments. In case of an accident, eye washes and showers should be used for eye contamination or a chemical spill that covers a student's body. Small chemical spills should only be contained and cleaned by the teacher. Kitty litter or a chemical spill kit should be used to clean spills. For large spills, the school administration and the local fire department should be notified. Biological spills should also be handled only by the teacher. Contamination with biological waste can be cleaned by using bleach, when appropriate.

Accidents and injuries should always be reported to the school administration and local health facilities. The severity of the accident or injury will determine the course of action to pursue.

It is the responsibility of the teacher to provide a safe environment for students. Proper supervision greatly reduces the risk of injury, and a teacher should never leave a class for any reason without providing alternate supervision. After an accident, two factors are considered: **foreseeability** and **negligence**. Foreseeability is the anticipation that an event may occur under certain circumstances. Negligence is the failure to exercise ordinary or reasonable care. Safety procedures should be a part of the science curriculum, and a well-managed classroom is important to avoid potential lawsuits.

Storing, Identifying and Disposing of Chemicals and Biological Materials
All laboratory solutions should be prepared as directed in the lab manual. Care should be taken to avoid contamination. All glassware should be rinsed thoroughly with distilled water before using and cleaned well after use. All solutions should be made with distilled water, as tap water contains dissolved particles that may affect the results of an experiment. Unused solutions should be disposed of according to local disposal procedures.

The "Right to Know Law" covers science teachers who work with potentially hazardous chemicals. Briefly, the law states that employees must be informed of potentially toxic chemicals. An inventory must be made available if requested. The inventory must contain information about the hazards and properties of the chemicals. This inventory is to be checked against the "Substance List". Training must be provided on the safe handling and interpretation of the Material Safety Data Sheet.

The following chemicals are potential carcinogens and are not allowed in school facilities: Acrylonitriel, Arsenic compounds, Asbestos, Bensidine, Benzene, Cadmium compounds, Chloroform, Chromium compounds, Ethylene oxide, Ortho-toluidine, Nickle powder and Mercury.

Chemicals should not be stored on bench tops or heat sources. They should be stored in groups, based on their reactivity with one another, and in protective storage cabinets. All containers within the lab must be labeled. Suspect and known carcinogens must be labeled as such and segregated within trays to contain leaks and spills.

Chemical waste should be disposed of in properly-labeled containers. Waste should be separated based on its reactivity with other chemicals.

Biological material should never be stored near food or water that is used for human consumption. All biological material should be appropriately labeled. All blood and body fluids should be put in a container with a secure lid to prevent leaking. All biological waste should be disposed of in biological hazardous waste bags.

Material safety data sheets are available for every chemical and biological substance. These are available directly from the company of acquisition or the Internet. The manuals for equipment used in the lab should be read and understood before using them.

Use of Live Specimens
No dissections may be performed on living mammalian vertebrates or birds. Lower order life and invertebrates may be used. Biological experiments may be done with all animals except mammalian vertebrates or birds. No physiological harm may result to the animal. All animals housed and cared for in the school must be handled in a safe and humane manner. Animals are not to remain on school premises during extended vacations unless adequate care is provided. Any instructor who intentionally refuses to comply with the laws may be suspended or dismissed.

Pathogenic organisms must never be used for experimentation. Students should adhere to the following rules at all times when working with microorganisms to avoid accidental contamination:

1. Treat all microorganisms as if they were pathogenic.
2. Maintain sterile conditions at all times.

Dissection and Alternatives to Dissection

Animals that are not obtained from recognized sources should not be used. Decaying animals, or those of unknown origin, may harbor pathogens and/or parasites. Specimens should be rinsed before handling. Latex gloves are desirable. If not available, students with sores or scratches should be excused from the activity. Formaldehyde is likely carcinogenic and should be avoided or disposed of according to district regulations. Students objecting to dissections for moral reasons should be given an alternative assignment. Interactive dissections are available online or from software companies for those students who object to performing dissections. There should be no penalty for those students who refuse to physically perform a dissection.

Skill 13.7   Identify ways to incorporate the Illinois Learning Standards in the areas of life and environmental science in the development of instruction and Individualized Education Programs (IEPs)

(See Skill 7.8.)

Skill 13.8   Identify strategies for selecting and using a wide range of instructional resources, modes of inquiry and technologies to support learning in life and environmental science

Knowledge of Appropriate Use of Laboratory Materials

Bunsen burners—hot plates should be used whenever possible to avoid the risk of burns or fire. If Bunsen burners are used, the following precautions should be followed:

1. Know the location of fire extinguishers and safety blankets, and train students in their use. Long hair and long sleeves should be secured and out of the way.
2. Turn the gas all the way on, and make a spark with the striker. The preferred method to light burners is to use strikers rather than matches.
3. Adjust the air valve at the bottom of the Bunsen burner until the flame shows an inner cone.
4. Adjust the flow of gas to the desired flame height by using the adjustment valve.
5. Do not touch the barrel of the burner. (It is hot.)

Graduated Cylinder–these are used for precise measurements. They should always be placed on a flat surface. The surface of the liquid will form a meniscus (lens-shaped curve). The measurement is read at the <u>bottom</u> of this curve.

Balance–electronic balances are easier to use, but more expensive. An electronic balance should always be tarred (returned to zero) before measuring and used on a flat surface. Substances should always be placed on a piece of paper to avoid spills and/or damage to the instrument. Triple beam balances must be used on a level surface. There are screws located at the bottom of the balance to make any adjustments. Start with the largest counterweight first, and proceed toward the last notch that does not tip the balance. Do the same with the next largest, etc. until the pointer remains at zero. The total mass is the total of all the readings on the beams. Again, use paper under the substance to protect the equipment.

Buret–a buret is used to dispense precisely measured volumes of liquid. A stopcock is used to control the volume of liquid being dispensed at a time.

Light microscopes–these are commonly used in laboratory experiments. Several procedures should be followed to properly care for this equipment:

- Clean all lenses with lens paper only.
- Carry microscopes with two hands: one on the arm and one on the base.
- Always begin focusing on low power; then, switch to high power.
- Store microscopes with the low power objective down.
- Always use a coverslip when viewing wet mount slides.
- Bring the objective down to its lowest position; then focus by moving up to avoid breaking the slide or scratching the lens.

Wet Mount Slides–should be made by placing a drop of water on the specimen and then putting a glass coverslip on top of the drop of water. Dropping the coverslip at a forty-five degree angle will help in avoiding air bubbles. Total magnification is determined by multiplying the ocular (usually 10X) and the objective (usually 10X on low, 40X on high).

Chromatography–uses the principles of capillarity to separate substances, such as plant pigments. Molecules of a larger size will move slower up the paper, whereas smaller molecules will move more quickly, producing lines of pigment.

An **indicator** is any substance used to assist in the classification of another substance. An example of an indicator is litmus paper. Litmus paper is a way to measure whether a substance is acidic or basic. Blue litmus turns pink when an acid is placed on it, and pink litmus turns blue when a base is placed on it. pH paper is a more accurate measure of pH, with the paper turning different colors depending on the pH value.

Spectrophotometry–measures percent of light at different wavelengths absorbed and transmitted by a pigment solution.

Centrifugation–involves spinning substances at a high speed. The more dense part of a solution will settle to the bottom of the test tube, where the lighter material will stay on top. Centrifugation is used to separate blood into blood cells and plasma, with the heavier blood cells settling to the bottom.

Electrophoresis–uses electrical charges of molecules to separate them according to their size. The molecules, such as DNA or proteins, are pulled through a gel towards either the positive end of the gel box (if the material has a negative charge) or the negative end of the gel box (if the material has a positive charge). DNA is negatively charged and moves towards the positive charge.

COMPETENCY 14.0   UNDERSTAND FUNDAMENTAL CONCEPTS AND PRINCIPLES RELATED TO PHYSICAL SCIENCE.

Skill 14.1   Recognize basic concepts related to matter and energy

Everything in our world is made up of **matter**, whether it is a rock, a building, an animal, or a person. Matter is defined by its characteristics: It takes up space, and it has mass.

Mass–a measure of the amount of matter in an object. Two objects of equal mass will balance each other on a simple balance scale, no matter where the scale is located. For instance, two rocks with the same amount of mass that are in balance on Earth will also be in balance on the moon. They will feel heavier on Earth than on the moon because of the gravitational pull of the Earth. So, although the two rocks have the same mass, they will have different **weight.**

Weight–measure of the Earth's pull of gravity on an object. It can also be defined as the pull of gravity between other bodies. The units of weight measurement commonly used are the pound (English measure) and the kilogram (metric measure).

In addition to mass, matter also has the property of volume. **Volume** is the amount of cubic space that an object occupies. Volume and mass together give a more exact description of the object. Two objects may have the same volume, but different mass, or the same mass but different volumes, etc. For instance, consider two cubes that are each one cubic centimeter, one made from plastic, one from lead. They have the same volume, but the lead cube has more mass. The measure that we use to describe the cubes takes into consideration both the mass and the volume. **Density** is the mass of a substance contained per unit of volume. If the density of an object is less than the density of a liquid, the object will float in the liquid. If the object is denser than the liquid, then the object will sink.

Density is stated in grams per cubic centimeter (g/cm^3), where the gram is the standard unit of mass. To find an object's density, you must measure its mass and its volume. Then divide the mass by the volume ($D = m/V$). To discover an object's density, first use a balance to find its mass. Then calculate its volume. If the object is a regular shape, you can find the volume by multiplying the length, width, and height together. However, if it is an irregular shape, you can find the volume by seeing how much water it displaces. Measure the water in the container before and after the object is submerged. The difference will be the volume of the object.

Specific Gravity–is the ratio of the density of a substance to the density of water. For instance, the specific density of one liter of turpentine is calculated by comparing its mass (0.81 kg) to the mass of one liter of water (1 kg):

$$\frac{\text{mass of 1 L alcohol}}{\text{mass of 1 L water}} = \frac{0.81 \text{ kg}}{1.00 \text{ kg}} = 0.81$$

Physical properties and chemical properties of matter describe the appearance or behavior of a substance. A **physical property** can be observed without changing the identity of a substance. For instance, you can describe the color, mass, shape, and volume of a book. **Chemical properties** describe the ability of a substance to be changed into new substances. Baking powder goes through a chemical change as it changes into carbon dioxide gas during the baking process.

Matter constantly changes. A **physical change** is a change that does not produce a new substance. The freezing and melting of water is an example of physical change. A **chemical change** (or chemical reaction) is any change of a substance into one or more other substances. Burning materials turn into smoke; a seltzer tablet fizzes into gas bubbles.

The **phase of matter** (solid, liquid, or gas) is identified by its shape and volume.

Solid–a definite shape and volume. A **liquid** has a definite volume, but no shape. A **gas** has no shape or volume because it will spread out to occupy the entire space of whatever container it is in.

While plasma is really a type of gas, its properties are so unique that it is considered a unique phase of matter. **Plasma is a gas that has been ionized**, meaning that at least one electron has been removed from some of its atoms. Plasma shares some characteristics with gas, specifically, the **high kinetic energy** of its molecules. Thus, plasma exists as a diffuse "cloud," though it sometimes includes tiny grains (termed dusty plasma). What most distinguishes plasma from gas is that it is **electrically conductive** and exhibits a strong response to electromagnetic fields. This property is a consequence of the **charged particles that result from the removal of electrons** from the molecules in the plasma.

Energy–the ability to cause change in matter. Applying heat to a frozen liquid changes it from solid back to liquid. Continue heating it and it will boil and give off steam, a gas.

Evaporation is the change in phase from liquid to gas. **Condensation** is the change in phase from gas to liquid.

Skill 14.2   Recognize the physical and chemical properties of matter

Atom–a nucleus surrounded by a cloud with moving electrons.

The **nucleus** is the center of the atom. The positive particles inside the nucleus are called **protons.** The mass of a proton is about 2,000 times that of the mass of an electron. The number of protons in the nucleus of an atom is called the **atomic number.** All atoms of the same element have the same atomic number.

Neutrons–type of particle in the nucleus. Neutrons and protons have about the same mass, but neutrons have no charge. Neutrons were discovered because scientists observed that not all atoms in neon gas have the same mass. They had identified isotopes. **Isotopes** of an element have the same number of protons in the nucleus, but have different masses. Neutrons explain the difference in mass. They have mass but no charge.

The mass of matter is measured against a standard mass, such as the gram. Scientists measure the mass of an atom by comparing it to that of a standard atom. The result is relative mass. The **relative mass** of an atom is its mass expressed in terms of the mass of the standard atom. The isotope of the element carbon is the standard atom. It has six (6) neutrons and is called carbon-12. It is assigned a mass of 12 atomic mass units (amu). Therefore, the **atomic mass unit (amu)** is the standard unit for measuring the mass of an atom. It is equal to the mass of a carbon atom.

The **mass number** of an atom is the sum of its protons and neutrons. In any element, there is a mixture of isotopes, some having slightly more or slightly fewer protons and neutrons. The **atomic mass** of an element is an average of the mass numbers of its atoms.

The following table summarizes the terms used to describe atomic nuclei:

Term	Example	Meaning	Characteristic
Atomic Number	# protons (p)	same for all atoms of a given element	Carbon (C) atomic number = 6 (6p)
Mass Number	# protons + # neutrons (p + n)	changes for different isotopes of an element	C-12 (6p + 6n) C-13 (6p + 7n)
Atomic Mass	average mass of the atoms of the element	usually not a whole number	atomic mass of carbon equals 12.011

Each atom has an equal number of electrons (negative) and protons (positive). Therefore, atoms are neutral. Electrons orbiting the nucleus occupy energy levels that are arranged in order, and the electrons tend to occupy the lowest energy level available. A **stable electron arrangement** is an atom that has all of its electrons in the lowest possible energy levels.

Each energy level holds a maximum number of electrons. However, an atom with more than one level does not hold more than 8 electrons in its outermost shell.

Level	Name	Max. # of Electrons
First	K shell	2
Second	L shell	8
Third	M shell	18
Fourth	N shell	32

This can help explain why chemical reactions occur. Atoms react with each other when their outer levels are unfilled. When atoms either exchange or share electrons with each other, these energy levels become filled, and the atom becomes more stable.

As an electron gains energy, it moves from one energy level to a higher energy level. The electron cannot leave one level until it has enough energy to reach the next level. **Excited electrons** are electrons that have absorbed energy and have moved farther from the nucleus.

Electrons can also lose energy. When they do, they fall to a lower level. However, they can only fall to the lowest level that has room for them. This explains why atoms do not collapse.

Skill 14.3 Demonstrate knowledge of characteristics of different forms of energy

Dynamics is the study of the relationship between motion and the forces affecting motion. **Force** causes motion.

Mass and weight are not the same quantities. An object's **mass** gives it a reluctance to change its current state of motion. It is also the measure of an object's resistance to acceleration. The force that the Earth's gravity exerts on an object with a specific mass is called the object's weight on Earth. Weight is a force that is measured in Newtons. Weight (W) = mass times acceleration due to gravity (**W = mg**). To illustrate the difference between mass and weight, picture two rocks of equal mass on a balance scale. If the scale is balanced in one place, it will be balanced everywhere, regardless of the gravitational field. However, the weight of the stones would vary on a spring scale, depending upon the gravitational field. In other words, the stones would be balanced both on Earth and on the moon. However, the weight of the stones would be greater on Earth than on the moon. Surfaces that touch each other have a certain resistance to motion. This resistance is **friction**:

- The materials that make up the surfaces will determine the magnitude of the frictional force.
- The frictional force is independent of the area of contact between the two surfaces.
- The direction of the frictional force is opposite to the direction of motion.
- The frictional force is proportional to the normal force between the two surfaces in contact.

Static Friction—describes the force of friction of two surfaces that are in contact but do not have any motion relative to each other, such as a block sitting on an inclined plane. **Kinetic friction** describes the force of friction of two surfaces in contact with each other when there is relative motion between the surfaces. When an object moves in a circular path, a force must be directed toward the center of the circle in order to keep the motion going. This constraining force is called **centripetal force**. Gravity is the centripetal force that keeps a satellite circling the earth.

Electrical force is the influential power resulting from electricity as an attractive or repulsive interaction between two charged objects. The electric force is determined using Coulomb's law. As shown below, the appropriate unit on charge is the Coulomb (C), and the appropriate unit on distance is meters (m). Use of these units will result in a force expressed in units of Newtons. The demand for these units emerges from the units on Coulomb's constant.

$$F_{elect} = k \cdot Q_1 \cdot Q_2 / d^2$$

There is something of a mystery as to how objects affect each other when they are not in mechanical contact. Newton wrestled with the concept of "action-at-a-distance" (as Electrical Force is now classified) and eventually concluded that it was necessary for there to be some form of ether, or intermediate medium, which made it possible for one object to transfer force to another. We now know that no ether exists. It is possible for objects to exert forces on one another without any medium to transfer the force. From our fluid notion of electrical forces, however, we still associate forces as being due to the exchange of something between the two objects. The electrical field force acts between two charges, in the same way that the gravitational field force acts between two masses.

Magnetic Force—magnetized items interact with other items in very specific ways. If a magnet is brought close enough to a ferromagnetic material (that is not magnetized itself) the magnet will strongly attract the ferromagnetic material, regardless of orientation. Both the north and south pole of the magnet will attract the other item with equal strength. In opposition, diamagnetic materials weakly repel a magnetic field. This occurs regardless of the north/south orientation of the field. Paramagnetic materials are weakly attracted to a magnetic field.

Calculating—the attractive or repulsive magnetic force between two magnets is, in the general case, an extremely complex operation, as it depends on the shape, magnetization, orientation and separation of the magnets.

In the **Nuclear Force**, the protons in the nucleus of an atom are positively charged. If protons interact, they are usually pushed apart by the electromagnetic force. However, when two or more nuclei come VERY close together, the nuclear force comes into play. The nuclear force is a hundred times stronger than the electromagnetic force, so the nuclear force may be able to "glue" the nuclei together so fusion can happen. The nuclear force is also known as the strong force. The nuclear force keeps together the most basic of elementary particles, the quarks. Quarks combine together to form the protons and neutrons in the atomic nucleus.

The **force of gravity** is the force at which the Earth, moon, or other massively large objects attract another object towards themselves. By definition, this is the weight of the object. All objects upon Earth experience a force of gravity that is directed "downward" towards the center of the Earth. The force of gravity on Earth is always equal to the weight of the object, as found by the equation:

Fgrav = m * g

where g = 9.8 m/s^2 (on Earth) and m = mass (in kg)

Skill 14.4   Analyze the interactions of matter and energy in a system, including transfers and transformations of energy and changes in matter

(See skill 14.3.)

Skill 14.5   Apply knowledge of principles and procedures (e.g., safety practices) related to the design and implementation of scientific investigations and processes to develop explanations of natural phenomena related to physical science

When completing any science procedure, you want to be sure to take the necessary safety precautions for your students. This may include: wearing protective gloves or glasses, limiting experiments due to the possible danger within the classroom, or demonstrating more complex or dangerous experiments, along with other common sense items. When in doubt, ask an administrator before completing an experiment.

Skill 14.6   Identify ways to develop lesson plans that incorporate physical science curriculum, instructional strategies and everyday applications into individualized education goals and benchmarks

(See Skill 7.8.)

Skill 14.7   Identify ways to incorporate the Illinois Learning Standards in the area of physical science in the development of instruction and Individualized Education Programs (IEPs)

(See Skill 7.8.)

Skill 14.8   Identify strategies for selecting and using a wide range of instructional resources, modes of inquiry and technologies to support learning in physical science

In any curriculum area, it is essential that when presenting content in the area, the teacher utilize a wide range of instructional resources and incorporate technology to ensure the success of the students.

Providing the students with hands-on models, acting out scenarios, using drama, experiments and other manipulatives can provide a key component to successful mastery of the content presented. The Internet provides a valuable resource with movies, clips, animated interactive representations, and a wealth of other information the students can access. WebQuests, or other interactive Internet activities, are generally fun learning experiences for the students.

COMPETENCY 15.0 UNDERSTAND FUNDAMENTAL CONCEPTS AND PRINCIPLES RELATED TO EARTH AND SPACE SCIENCE.

Skill 15.1   Demonstrate knowledge of the geological composition and history of the earth

A fossil is the remains or trace of an ancient organism that has been preserved naturally in the Earth's crust. Sedimentary rocks usually are rich sources of fossil remains. Those fossils found in layers of sediment were embedded in the slowly forming sedimentary rock strata. The oldest fossils known are the traces of 3.5 billion-year-old bacteria found in sedimentary rocks. Few fossils are found in metamorphic rock, and virtually none are found in igneous rocks. The magma is so hot that any organism trapped in the magma is destroyed.

The fossil remains of a woolly mammoth embedded in ice were found by a group of Russian explorers. However, the best-preserved animal remains have been discovered in natural tar pits. When an animal accidentally fell into the tar, it became trapped, sinking to the bottom. Preserved bones of the saber-toothed cat have been found in tar pits.

Prehistoric insects have been found trapped in ancient amber or fossil resin that was excreted by some extinct species of pine trees.

Fossil molds are the hollow spaces in a rock previously occupied by bones or shells. A fossil cast is a fossil mold that fills with sediments or minerals that later hardens, forming a cast.

Fossil tracks are the imprints in hardened mud left behind by birds or animals.

The three major subdivisions of rocks are sedimentary, metamorphic and igneous.

Lithification of Sedimentary Rocks
When fluid sediments are transformed into solid sedimentary rocks, the process is known as lithification. One very common process affecting sediments is compaction where the weights of overlying materials compress and compact the deeper sediments. The compaction process leads to cementation. Cementation is when sediments are converted to sedimentary rock.

Factors in Crystallization of Igneous Rocks
Igneous rocks can be classified according to their texture, their composition and the way they formed.

Molten rock is called magma. When molten rock pours out onto the surface of Earth, it is called lava. As magma cools, the elements and compounds begin to form crystals. The slower the magma cools, the larger the crystals grow. Rocks with large crystals are said to have a coarse-grained texture. Granite is an example of a coarse-grained rock. Rocks that cool rapidly before any crystals can form have a glassy texture, such as obsidian, also commonly known as volcanic glass.

Metamorphic rocks are formed by high temperatures and great pressures. The process by which the rocks undergo these changes is called metamorphism. The outcomes of metamorphic changes include deformation by extreme heat and pressure, compaction, destruction of the original characteristics of the parent rock, bending and folding while in a plastic stage, and the emergence of completely new and different minerals due to chemical reactions with heated water and dissolved minerals.

Metamorphic rocks are classified into two groups, foliated (leaf-like) rocks and unfoliated rocks. Foliated rocks consist of compressed, parallel bands of minerals, which give the rocks a striped appearance. Examples of such rocks include slate, schist, and gneiss. Unfoliated rocks are not banded, and examples of such include quartzite, marble, and anthracite rocks.

Minerals are natural, non-living solids with a definite chemical composition and a crystalline structure. Ores are minerals or rock deposits that can be mined for a profit. Rocks are earth materials made of one or more minerals. A Rock Facies is a rock group that differs from comparable rocks (as in composition, age, or fossil content).

Characteristics by which Minerals are Classified
Minerals must adhere to five criteria. They must be (1) non-living, (2) formed in nature, (3) solid in form, (4) contain atoms that form a crystalline pattern, and (5) have a chemical composition that is fixed within narrow limits.

There are over 3000 minerals in Earth's crust. Minerals are classified by composition. The major groups of minerals are silicates, carbonates, oxides, sulfides, sulfates, and halides. The largest group of minerals is the silicates. Silicates are made of silicon, oxygen, and one or more other elements.

Soil
Soils are composed of particles of sand, clay, various minerals, tiny living organisms, and humus, plus the decayed remains of plants and animals. Soils are divided into three classes, according to their texture. These classes are sandy soils, clay soils and loamy soils.

Sandy soils are gritty, and their particles do not bind together firmly. Sandy soils are porous—water passes through them rapidly. Sandy soils do not hold much water.

Clay soils are smooth and greasy; their particles bind together firmly. Clay soils are moist and usually do not allow water to pass through easily.

Loamy soils feel somewhat like velvet, and their particles clump together. Loamy soils are made up of sand, clay, and silt. Loamy soils hold water, but some water can pass through.

In addition to three main classes, soils are further grouped into three major types, based upon their composition. These groups are pedalfers, pedocals and laterites.

Pedalfers form in the humid, temperate climate of the eastern United States. Pedalfer soils contain large amounts of iron oxide and aluminum-rich clays, making the soil a brown to reddish brown color. This soil supports forest type vegetation.

Pedocals are found in the western United States, where the climate is dry and temperate. These soils are rich in calcium carbonate. This type of soil supports grasslands and brush vegetation.

Laterites are found where the climate is wet and tropical. Large amounts of water flow through this soil. Laterites are red-orange soils rich in iron and aluminum oxides. There is little humus, and this soil is not very fertile.

Minerals

Minerals are natural inorganic compounds. They are solid, with homogenous crystal structures. Crystal structures are the 3-D geometric arrangements of atoms within minerals. Though these mineral grains are often too small to see, they can be visualized by X-ray diffraction. Both chemical composition and crystal structure determine mineral type. The chemical composition of minerals can vary from purely elemental to simple salts to complex compounds. However, it is possible for two or more minerals to have identical chemical composition, but varied crystal structure. Such minerals are known as polymorphs. One example of polymorphs demonstrates how crystal structures influence the physical properties of minerals with the same chemical composition: diamonds and graphite. Both are made from carbon, but diamonds are extremely hard because the carbon atoms are arranged in a strong 3-D network, while graphite is soft because the carbon atoms are present in sheets that slide past one another.

There are over 4,400 minerals on Earth, which are organized into the following classes:

Silicate Minerals—composed mostly of silicon and oxygen. This is the most abundant class of minerals on Earth and includes quartz, garnets, micas, and feldspars.

Carbonate Class Minerals –formed from compounds, including carbonate ions (e.g., calcium carbonate, magnesium carbonate and iron carbonate). They are common in marine environments, in caves (stalactite and stalagmites), and anywhere minerals can form via dissolution and precipitation. Nitrate and borate minerals are also in this class.

Sulfate minerals contain sulfate ions and are formed near bodies of water where slow evaporation allows precipitation of sulfates and halides. Sulfates include celestite, barite and gypsum.

Halide minerals include all minerals formed from natural salts, including calcium fluoride, sodium chloride, and ammonium chloride. Like the sulfides, these minerals are typically formed in evaporative settings. Minerals in this class include fluorite, halite and sylvite.

Oxide class minerals contain oxide compounds, including iron oxide, magnetite oxide, and chromium oxide. They are formed by various processes, including precipitation and oxidation of other minerals. These minerals form many ores and are important in mining. Hematite, chromite, rutile and magnetite are all examples of oxide minerals.

Sulfide Minerals—formed from sulfide compounds, such as iron sulfide, nickel iron sulfide, and lead sulfide. Several important metal ores are members of this class. Minerals in this class include pyrite (fool's gold) and galena.

Phosphate Class Minerals—include not only those containing phosphate ions, but any mineral with a tetrahedral molecular geometry in which an element is surrounded by four oxygen atoms. This can include elements such as phosphorous, arsenic, and antimony. Minerals in this class are important biologically, as they are common in teeth and bones. Phosphate, arsenate, vanadate and antimonite minerals are all in this class.

Element class minerals are formed from pure elements, whether they are metallic, semi-metallic, or non-metallic. Accordingly, minerals in this class include gold, silver, copper, bismuth, and graphite, as well as natural alloys, such as electrum and carbides.

Rocks

Rocks are simply aggregates of minerals. Rocks are classified by their differences in chemical composition and mode of formation. Generally, three classes are recognized: igneous, sedimentary and metamorphic. However, it is common that one type of rock is transformed into another, and this is known as the rock cycle.

Igneous rocks are formed from molten magma. There are two types of igneous rock: volcanic and plutonic. As the name suggests, volcanic rock is formed when magma reaches the Earth's surface as lava. Plutonic rock is also derived from magma, but it is formed when magma cools and crystallizes beneath the surface of the Earth. Thus, both types of igneous rock are magma that has cooled either above (volcanic) or below (plutonic) the Earth's crust. Examples of this type of rock include granite and obsidian glass.

Sedimentary rocks are formed by the layered deposition of inorganic and/or organic matter. Layers, or strata, of rock are laid down horizontally to form sedimentary rocks. Sedimentary rocks that form as mineral solutions (i.e., sea water) evaporate are called precipitate. Those that contain the remains of living organisms are termed biogenic. Finally, those that form from the freed fragments of other rocks are called clastic. Because the layers of sedimentary rocks reveal chronology and often contain fossils, these types of rock have been key in helping scientists understand the history of the Earth. Chalk, limestone, sandstone and shale are all examples of sedimentary rock.

Metamorphic rocks are created when rocks are subjected to high temperatures and pressures. The original rock, or protolith, may have been igneous, sedimentary, or even an older metamorphic rock. The temperatures and pressures necessary to achieve transformation are higher than those observed on the Earth's surface and are high enough to alter the minerals in the protolith. Because these rocks are formed within the Earth's crust, studying metamorphic rocks gives us clues to conditions in the Earth's mantle. In some metamorphic rocks, different colored bands are apparent. These result from strong pressures being applied from specific directions and is termed foliation. Examples of metamorphic rock include slate and marble.

Skill 15.2 Analyze the major features of the Earth in terms of the natural processes that shape them

Orogeny is the term given to natural mountain building.

A mountain is terrain that has been raised high above the surrounding landscape by volcanic action, or some form of tectonic plate collisions. The plate collisions could be intercontinental or ocean floor collisions with a continental crust (subduction). The physical composition of mountains would include igneous, metamorphic or sedimentary rocks; some may have rock layers that are tilted or distorted by plate collision forces.

There are many different types of mountains. The physical attributes of a mountain range depends upon the angle at which plate movement thrust layers of rock to the surface. Many mountains (Adirondacks, Southern Rockies) were formed along high angle faults.

Folded mountains (Alps, Himalayas) are produced by the folding of rock layers during their formation. The Himalayas are the highest mountains in the world and contain Mount Everest, which rises almost 9 km above sea level. The Himalayas were formed when India collided with Asia. The movement that created this collision is still in process at the rate of a few centimeters per year.

Fault-block mountains (Utah, Arizona and New Mexico) are created when plate movement produces tension forces instead of compression forces. The area under tension produces normal faults, and rock along these faults is displaced upward.

Dome mountains are formed as magma tries to push up through the crust but fails to break the surface. Dome mountains resemble a huge blister on the Earth's surface.

Upwarped mountains (Black Hills of S.D.) are created in association with a broad arching of the crust. They can also be formed by rock thrust upward along high angle faults.

Volcanism is the term given to the movement of magma through the crust and its emergence as lava onto the Earth's surface. Volcanic mountains are built up by successive deposits of volcanic materials.

An active volcano is one that is presently erupting or building to an eruption. A dormant volcano is one that is between eruptions but still shows signs of internal activity that might lead to an eruption in the future. An extinct volcano is said to be no longer capable of erupting. Most of the world's active volcanoes are found along the rim of the Pacific Ocean, which is also a major earthquake zone. This curving belt of active faults and volcanoes is often called the Ring of Fire.

The world's best known volcanic mountains include: Mount Etna in Italy and Mount Kilimanjaro in Africa. The Hawaiian Islands are actually the tops of a chain of volcanic mountains that rise from the ocean floor.

There are three types of volcanic mountains: shield volcanoes, cinder cones, and composite volcanoes.

Shield Volcanoes—associated with quiet eruptions. Lava emerges from the vent or opening in the crater and flows freely out over the Earth's surface until it cools and hardens into a layer of igneous rock. A repeated lava flow builds this type of volcano into the largest volcanic mountain. Mauna Loa, found in Hawaii, is the largest volcano on Earth.

Cinder Cone Volcanoes—associated with explosive eruptions as lava is hurled high into the air in a spray of droplets of various sizes. These droplets cool and harden into cinders and particles of ash before falling to the ground. The ash and cinder pile up around the vent to form a steep, cone-shaped hill called the cinder cone. Cinder cone volcanoes are relatively small but may form quite rapidly.

Composite Volcanoes—described as being built by both lava flows and layers of ash and cinders. Mount Fuji in Japan, Mount St. Helens in Washington, USA and Mount Vesuvius in Italy are all famous composite volcanoes.

Mechanisms of Producing Mountains
Mountains are produced by different types of mountain-building processes. Most major mountain ranges are formed by the processes of folding and faulting.

Folded Mountains—produced by the folding of rock layers. Crustal movements may press horizontal layers of sedimentary rock together from the sides, squeezing them into wavelike folds. Up-folded sections of rock are called anticlines; down-folded sections of rock are called synclines. The Appalachian Mountains are an example of folded mountains, with long ridges and valleys in a series of anticlines and synclines formed by folded rock layers.

Faults—fractures in the Earth's crust that have been created by either tension or compression forces transmitted through the crust. These forces are produced by the movement of separate blocks of crust.

Faultings are categorized on the basis of the relative movement between the blocks on both sides of the fault plane. The movement can be horizontal, vertical, or oblique.

A Dip-Slip Fault—occurs when the movement of the plates is vertical and opposite. The displacement is in the direction of the inclination, or dip, of the fault. Dip-slip faults are classified as normal faults when the rock above the fault plane moves down relative to the rock below.

Reverse Faults—created when the rock above the fault plane moves up relative to the rock below. Reverse faults having a very low angle to the horizontal are also referred to as thrust faults.

Faults in which the dominant displacement is horizontal movement along the trend or strike (length) of the fault are called **strike-slip faults**. When a large strike-slip fault is associated with plate boundaries, it is called a **transform fault**. The San Andreas Fault in California is a well-known transform fault.

Faults that have both vertical and horizontal movement are called **oblique-slip faults**.

When lava cools, igneous rock is formed. This formation can occur either above ground or below ground.

Intrusive Rock—includes any igneous rock that was formed below the Earth's surface. Batholiths are the largest structures of intrusive type rock and are composed of near granite materials; they are the core of the Sierra Nevada Mountains.

Extrusive Rock—includes any igneous rock that was formed at the Earth's surface.

Dikes—old lava tubes formed when magma entered a vertical fracture and hardened. Sometimes magma squeezes between two rock layers and hardens into a thin horizontal sheet called a **sill**. A **laccolith** is formed in much the same way as a sill, but the magma that creates a laccolith is very thick and does not flow easily. It pools and forces the overlying strata, creating an obvious surface dome.

A **caldera** is normally formed by the collapse of the top of a volcano. This collapse can be caused by a massive explosion that destroys the cone and empties most, if not all, of the magma chamber below the volcano. The cone collapses into the empty magma chamber, forming a caldera.

An inactive volcano may have magma solidified in its pipe. This structure, called a volcanic neck, is resistant to erosion and today may be the only visible evidence of the past presence of an active volcano.

Glaciation

A continental glacier covered a large part of North America during the most recent ice age. Evidence of this glacial coverage remains as abrasive grooves, large boulders from northern environments dropped in southerly locations, glacial troughs created by the rounding out of steep valleys by glacial scouring, and the remains of glacial sources called cirques that were created by frost wedging the rock at the bottom of the glacier. Remains of plants and animals found in warm climates have been discovered in the moraines and outwash plains and they help to support the theory of periods of warmth during the past ice ages.

The Ice Age began about 2 -3 million years ago. This age saw the advancement and retreat of glacial ice over millions of years. Theories relating to the origin of glacial activity include Plate Tectonics, where it can be demonstrated that some continental masses, now in temperate climates, were at one time blanketed by ice and snow. Another theory involves changes in the Earth's orbit around the sun, changes in the angle of the Earth's axis, and the wobbling of the Earth's axis. Support for the validity of this theory has come from deep ocean research that indicates a correlation between climatic sensitive microorganisms and the changes in the Earth's orbital status.

About 12,000 years ago, a vast sheet of ice covered a large part of the northern United States. This huge, frozen mass had moved southward from the northern regions of Canada as several large bodies of slow-moving ice, or glaciers. A time period in which glaciers advance over a large portion of a continent is called an ice age. A glacier is a large mass of ice that moves or flows over the land in response to gravity. Glaciers form among high mountains and in other cold regions.

There are two main types of glaciers: valley glaciers and continental glaciers. Erosion by valley glaciers is characteristic of U-shaped erosion. They produce sharp peaked mountains such as the Matterhorn in Switzerland. Erosion by continental glaciers often rides over mountains in their paths, leaving smoothed, rounded mountains and ridges.

Skill 15.3   Demonstrate knowledge of the water cycle

Water is conserved, except for chemical or nuclear reactions, and any drop of water could circulate through clouds, rain, ground water and surface water.

All natural chemical cycles, including the Water Cycle, depend on the principle of Conservation of Mass. (For water, unlike for elements such as Nitrogen, chemical reactions may cause sources or sinks of water molecules.) Any drop of water may circulate through the hydrologic system, ending up in a cloud, as rain, or as surface or ground water.

Air Masses—moving toward or away from the Earth's surface are called air currents. Air moving parallel to Earth's surface is called **wind**. Weather conditions are generated by winds and air currents carrying large amounts of heat and moisture from one part of the atmosphere to another. Wind speeds are measured by instruments called anemometers.

The wind belts in each hemisphere consist of convection cells that encircle Earth like belts. There are three major wind belts on Earth: (1) trade winds, (2) prevailing westerlies, and (3) polar easterlies. Wind belt formation depends on the differences in air pressures that develop in the doldrums, the horse latitudes, and the polar regions. The Doldrums surround the equator. Within this belt, heated air usually rises straight up into Earth's atmosphere. The Horse latitudes are regions of high barometric pressure with calm and light winds, and the Polar Regions contain cold dense air that sinks to the Earth's surface.

Winds caused by local temperature changes include sea breezes and land breezes.

Sea Breezes—caused by the unequal heating of the land and an adjacent large body of water. Land heats up faster than water. The movement of cool ocean air toward the land is called a sea breeze. Sea breezes usually begin blowing about mid-morning, ending about sunset.

A breeze that blows from the land to the ocean or a large lake is called a **land breeze.**

Monsoons—huge wind systems that cover large geographic areas and that reverse direction seasonally. The monsoons of India and Asia are examples of these seasonal winds. They alternate wet and dry seasons. As denser, cooler air over the ocean moves inland, a steady seasonal wind, called a summer or wet monsoon, is produced.

Skill 15.4   Recognize fundamental weather processes and phenomena and the factors that influence them

Earthquakes

An earthquake is a destructive force, brought about by the interactions and movements between the Earth's tectonic plates. Often occurring among the plate edges, earthquakes range from being destructive to barely noticeable. If the intensity is high, there could be loss of life and damage to properties.

Factors Influencing the Location of Earthquakes

1. **Plate Convergence, Divergence or Sliding Past One Another**: These are the most important reasons for earthquakes to occur.
2, **Volcanic Activity**: Areas with earthquakes coincide with areas with volcanic activity.
3, **Percent Distribution of Earthquakes**: 70% of the earthquakes occur in the Circum-Pacific region, and 20% in the belt stretching from the Himalayan mountains to the Mediterranean Sea. The remaining 10% occur in divergent plate boundaries, such as the Mid-Atlantic Ridge.

Factors Influencing the Intensity of the Earthquakes

1. **Magnitude of Earthquakes**: of the estimated 6000 earthquakes a year, only 50 cause huge damage to people and properties, and these are above 6.0 on the Richter scale.
2. **Depth of Focus**: earthquakes which have a focus around 70 Km deep are the most devastating and destructive.
3. **Proximity to the Epicenter**: areas closer to the epicenter suffer huge damages compared with areas farther away.
4. **Geology of Epicenter**: an epicenter made of soft rocks will suffer more damage than an epicenter made of hard rocks.
5. **Types of Buildings**: weaker and older buildings are a threat to many lives, as opposed to buildings reinforced to withstand earthquakes.

Plate Tectonics

Plate tectonics is a theory of geology that was developed to explain the observed evidence for large scale motion within the Earth's crust. This theory superseded the older theory of Continental Drift by Alfred Wagener of Germany.

The outermost part of the Earth's crust is made up of two layers. Above is the lithosphere, comprising the rigid uppermost part of the mantle. Below the lithosphere lies the athenosphere, which is a more viscous zone of the mantle.

The influence of plate tectonics on climate, geography, and distribution of organisms:

Plate boundaries are commonly associated with geological events, such as earthquakes, mountains, volcanoes and oceanic trenches.

The left or right lateral motion of one plate against another along transform faults can cause highly-visible surface effects, such as earthquakes along transform boundaries. A good example of this is the San Andreas Fault in North America.

The evidence for the movement of plates is found in the observations of the distribution of the same species of plants in areas like western Africa and the eastern part of South America. The same type of fossils and fauna were also found in areas, which were supposed to be one piece before the continents drifted away. Similar observations were recorded regarding the climate.

Basing on all these, we can conclude that the Earth is made up of several plates, and the plates were separated and are in the present form as continents. We also has evidences in the distribution of flora and fauna.

El Niño refers to a sequence of changes in the ocean and atmospheric circulation across the Pacific Ocean. The water around the equator is unusually hot every two to seven years. Trade winds normally blow east to west across the equatorial latitudes, piling warm water into the western Pacific. A huge mass of heavy thunderstorms usually forms in the area and produces vast currents of rising air that displace heat poleward. This helps create the strong mid-latitude jet streams. The world's climate patterns are disrupted by this change in location of thunderstorm activity.

Air Masses–moving toward or away from the Earth's surface are called air currents. Air moving parallel to Earth's surface is called **wind**. Weather conditions are generated by winds and air currents carrying large amounts of heat and moisture from one part of the atmosphere to another. Wind speeds are measured by instruments called anemometers.

The wind belts in each hemisphere consist of convection cells that encircle Earth like belts. There are three major wind belts on Earth: (1) trade winds, (2) prevailing westerlies, and (3) polar easterlies. Wind belt formation depends on the differences in air pressures that develop in the doldrums, the horse latitudes, and the Polar Regions. The Doldrums surround the equator. Within this belt, heated air usually rises straight up into Earth's atmosphere. The Horse latitudes are regions of high barometric pressure with calm and light winds, and the Polar Regions contain cold dense air that sinks to the Earth's surface.

Winds caused by local temperature changes include sea breezes and land breezes.

Sea Breezes–caused by the unequal heating of the land and an adjacent large body of water. Land heats up faster than water. The movement of cool ocean air toward the land is called a sea breeze. Sea breezes usually begin blowing about mid-morning, ending about sunset.

A breeze that blows from the land to the ocean or a large lake is called a **land breeze**.

Monsoons–huge wind systems that cover large geographic areas and that reverse direction seasonally. The monsoons of India and Asia are examples of these seasonal winds. They alternate wet and dry seasons. As denser, cooler air over the ocean moves inland, a steady seasonal wind, called a summer or wet monsoon, is produced.

The air temperature at which water vapor begins to condense is called the **dew point.**

Relative Humidity–is the actual amount of water vapor in a certain volume of air, compared to the maximum amount of water vapor this air could hold at a given temperature.

Knowledge of Types of Storms

A **thunderstorm** is a brief, local storm produced by the rapid upward movement of warm, moist air within a cumulonimbus cloud. Thunderstorms always produce lightning and thunder and are accompanied by strong wind gusts and heavy rain or hail.

A severe storm with swirling winds that may reach speeds of hundreds of kilometers per hour is called a **tornado**. Such a storm is also referred to as a "twister". The sky is covered by large cumulonimbus clouds and violent thunderstorms, and a funnel-shaped swirling cloud may extend downward from a cumulonimbus cloud and reach the ground. Tornadoes are storms that leave a narrow path of destruction on the ground.

A swirling, funnel-shaped cloud that **extends** downward and touches a body of water is called a **waterspout.**

Hurricanes–storms that develop when warm, moist air carried by trade winds rotates around a low-pressure "eye." A large, rotating, low-pressure system accompanied by heavy precipitation and strong winds is called a tropical cyclone (better known as a hurricane). In the Pacific region, a hurricane is called a typhoon.

Storms that occur only in the winter are known as blizzards or ice storms. A **blizzard** is a storm with strong winds, blowing snow and frigid temperatures. An **ice storm** consists of falling rain that freezes when it strikes the ground, covering everything with a layer of ice.

Skill 15.5 Demonstrate knowledge of the basic components and structure of the solar system

There are eight established planets in our solar system: Mercury, Venus, Earth, Mars, Jupiter, Saturn, Uranus and Neptune. Pluto was an established planet in our solar system, but as of Summer 2006, its status is being reconsidered. The planets are divided into two groups based on distance from the sun. The inner planets include: Mercury, Venus, Earth and Mars. The outer planets include: Jupiter, Saturn, Uranus, and Neptune.

Mercury is the closest planet to the sun. Its surface has craters and rocks. The atmosphere is composed of hydrogen, helium and sodium. Mercury was named after the Roman messenger god.

Venus has a slow rotation when compared to Earth. Venus and Uranus rotate in opposite directions from the other planets. This opposite rotation is called retrograde rotation. The surface of Venus is not visible, due to the extensive cloud cover. The atmosphere is composed mostly of carbon dioxide. Sulfuric acid droplets in the dense cloud cover give Venus a yellow appearance. Venus has a greater greenhouse effect than observed on Earth. The dense clouds, combined with carbon dioxide and trap heat. Venus was named after the Roman goddess of love.

Earth is considered a water planet, with 70% of its surface covered by water. Gravity holds the masses of water in place. The different temperatures observed on Earth allow for the different states (solid, liquid, gas) of water to exist. The atmosphere is composed mainly of oxygen and nitrogen. Earth is the only planet that is known to support life.

Mars' surface contains numerous craters, active and extinct volcanoes, ridges, and valleys with extremely deep fractures. Iron oxide found in the dusty soil makes the surface seem rust colored and the skies seem pink in color. The atmosphere is composed of carbon dioxide, nitrogen, argon, oxygen and water vapor. Mars has Polar Regions with ice caps composed of water. Mars has two satellites. Mars was named after the Roman war god.

Jupiter is the largest planet in the solar system. Jupiter has 16 moons. The atmosphere is composed of hydrogen, helium, methane, and ammonia. There are white-colored bands of clouds, indicating rising gas and dark-colored bands of clouds, indicating descending gases. The gas movement is caused by heat resulting from the energy of Jupiter's core. Jupiter has a Great Red Spot that is thought to be a hurricane-type cloud. Jupiter has a strong magnetic field.

Saturn–second largest planet in the solar system. Saturn has rings of ice, rock, and dust particles circling it. Saturn's atmosphere is composed of hydrogen, helium, methane, and ammonia. Saturn has 20 plus satellites. Saturn was named after the Roman god of agriculture.

Uranus–second largest planet in the solar system with retrograde revolution. Uranus is a gaseous planet. It has 10 dark rings and 15 satellites. Its atmosphere is composed of hydrogen, helium, and methane. Uranus was named after the Greek god of the heavens.

Neptune–gaseous planet, with an atmosphere consisting of hydrogen, helium, and methane. Neptune has 3 rings and 2 satellites. Neptune was named after the Roman sea god because its atmosphere is the same color as the seas.

Pluto–once considered the smallest planet in the solar system; its status as a planet is being reconsidered . Pluto's atmosphere probably contains methane, ammonia, and frozen water. Pluto has 1 satellite. Pluto revolves around the sun every 250 years. Pluto was named after the Roman god of the underworld.

Comets, Asteroids and Meteors
Astronomers believe that rocky fragments may have been the remains of the birth of the solar system that never formed into a planet. **Asteroids** are found in the region between Mars and Jupiter.

Comets–masses of frozen gases, cosmic dust and small rocky particles. Astronomers think that most comets originate in a dense comet cloud beyond Pluto. A comet consists of a nucleus, a coma, and a tail. A comet's tail always points away from the sun. The most famous comet, **Halley's Comet**, is named after the person whom first discovered it in 240 B.C. It returns to the skies near Earth every 75 to 76 years.

Meteoroids–composed of particles of rock and metal of various sizes. When a meteoroid travels through the Earth's atmosphere, friction causes its surface to heat up, and it begins to burn. The burning meteoroid falling through the Earth's atmosphere is called a **meteor** (also known as a "shooting star").

Meteorites are meteors that strike the Earth's surface. A physical example of a meteorite's impact on the Earth's surface can be seen in Arizona. The Barringer Crater is a huge meteor crater. There are many other meteor craters throughout the world.

Oort Cloud and Kuiper Belt

The **Oort Cloud** is a hypothetical spherical cloud surrounding our solar system. It extends approximately 3 light years, or 30 trillion kilometers, from the sun. The cloud is believed to be made up of materials ejected out of the inner solar system because of interaction with Uranus and Neptune, but is gravitationally bound to the sun. It is named the Oort Cloud after Jan Oort, who suggested its existence in 1950. Comets from the Oort Cloud exhibit a wide range of sizes, inclinations, and eccentricities and are often referred to as Long-Period Comets because they have a period of greater than 200 years.

It seems that the Oort Cloud objects were formed closer to the sun than the Kuiper Belt objects. Small objects formed near the giant planets would have been ejected from the solar system by gravitational encounters. Those that didn't escape entirely formed the distant Oort Cloud. Small objects formed farther out had no such interactions and remained as the Kuiper Belt objects.

The **Kuiper Belt** is the name given to a vast population of small bodies orbiting the sun beyond Neptune. There are more than 70,000 of these small bodies, with diameters larger than 100 km, extending outwards from the orbit of Neptune to 50AU. They exist mostly within a ring or belt surrounding the sun. It is believed that the objects in the Kuiper Belt are primitive remnants of the earliest phases of the solar system. It is also believed that the Kuiper Belt is the source of many Short-Period Comets (periods of less then 200 years). It is a reservoir for the comets in the same way that the Oort Cloud is a reservoir for Long-Period Comets.

Occasionally, the orbit of a Kuiper Belt object will be disturbed by the interactions of the giant planets in such a way as to cause the object to cross the orbit of Neptune. It will then very likely have a close encounter with Neptune, sending it out of the solar system or into an orbit crossing those of the other giant planets or even into the inner solar system. Prevailing theory states that scattered disk objects began as Kuiper belt objects, which were scattered through gravitational interactions with the giant planets.

Skill 15.6 **Demonstrate knowledge of general principles and basic concepts of Earth and space science with regard to the composition, motions and interactions of the objects in the universe**

Earth is the third planet away from the sun in our solar system. Earth's numerous types of motion and states of orientation greatly affect global conditions, such as seasons, tides and lunar phases. The Earth orbits the sun with a period of 365 days. During this orbit, the average distance between the Earth and sun is 93 million miles. The shape of the Earth's orbit around the sun only deviates slightly from the shape of a circle. This deviation, known as the Earth's eccentricity, has a very small effect on the Earth's climate. The Earth is closest to the sun at perihelion, occurring around January 2nd of each year, and farthest from the sun at aphelion, occurring around July 2nd. Because the Earth is closest to the sun in January, the northern winter is slightly warmer than the southern winter.

Seasons
The rotation axis of the Earth is not perpendicular to the orbital (ecliptic) plane. The axis of the Earth is tilted 23.45° from the perpendicular. The tilt of the Earth's axis is known as the obliquity of the ecliptic and is mainly responsible for the four seasons of the year by influencing the intensity of solar rays received by the Northern and Southern Hemispheres. The four seasons—spring, summer, fall and winter—are extended periods of characteristic average temperature, rainfall, storm frequency, and vegetation growth or dormancy. The effect of the Earth's tilt on climate is best demonstrated at the solstices, the two days of the year when the sun is farthest from the Earth's equatorial plane. At the Summer Solstice (June Solstice), the Earth's tilt on its axis causes the Northern Hemisphere to the lean toward the sun, while the southern hemisphere leans away. Consequently, the Northern Hemisphere receives more intense rays from the sun and experiences summer during this time, while the Southern Hemisphere experiences winter. At the Winter Solstice (December Solstice), it is the Southern Hemisphere that leans toward the sun and thus experiences summer. Spring and fall are produced by varying degrees of the same leaning toward or away from the sun.

Tides
The orientation of, and gravitational interaction between, the Earth and the Moon are responsible for the ocean tides that occur on Earth. The term "tide" refers to the cyclic rise and fall of large bodies of water. Gravitational attraction is defined as the force of attraction between all bodies in the universe. At the location on Earth closest to the Moon, the gravitational attraction of the Moon draws seawater toward the Moon in the form of a tidal bulge. On the opposite side of the Earth, another tidal bulge forms in the direction away from the Moon because at this point, the Moon's gravitational pull is the weakest.

"Spring tides" are especially strong tides that occur when the Earth, Sun and Moon are in line, allowing both the Sun and the Moon to exert gravitational force on the Earth and increase tidal bulge height. These tides occur during the full moon and the new moon. "Neap tides" are especially weak tides, occurring when the gravitational forces of the Moon and the Sun are perpendicular to one another. These tides occur during quarter moons.

Lunar Phases

The Earth's orientation, in respect to the solar system, is also responsible for our perception of the phases of the moon. As the Earth orbits the Sun with a period of 365 days, the Moon orbits the Earth every 27 days. As the moon circles the Earth, its shape in the night sky appears to change. The changes in the appearance of the Moon from Earth are known as "lunar phases." These phases vary cyclically, according to the relative positions of the Moon, the Earth, and the Sun. At all times, half of the Moon is facing the Sun, and is thus illuminated by reflecting the Sun's light. As the Moon orbits the Earth, and the Earth orbits the Sun, the half of the moon that faces the Sun changes. However, the Moon is in synchronous rotation around the Earth, meaning that nearly the same side of the moon faces the Earth at all times. This side is referred to as the near side of the moon. Lunar phases occur as the Earth and Moon orbit the Sun, and the fractional illumination of the Moon's near side changes.

When the Sun and Moon are on opposite sides of the Earth, observers on Earth perceive a "full moon," meaning the moon appears circular because the entire illuminated half of the moon is visible. As the Moon orbits the Earth, the Moon "wanes" as the amount of the illuminated half of the Moon that is visible from Earth decreases. A gibbous moon is between a full moon and a half moon, or between a half moon and a full moon. When the Sun and the Moon are on the same side of Earth, the illuminated half of the moon is facing away from Earth, and the moon appears invisible. This lunar phase is known as the "new moon." The time between each full moon is approximately 29.53 days.

A list of all **lunar phases** includes:
- **New Moon**: The moon is invisible, or the first signs of a crescent appear.
- **Waxing Crescent**: The right crescent of the moon is visible.
- **First Quarter**: The right quarter of the moon is visible.
- **Waxing Gibbous**: Only the left crescent is not illuminated.
- **Full Moon**: The entire illuminated half of the moon is visible.
- **Waning Gibbous**: Only the right crescent of the moon is not illuminated.
- **Last Quarter**: The left quarter of the moon is illuminated.
- **Waning Crescent**: Only the left crescent of the moon is illuminated.

Viewing the moon from the Southern Hemisphere would cause these phases to occur in the opposite order.

Skill 15.7   **Apply knowledge of principles and procedures (e.g., safety practices) related to the design and implementation of scientific investigations and processes to develop explanations of natural phenomena related to Earth and space science**

(See Skill 14.5.)

Skill 15.8   **Identify ways to develop lesson plans that incorporate Earth and space science curriculum, instructional strategies, and everyday applications into individualized education goals and benchmarks**

(See Skill 7.8.)

Skill 15.9   **Identify ways to incorporate the Illinois Learning Standards in the areas of Earth and space science in the development of instruction and Individualized Education Programs (IEPs)**

(See Skill 7.8.)

Skill 15.10   **Identify strategies for selecting and using a wide range of instructional resources, modes of inquiry, and technologies to support learning in Earth and space science**

(See Skill 14.8.)

COMPETENCY 16.0 UNDERSTAND FUNDAMENTAL CONCEPTS AND PRINCIPLES RELATED TO GOVERNMENT, POLITICS, CITIZENSHIP, CIVICS, AND ECONOMICS.

Skill 16.1   Recognize basic purposes and concepts of government, including the constitutional principles and democratic foundations of the U.S. government and basic principles of law in the Illinois and U.S. constitutional systems

Articles of Confederation–this was the first political system under which the newly independent colonies tried to organize themselves. It was drafted after the Declaration of Independence in 1776, was passed by the Continental Congress on November 15, 1777, ratified by the thirteen states, and took effect on March 1, 1781. The Articles gave Congress the power to declare war, appoint military officers, and coin money. The Articles of Confederation limited the powers of Congress by giving the states final authority. Although Congress could pass laws, at least nine of the thirteen states had to approve a law before it went into effect. To get money, Congress had to ask each state for it; no state could be forced to pay. Thus, the Articles created a loose alliance among the thirteen states. The national government was weak, in part, because it didn't have a strong chief executive to carry out laws passed by the legislature. Many different disputes arose, and there was no way of settling them. Thus, the delegates went to meet again to try to fix the Articles; instead, they ended up scrapping them and created a new **Constitution** based on what was learned from these earlier mistakes.

The central government of the new United States of America consisted of a Congress of two to seven delegates from each state, with each state having just one vote. Some of its powers included: borrowing and coining money, directing foreign affairs, declaring war and making peace, building and equipping a navy, regulating weights and measures, and asking the states to supply men and money for an army. The delegates to Congress had no real authority, as each state carefully and jealously guarded its own interests and limited powers under the Articles. Also, the delegates to Congress were paid by their states and had to vote as directed by their state legislatures.

The serious weaknesses were the lack of power: to regulate finances, over interstate trade, over foreign trade, to enforce treaties, and over the military. Something better and more efficient was needed. In May of 1787, delegates from all states, except Rhode Island, began meeting in Philadelphia. At first, they met to revise the Articles of Confederation as instructed by Congress, but they soon realized that much more was needed. Abandoning the instructions, they set out to write a new Constitution, the foundation of all government in the United States, and a model for representative government throughout the world.

All these ideas found their final expression in the United States Constitution's first ten amendments, known as the **Bill of Rights.** In 1789, the first Congress passed these first amendments, and by December 1791, three-fourths of the states at that time had ratified them. The Bill of Rights protects certain liberties and basic rights. James Madison, who wrote the amendments, said that the Bill of Rights does not give Americans these rights.

Skill 16.2   Demonstrate knowledge of the basic structures and functions of federal, state, and local government in the United States and basic democratic principles, rights, values, and beliefs and their significance for individuals, groups and society.

In the United States, the three branches of the federal government—the **Executive**, the **Legislative** and the **Judicial**—divide their powers thus:

Legislative—Article I of the Constitution established the legislative, or law-making, branch of the government called the Congress. It is made up of two houses, the House of Representatives and the Senate. Voters in all states elect the members who serve in each respective house of Congress. The Legislative branch is responsible for making laws, raising and printing money, regulating trade, establishing the postal service and federal courts, approving the President's appointments, declaring war, and supporting the armed forces. The Congress also has the power to change the Constitution itself and to impeach (bring charges against) the president. Charges for impeachment are brought by the House of Representatives and are tried in the Senate.

Executive—Article II of the Constitution created the Executive branch of the government, headed by the president, who leads the country, recommends new laws, and can veto bills passed by the Legislative branch. As the chief of state, the president is responsible for carrying out the laws of the country and the treaties and declarations of war passed by the Legislative branch. The president also appoints federal judges and is Commander in Chief of the military when it is called into service. Other members of the Executive branch include the vice-president, who is also elected, and various cabinet members as he might appoint: ambassadors, presidential advisers, members of the armed forces, and other appointed and civil servants of government agencies, departments, and bureaus. Though the President appoints them, they then must be approved by the legislative branch.

Judicial—Article III of the Constitution established the Judicial branch of government, which is headed by the Supreme Court. The Supreme Court has the power to rule that a law passed by the Legislature, or an act of the Executive branch, is illegal and unconstitutional. In an appeal capacity, citizens, businesses, and government officials can also ask the Supreme Court to review a decision made in a lower court if someone believes that the ruling by a judge is unconstitutional. The Judicial branch also includes lower federal courts, known as federal district courts, which have been established by the Congress. The courts try lawbreakers and review cases refereed from other courts.

Bill Of Rights—the first ten amendments to the United States Constitution deal with civil liberties and civil rights. James Madison was credited with writing a majority of them. They are in brief:

1. Freedom of Religion.
2. Right To Bear Arms.
3. Security from the quartering of troops in homes.
4. Right against unreasonable search and seizures.
5. Right against self-incrimination.
6. Right to trial by jury; right to legal council.
7. Right to jury trial for civil actions.
8. No cruel or unusual punishment allowed.
9. These rights shall not deny other rights the people enjoy.
10. Powers not mentioned in the Constitution shall be retained by the states or the people.

Skill 16.3   **Demonstrate knowledge of the political process and the role of political parties in the United States; responsibilities of U.S. citizens, including classroom, school and community applications; the skills, knowledge, and attitudes necessary for successful participation in civic life; and strategies for modeling the rights and responsibilities of citizenship in a democratic society**

Article III of the U.S. Constitution created a Supreme Court and authorized Congress to create other federal courts as it deemed necessary. In 1789, Congress passed the Judiciary Act, which set the number of Supreme Court justices at six, with one Chief Justice and five associates. The Judiciary Act also created 13 judicial districts, each with one district judge who was authorized to hear maritime cases and other types of cases. In 1793, Congress changed the circuit court to one Supreme Court justice and the local district judge.

Checks and Balances—a system set up by the Constitution in which each branch of the federal government has the power to check, or limit, the actions of other branches.

Separation of Powers—a system of American government in which each branch of government has its own specifically designated powers and cannot interfere with the powers of another.

Federalism in colonial America meant belief in a strong central government. The Articles of Confederation provided for a weak central government, and lawmakers and citizens alike saw the unlikelihood of such an idea. One of the debates that shaped the ratification of the Constitution was the idea that the national government would be superior in status to state and local governments. Indeed, the national government is often called the federal government as well. In this historical political debate, those who favored a strong federal government were called Federalists, and those opposed styled themselves anti-Federalists.

Beginning with opinions written by Chief Justice John Marshall (including Gibbons v. Ogden and McCulloch v. Maryland), a series of Supreme Court decisions affirmed the supremacy of the federal government over that of the states. After all, if a state could tax the federal government, as was argued in McCulloch, then the federal government could theoretically yield its authority to that state, giving it supremacy over every other state, and that would undermine the authority of the federal government, not only in the minds of the judges of the federal and state courts, but also in the hearts and minds of the people, of both the United States and other countries. This tradition has continued to the present day, with states being unable to sue the federal government, disputes between states being settled by federal courts, and foreign threats being answered by a national defense force. In today's political discussions, the idea of states superseding the federal government seems foreign indeed.

The two parties that developed through the early 1790s were led by Jefferson, as the Secretary of State, and Alexander Hamilton, as the Secretary of the Treasury. Jefferson and Hamilton were different in many ways. Hamilton wanted the federal government to be stronger than the state governments. Jefferson believed that the state governments should be stronger. Hamilton supported the creation of the first **Bank of the United States**; Jefferson opposed it because he felt that it gave too much power to wealthy investors who would help run it. Jefferson interpreted the Constitution strictly; he argued that nowhere did the Constitution give the federal government the power to create a national bank. Hamilton interpreted the Constitution much more loosely. He pointed out that the Constitution gave Congress the power to make all laws "necessary and proper" to carry out its duties. He reasoned that since Congress had the right to collect taxes, then Congress had the right to create the bank. Hamilton wanted the government to encourage economic growth. He favored the growth of trade, manufacturing, and the rise of cities as the necessary parts of economic growth. He favored the business leaders and mistrusted the common people. Jefferson believed that the common people, especially the farmers, were the backbone of the nation. He thought that the rise of big cities and manufacturing would corrupt American life.

The political party system in the U.S. has five main objects or lines of action:

- To influence government policy.
- To form or shape public opinion.
- To win elections.
- To choose between candidates for office.
- To procure salaried posts for party leaders and workers.

Skill 16.4   Recognize fundamental concepts and principles of economics (e.g., supply and demand); key features of different economic systems (e.g., command, market and mixed); and major features of the U.S. economic system, including the role of consumers and producers and types of economic resources

Economics–defined as a study of how scarce resources are allocated to satisfy unlimited wants. Resources refer to the four factors of production: **labor, capital, land and entrepreneurship**.

Scarcity–means that choices have to be made. If society decides to produce more of one good, this means that there are fewer resources available for the production of other goods.

Opportunity Cost–the value of the sacrificed alternative, i.e., the value of what had to be given up in order to have the output of goods. Opportunity cost does not just refer to production. Your opportunity cost of studying with this guide is the value of what you are not doing because you are studying, whether it is watching TV, spending time with family, working, or whatever. Every choice has an opportunity cost.

Marginal Analysis–used greatly in the study of economics. The term marginal always means "the change in." There are benefits and costs associated with every decision. The benefits are the gains or the advantages of a decision or action.

Production Costs–involve the cost of the resources involved and the cost of their alternative uses.

Marginal Cost–the increase in costs from producing one more unit of output, or the change in total cost divided by the change in quantity of output. Looking at costs and benefits in this way is referred to as making decisions at the margin, and this is the methodology used in the study of economics.

Market Economy–functions on the basis of the financial incentive. Firms use society's scarce resources to produce the goods that consumers want.

In a **planned economy**, particularly one based on public ownership of the means of production, a planning entity substitutes for the market, to varying degrees, from partial to total. Instead of consumers voting with their dollars, they have a bureaucratic entity trying to substitute for the functions of supply and demand in making production decisions.

Supply—defined as the quantity of a good or service that a producer is willing to make available at different prices during a specified period of time.

Demand—defined as the quantity of goods and services that a buyer is willing and able to buy at different prices during a specified period of time.

Market Equilibrium—occurs where the selling decisions of producers are equal to the buying decisions of consumers, or where the supply and demand curves intersect.

Incentives and **Substitutes**—affect the market situation. Incentives for consumers are things like sales, coupons, rebates, etc. The incentives result in increased sales for the firm even though there is a cost to the incentives.

Skill 16.5   Recognize key features and historical developments associated with different types of political systems; the interrelationships of economic and political systems; and their relationship to historical and contemporary developments in Illinois, the United States and the world

The reasons for the decline of the Roman Empire are still a matter of debate, but they fall into the categories of political, economic, and biological/ecological/social:

1. **Political**: a period of anarchy and military emperors led to war and destruction.
2. **Economic**: the rise of large villas owned and controlled by landlords, who settled poor people on the land as hereditary tenants who lived under conditions of partial servitude; use of wasteful agricultural methods; a decline of commerce; skilled workers were bound to jobs and were forced to accept government wages and prices; corruption, lack of productivity, and inadequate investment of capital; and the draining of gold from the western part of the empire through unfavorable trade balances with the East.
3. **Biological, ecological, and social**: these factors include deforestation, bad agricultural methods, diseases (particularly malaria), earthquakes, immorality, brutalization of the masses in the cities, demoralization of the upper classes. This was accompanied by the decay of pagan beliefs and Roman ideals with the rise of Christianity.

The beginning of the barbarian infiltrations and invasions further weakened the sense of Roman identity. All of these factors contributed to an empire that was ill- equipped to contend with invaders.

With the increase in trade and travel, cities sprang up and began to grow. Craft workers in the cities developed their skills to a high degree, eventually organizing guilds to protect the quality of the work and to regulate the buying and selling of their products. City government developed and flourished centered on strong town councils. The end of the feudal manorial system was sealed by the outbreak and spread of the infamous **Black Death**, which killed over one third of the total population of Europe. Those who survived and were skilled in any job or occupation were in demand, and many serfs or peasants found freedom and, for that time, a decidedly improved standard of living. Strong **nation-states** became powerful, and people developed a renewed interest in life and learning.

The first phase of the **Industrial Revolution** (1750-1830) saw the mechanization of the textile industry; vast improvements in mining, with the invention of the steam engine; and numerous improvements in transportation, with the development and improvement of turnpikes, canals, and the invention of the railroad.

The second phase (1830-1910) resulted in vast improvements in a number of industries that had already been mechanized through such inventions as the Bessemer steel process and the invention of steam ships. New industries arose as a result of the new technological advances, such as photography, electricity, and chemical processes. New sources of power were harnessed and applied, including petroleum and hydroelectric power. Precision instruments were developed, and engineering was launched. It was during this second phase that the industrial revolution spread to other European countries, to Japan and to the United States.

The direct results of the industrial revolution, particularly as they affected industry, commerce, and agriculture, included:
- Enormous increases in productivity.
- Huge increases in world trade.
- Specialization and division of labor.
- Standardization of parts and mass production.
- Growth of giant business conglomerates and monopolies.
- A new revolution in agriculture, facilitated by the steam engine, machinery, chemical fertilizers, processing, canning and refrigeration.

The political results included:

- Growth of complex government by technical experts.
- Centralization of government, including regulatory administrative agencies.
- Advantages to democratic development, including extension of franchise to the middle class, and later to all elements of the population; mass education to meet the needs of an industrial society; and the development of media of public communication, including radio, television and cheap newspapers.
- Dangers to democracy included the risk of manipulation of the media of mass communication, facilitation of dictatorial centralization and totalitarian control, subordination of the legislative function to administrative directives, efforts to achieve uniformity and conformity, and social impersonalization.

The economic results were numerous:

- The conflict between free trade and low tariffs and protectionism.
- The issue of free enterprise against government regulation.
- Struggles between labor and capital, including the trade-union movement.
- The rise of socialism.
- The rise of the utopian socialists.
- The rise of Marxian or scientific socialism.

The social results of the Industrial Revolution include:

- Increase of population, especially in industrial centers.
- Advances in science applied to agriculture, sanitation and medicine.
- Growth of great cities.
- Disappearance of the difference between city dwellers and farmers.
- Faster tempo of life and increased stress from the monotony of the work routine.
- The emancipation of women.
- The decline of religion.
- Rise of scientific materialism.
- Darwin's theory of evolution.

Skill 16.6 **Demonstrate knowledge of the relationships among government, politics, citizenship, civics and economics and other social sciences and learning areas**

Government ultimately began as a form of protection. A strong person, usually one of the best warriors, or someone who had the support of many strong men, assumed command of a people, a city, or a land. The power to rule those people rested in his hands. **Laws** existed, insofar as the pronouncements and decisions of the ruler, and were not, in practice, written down, leading to inconsistency Religious leaders had a strong hand in governing the lives of people. In many instances, the political leader was also the primary religious figure.

First in Greece, and then in Rome, and then in other places throughout the world, the idea of government by more than one person, or more than just a handful, came to the fore. These governments still existed to keep the peace and protect their people from encroachments by both inside and outside forces.

Through the Middle Ages and on into even the twentieth century, many countries still had **monarchs** as their heads of state. These monarchs made laws (or, later, upheld laws), but the laws were still designed to protect the welfare of the people—and the state.

In the modern day, people are subject to **laws** made by many levels of government. Local governments, such as city and county bodies, are allowed to pass ordinances covering certain local matters, such as property taxation, school districting, civil infractions and business licensing.

State governments in the United States are mainly patterned after the federal government, with an elected legislative body, a judicial system and a governor who oversees the executive branch. Like the federal government, state governments derive their authority from **constitutions**. State legislation applies to all residents of that state, and local laws must conform. State government funding is frequently from state income tax and sales taxes.

The national or federal government of the United States derives its power from the U.S. Constitution and has three branches, the legislative, executive and judicial branches. The federal government exists to make national policy and to legislate matters that affect the residents of all states and to settle matters between states. National income tax is the primary source for federal funding.

Anarchism—a political movement believing in the elimination of all government and its replacement by a cooperative community of individuals. Sometimes it has involved political violence, such as assassinations of important political or governmental figures. The historical banner of the movement is a black flag.

Communism–a belief, as well as a political system, characterized by the ideology of class conflict and revolution, one party state and dictatorship, repressive police apparatus, and government ownership of the means of production and distribution of goods and services. It is a revolutionary ideology that preaches the eventual overthrow of all other political orders and the establishment of a one world Communist government.

Dictatorship–rule by an individual or small group of individuals (oligarchy) that centralizes all political control in itself and enforces its will with a terrorist police force.

Fascism–a belief, as well as a political system, opposed ideologically to Communism, though similar in basic structure with a one party state, centralized political control and a repressive police system. It, however, tolerates private ownership of the means of production, though it maintains tight overall control. Central to its belief is the idolization of the Leader, a "Cult of the Personality," and most often an expansionist ideology. Examples have been German Nazism and Italian Fascism.

Monarchy–the rule of a nation by a Monarch, a non-elected, usually hereditary leader, who is most often a king or queen. It may or may not be accompanied by some measure of democratic open institutions and elections at various levels. A modern example is Great Britain, where it is called a Constitutional Monarchy.

Parliamentary System–a system of government with a legislature, usually involving a multiplicity of political parties and often coalition politics. There is division between the head of state and head of government. Head of government is usually known as a Prime Minister, who is also usually the head of the largest party. The head of government and cabinet usually both sit and vote in the parliament. Head of state is most often an elected president, though in the case of a constitutional monarchy, like Great Britain, the sovereign may take the place of a president as head of state.

Presidential System–a system of government with a legislature, can involve few or many political parties, and has no division between head of state and head of government. The president serves in both capacities. The president is elected either by direct or indirect election. A president and cabinet usually do not sit or vote in the legislature, and the president may or may not be the head of the largest political party. A president can thus rule even without a majority in the legislature.

Socialism–a political belief and system in which the state takes a guiding role in the national economy and provides extensive social services to its population. It may or may not own outright means of production, but even where it does not, it exercises tight control.

Skill 16.7   Identify ways to develop lesson plans that incorporate government, politics, citizenship, civics and economics curriculum and instructional strategies with individualized education goals and benchmarks

(See Skill 7.8.)

Skill 16.8   Demonstrate knowledge of ways to incorporate the Illinois Learning Standards in the areas of government, politics, citizenship, civics and economics in the development of instruction and Individualized Education Programs (IEPs)

(See Skill 7.8.)

Skill 16.9   Identify strategies for selecting and using a wide range of instructional resources, modes of inquiry, and technologies to support learning related to government, politics, citizenship, civics and economics

(See Skill 14.8.)

Sample Test

Reading, Language & Literature

1. **If a student has a poor vocabulary the teacher should recommend that:**
    (Skill 1.01) (Hard Rigor)

    A. the student read newspapers, magazines and books on a regular basis.

    B. the student enroll in a Latin class.

    C. the student writes the words repetitively after looking them up in the dictionary.

    D. the student use a thesaurus to locate synonyms and incorporate them into his/her vocabulary.

2. **Which of the following is not a technique of prewriting?**
    (Skill 1.01) (Easy Rigor)

    A. Clustering

    B. Listing

    C. Brainstorming

    D. Proofreading

3. **All of the following are true about phonological awareness EXCEPT:**
    (Skill 1.02) (Average Rigor)

    A. It may involve print.

    B. It is a prerequisite for spelling and phonics.

    C. Activities can be done by the children with their eyes closed.

    D. Starts before letter recognition is taught.

4. **Unlike phonemic awareness, the study of phonics:**
    (Skill 1.02) (Average Rigor)

    A. Is solely based on comprehension.

    B. Must be done with the eyes open.

    C. Is the basis of understanding spoken language.

    D. Must be paired with Whole-word Instruction.

5. **Which of the following is a complex sentence?**
    (Skill 1.02) (Average Rigor)

    A. Anna and Margaret read a total of fifty-four books during summer vacation.

    B. The youngest boy on the team had the best earned run average, which mystifies the coaching staff.

    C. Earl decided to attend Princeton; his twin brother Roy, who aced the ASVAB test, will be going to Annapolis.

    D. "Easy come, easy go," Marcia moaned.

6. **The arrangement and relationship of verbal and nonverbal cues in structure best describe:**
    (Skill 1.03) (Rigorous)

    A. style.

    B. discourse.

    C. thesis.

    D. syntax.

7. **A strategy that can assist in the comprehension of silent reading is:** *(Skill 1.03) (Average Rigor)*

    A. Interrupting the class silent reading time and asking detail questions.

    B. Waiting until the students have finished reading a passage to give a definition.

    C. Reading the passage aloud after students have read silently

    D. Preparing activities related to the printed passage, some may look for specific details, others may look for creative expression.

8. **A major difficulty the English Language Learners have is:** *(Skill 1.04) (Average Rigor)*

    A. Some languages having missing phonemes and may have phonemes not present in English.

    B. Word wall organization.

    C. singing.

    D. reading.

9. **The below listed activities all promote phonemic awareness, except?**
(Skill 2.01) (Easy Rigor)

   A. Using visual cues and movements to help children understand when the speaker goes from one sound to another.

   B. Incorporating oral segmentation activities which focus on easily- distinguished syllables rather than sounds.

   C. Singing familiar songs (e.g., Happy Birthday, Knick Knack Paddy Wack) and replacing key words with words with a different ending or middle sound (oral segmentation).

   D. All of the above.

10. **A structural analysis activity of words would involve:**
(Skill 2.2) (Hard Rigor)

   A. Getting together in discussion groups after a reading to discuss a passage.

   B. A group of ELL students discussing the different sounds for a word.

   C. A group selected by a teacher to focus on the relationship between spelling patterns and their consonant sounds.

   D. Encouraging students to compose a list of words they have learned or are interested in learning.

11. **One activity that is not encouraged by some in the field of reading is:**
(Skill 2.4) (Easy Rigor)

   A. Checking for understanding

   B. Story mapping

   C. Using the dictionary to look up new words

   D. Story illustration

12. **Effective teachers encourage the development of vocabulary by:**
(Skill 3.1) (Easy Rigor)

   A. Having student draw pictures of keywords that highlight their meaning

   B. Diagramming words show the prefix, root and suffix

   C. Teacher led discussions about the meaning of a word.

   D. Accepting consistency is good but vocabulary is best developed by using multiple methods.

13. **Followers of Piaget's learning theory believe that adolescents in the formal operations period:**
(Skill 3.3) (Average Rigor)

   A. behave properly from fear of punishment rather than from a conscious decision to take a certain action.

   B. see the past more realistically and can relate to people from the past more than preadolescents.

   C. are less self-conscious and thus more willing to project their own identities into those of fictional characters.

   D have not yet developed a symbolic imagination.

14. **Which aspect of language is innate?** *(Skill 3.4)*
(Average Rigor)

   A. Biological capability to articulate sounds understood by other humans

   B. Cognitive ability to create syntactical structures

   C. Capacity for using semantics to convey meaning in a social environment

   D. Ability to vary inflections and accents

15. **English Language Learners have difficulty with stories because:**
(Skill 4.1) (Hard Rigor)

   A. They can sound out the words to a story but not understand it.

   B. They understand the story only when it is read to them aloud.

   C. Stories must be culturally relevant.

   D. Cognitive ability to process two languages at the same time may be hampered.

16. **The following is NOT an example of Inferential Comprehension:** *(Skill 4.3) (Easy Rigor)*

    A. Predicting outcomes

    B. Visually displaying the details of a story.

    C. Looking for the moral of the story.

    D. Inferring cause and effect relationships

17. **Which of the following is NOT a benefit of using traditional language to teach reading?** *(Skill 5.1) (Rigorous)*

    A. reader interest stimulated by fanciful/superhuman beings.

    B. repetitive elements.

    C. moral teaching creating predictive literature.

    D. moral message derived at the end of a reading.

18. **The children's literature genre came into its own in the:** *(Skill 5.1) (Rigorous)*

    A. seventeenth century

    B. eighteenth century

    C. nineteenth century

    D. twentieth century

19. **Which of the following is NOT a consideration that should be met in order for a teacher to select a "just right" book for a student?** *(Skill 5.3) (Rigorous)*

    A. Analysis of reading behavior

    B. Syllabic readiness

    C. Illustration level

    A. Book length

20. **Which of the following questions most directly evaluates the utility of instructional material?** *(Skill 5.4) (Rigorous)*

    A. Is the cost within budgetary means?

    B. Can the materials withstand handling by students?

    C. Are the materials organized in a useful manner?

    D. Are the needs of the students met by the use of the materials?

21. **Which is NOT a rule to use when choosing appropriate technology for your classroom?**
(Skill 5.5) (Average Rigor)

   A. Does it meet the developmental level of your students?

   B. Will the item assist the students learning?

   C. Will your students understand this better than you do?

   D. Is it feasible?

22. **Which of the following indicates that a student is a fluent reader?**
(Skill 6.2) (Easy Rigor)

   A. reads texts with expression or prosody.

   B. reads word-to-word and haltingly.

   C. must intentionally decode a majority of the words.

   D. in a writing assignment, sentences are poorly-organized structurally.

23. **All of the following are examples of ongoing informal assessment techniques used to observe student progress EXCEPT:**
(Skill 6.3) (Hard Rigor)

   A. analyses of student work product

   B. collection of data from assessment tests

   C. effective questioning

   D. observation of students

24. **Which of the following is a formal reading level assessment?**
(Skill 6.4) (Easy Rigor)

   A. a standardized reading test

   B. a teacher-made reading test

   C. an interview

   D. a reading diary.

25. **Which of the following is an essential characteristic of effective assessment?**
(Skill 6.4) (Easy Rigor)

   A. Students are the ones being tested; they are not involved in the assessment process.

   B. Testing activities are kept separate from the teaching activities.

   C. Assessment should reflect the actual reading the classroom instruction has prepared the student for.

   D. Tests should use entirely different materials than those used in teaching so the result will be reliable.

26. **For which of the following uses are individual tests MOST appropriate?**
(Skill 6.4) (Rigorous)

   A. Screening students to determine possible need for special education services

   B. Evaluation of special education curricula

   C. Tracking of gifted students

   D. Evaluation of a student for eligibility and placement, or individualized program planning, in special education

27. **Which of the following is an advantage of giving individual rather than group tests?**
(Skill 6.4) (Easy Rigor)

   A. The test administrator can control the tempo of an individual test, giving breaks when needed.

   B. The test administrator can clarify or rephrase questions.

   C. Individual tests provide for the gathering of both qualitative and quantitative results.

   D. All of the above

28. **Safeguards against bias and discrimination in the assessment of children include:**
(Skill 6.4) (Average Rigor)

   A. The testing of a child in Standard English

   B. The requirement for the use of one standardized test

   C. The use of evaluative materials in the child's native language or other mode of communication

   D. All testing performed by a certified, licensed psychologist

29. It is important that teachers should do the following when teaching students how to read from an expository text. (Skill 7.3) (Rigorous)

A. Model the desired behavior.

B. Provide a set of guidelines for reading the text.

C. Show the student the parts of the text (i.e. sub topic headings, illustrations, Table of Contents, index)

D. All of the above

30. Which of the following is typical of a Middle School student's developmental reading?
(Skill 7.5) (Rigorous)

A. Students begin to comprehend books by using context clues.

B. Students begin to analyze literature.

C. Students begin to utilize sight word vocabulary of 500 words

D. Interpretive literature is read and discussed.

31. A good strategy to utilize when teaching literature to young gifted students is:
(Skill 7.6)(Rigorous)

A. KWL

B. Reflection/Summarization

C. Illustration

D. Literature Circles

32. You are evaluating Karrie's number sense development. You learn that she has difficulty telling left from right, but she can count from one to ten and pair objects like shoes and gloves with their owners. What number sense is Karrie having difficulty with?
(Skill 8.1) (Average Rigor)

A. Linear

B. One-to-one correspondence

C. Temporal

D. Spatial relations

33. A teaching strategy appropriate for developing the cardinality number sense is:
(Skill 8.1) (Rigorous)

   A. Rearranging the same number of items and having students confirm that the number has not changed.

   B. Providing a bag of marbles and having the students count out the blue ones.

   C. Providing students with two cookies. Removing the cookies and asking how much they have left.

   D. Singing a number song with the class.

34. $\left(\dfrac{-4}{9}\right)+\left(\dfrac{-7}{10}\right)=$
(Skill 8.4) (Easy Rigor)

   A. $\dfrac{23}{90}$

   B. $\dfrac{-23}{90}$

   C. $\dfrac{103}{90}$

   D. $\dfrac{-103}{90}$

35. $(5.6)\times\left(-0.11\right)=$
(Skill 8.4) (Easy Rigor)

   A. -0.616

   B. 0.616

   C. -6.110

   D. 6.110

36. An item that sells for $375 is put on sale at $120. What is the percent of decrease?
(Skill 8.4) (Easy Rigor)

   A. 25%

   B. 28%

   C. 68%

   D. 34%

37. Two mathematics classes have a total of 410 students. The 8:00 am class has 40 more than the 10:00 am class. How many students are in the 10:00 am class?
(Skill 8.4) (Average Rigor)

   A. 123.3

   B. 370

   C. 185

   D. 330

38. According to a recipe for 4 people you need 1 2/3 cup of flour but you are expecting 10 people. How much flour do you need? Pick the closest answer.
(Skill 8.4) (Rigorous)

A. 3 2/3 cups

B. 4 1/5 cups

C. 3 5/3 cups

D. 4 2/3 cups

39. If $4x - (3 - x) = 7(x - 3) + 10$, then
(Skill 8.4) (Average Rigor)

A. x = 8

B. x = -8

C. x = 4

D. x = -4

40. A sofa sells for $520. If the retailer makes a 30% profit, what was the wholesale price?
(Skill 8.4) (Average Rigor)

A. $400

B. $676

C. $490

D. $364

41. Given a drawer with 5 black socks, 3 blue socks, and 2 red socks, what is the probability that you will draw two black socks in two draws in a dark room?
(Skill 8.4) (Average Rigor)

A. 2/9

B. 1/4

C. 17/18

D. 1/18

42. 303 is what percent of 600?
(Skill 8.4) (Average Rigor)

A. 0.505%

B. 5.05%

C. 505%

D. 50.5%

43. Given the formula *d =rt*, (where *d* = distance, *r* =rate, and *t* =time), calculate the time required for a vehicle to travel 585 miles at a rate of 65 miles per hour.
(Skill 9.2) (Average Rigor)

A. 8.5 hours

B. 6.5 hours

C. 9.5 hours

D. 9 hours

44. Solve for x: $|2x +3| > 4$
    (Skill 9.2) (Rigorous)

    A. $-\frac{7}{2} > x > \frac{1}{2}$

    B. $-\frac{1}{2} > x > \frac{7}{2}$

    C. $x < \frac{7}{2}$ or $x < -\frac{1}{2}$

    D. $x < -\frac{7}{2}$ or $x > \frac{1}{2}$

45. Graph the solution:
    $|x| + 7 < 13$
    (Skill 9.2) (Average Rigor)

    A.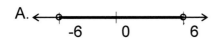

    B.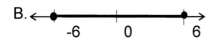

    C.

    D.

46. Given segment AC with B as its midpoint find the coordinates of C if A = (5,7) and B = (3, 6.5).
    (Skill 9.2) (Average Rigor)

    A. (4, 6.5)

    B. (1, 6)

    C. (2, 0.5)

    D. (16, 1)

47. In similar polygons, if the perimeters are in a ratio of x:y, the sides are in a ratio of
    (Skill 9.2) (Rigorous)

    A. $x : y$

    B. $x^2 : y^2$

    C. $2x : y$

    D. $1/2\ x : y$

48. Find the midpoint of (2,5) and (7,-4).
    (Skill 9.2) (Average Rigor)

    A. (9,-1)

    B. (5,9)

    C. (9/2 , -1/2)

    D. (9/2, 1/2)

49. Which of the following is an acute triangle?
    (Skill 9.3) (Easy Rigor)

    A.

    B.

    C.

50. The measure of the interior angles of a polygon can be found by using what formula?
(Skill 9.3) (Rigorous)

A. Measure of $\angle = 180 (n-2)$

A. Measure of $\angle = \dfrac{180(n-2)}{4}$

C. Measure of $\angle = \dfrac{180(n-2)}{n}$

D. Measure of $\angle = \dfrac{360(n-2)}{n-4}$

51. You want to get a new rug for your bedroom which is a combined shape of a square and a trapezoid, the only measurements you have are below. How much do you need to order?

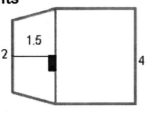

(Skill 9.4) (Rigorous)

A. 16.5 square feet

B. 20.5 square feet

C. 18 square feet

D. 21.5 square feet

52. Find the area of this trapezoid.
(Skill 9.4) (Rigorous)

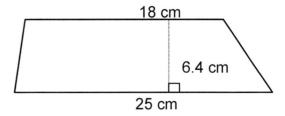

A. 100 cm^2

B. 105.6 cm^2

C. 131.8 cm^2

D. 211.2 cm^2

53. What measure could be used to report the distance traveled in walking around a track?
(Skill 10.1) (Rigorous)

A. degrees

B. square meters

C. kilometers

D. cubic feet

54. What is the closes equivalent to 1 gram?
(Skill 10.1) (Easy Rigor)

A. 1 pint

B. 1 Quart

C. 1 ounce

D. 1 millimeter

55. 3 km is equivalent to
(Skill 10.2) (Easy Rigor)

A. 300 cm

B. 300 m

C. 3000 cm

D. 3000 m

56. The mass of a cookie is
closest to: (Skill 10.2)
(Average Rigor)

A. 0.5 kg

B. 0.5 grams

C. 15 grams

D. 1.5 grams

57. A car gets 25.36 miles per
gallon. The car has been
driven 83,310 miles. What is
a reasonable estimate for the
number of gallons of gas
used?
(Skill 10.2) (Average Rigor)

A. 2,087 gallons

B. 3,000 gallons

C. 1,800 gallons

D. 164 gallons

58. What is the probability of
drawing 2 consecutive aces from
a standard deck of cards?
(Skill 10.3) (Average Rigor)

A. $\dfrac{3}{51}$

B. $\dfrac{1}{221}$

C. $\dfrac{2}{104}$

D. $\dfrac{2}{52}$

59. What is the median of the
following? (Skill 10.3) (Average
Rigor)

83, 75, 12, 65, 69, 90, 12, 73, 77, 80

A. 73

B. 70

C. 12

D. 74

60. Corporate salaries are listed for
several employees. Which would
be the best measure of central
tendency?
(Skill 10.3) (Rigorous)

$24,000 $24,000 $26,000
$28,000 $30,000 $120,000

A. Mean

B. median

C. mode

D. no difference

61. **Which statement is true about George's budget?**
(Skill 10.4) (Easy Rigor)

A. George spends the greatest portion of his income on food.

B. George spends twice as much on utilities as he does on his mortgage.

C. George spends twice as much on utilities as he does on food.

D. George spends the same amount on food and utilities as he does on mortgage.

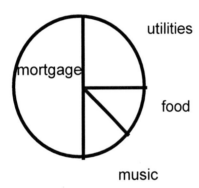

62. **A person whose test score falls in the 60th percentile has:**
(Skill 10.5) (Average Rigor)

A. scored a 60 on the test.

B. Has outperformed 60% of those who took the test.

C. Has out performed 40% of those who took the test

D. Has failed the test

63. **A good reason to use manipulatives when teaching math concepts is because:**
(Skill 11.2)(Average Rigor)

A. Alternate presentation of math problems

B. Concrete model

C. Both A and B

D. Abstract presentation of math concepts

64. **Which of the following is NOT considered a necessary skill for problem solving?**
(Skill11.3) (Average Rigor)

A. Identify the main idea

B. Identify the important facts

C. Ability to perform the computation.

D. Understanding of substitution

65. **Individualizing instruction for a student within an inclusive math environment should require the teacher to:**
(Skill 12.3) (Rigorous)

A. Assess the current strengths and weaknesses of the student

B. Shorten the assignment

C. Observe student needs of all students

D. To understand the current goals on the IEP.

66. **What cell organelle contains the cell's stored food?**
(Skill 13.1) (Rigorous)

   A. Vacuoles

   B. Golgi Apparatus

   C. Ribosomes

   D. Lysosomes

67. **Identify the correct sequence of organization of living things from lower to higher order:**
(Skill 13.2) (Easy Rigor)

   A. Cell, Organelle, Organ, Tissue, System, Organism.

   B. Cell, Tissue, Organ, Organelle, System, Organism.

   C. Organelle, Cell, Tissue, Organ, System, Organism.

   D. Organelle, Tissue, Cell, Organ, System, Organism.

68. **Autotrophs are:**
(Skill 13.3) (Rigorous)

   A. Tertiary Consumers

   B. Producers

   C. Primary Consumers

   D. Decomposers

69. **A good definition of a "parasite is:**
(Skill 13.4) (Average Rigor)

   A. A host that has a being eating of its sustenance.

   B. A predator living on a host causing negative effects to the host.

   C. A predator that lives on a host leaving positive effects to the host.

   D. A species that competes for sustenance against the direct community

70. **A possible detrimental effect of disturbing a bat's niche is:**
(Skill 13.4) (Rigorous)

   A. An increase in population of insects

   B. The negative effects of Bat guano

   C. Necessary relocation of a bat lair.

   D. The density-dependency factor created on small animals.

71. **Which of the following is a correct description of 'evolution' theory?**
(Skill 13.5) (Average Rigor)

   A. Giraffes need to reach higher for leaves to eat, so their necks stretch. The giraffe babies are then born with longer necks. Eventually, there are more long-necked giraffes in the population.

   B. Giraffes with longer necks are able to reach more leaves, so they eat more and have more babies than other giraffes. Eventually, there are more long-necked giraffes in the population.

   C. Giraffes want to reach higher for leaves to eat, so they release enzymes into their bloodstream, which in turn causes fetal development of longer-necked giraffes. Eventually, there are more long-necked giraffes in the population.

   D. Giraffes with long necks are more attractive to other giraffes, so they get the best mating partners and have more babies. Eventually, there are more long-necked giraffes in the population.

72. **Accepted procedures for preparing solutions should be made with _____ .**
(Skill 13.6) (Rigorous)

   A. alcohol.

   B. hydrochloric acid.

   C. distilled water.

   D. tap water.

73. **Chemicals should be stored:**
(Skill 13.6) (Rigorous)

   A. in the principal's office.

   B. in a dark room.

   C. according to their reactivity with other substances.

   D. in a double locked room

74. **Computer simulations are most appropriate for:**
(Skill 13.6) (Easy Rigor)

   A. replicating dangerous experiments.

   B. mastering basic facts.

   C. emphasizing competition and entertainment.

   D. providing motivational feedback.

75. **Density is determined by:**
(Skill 14.1) (Rigorous).

A. dividing mass by volume

B. dividing volume by mass

C. using a scale

D. Determining water displacement

76. **Plasma is considered a:**
(Skill 14.1) (Average Rigor)

A. Gas

B. Solid

C. Liquid

D. Form of energy

77. **The Atomic number of an element represents:**
(Skill 14.2) (Rigorous)

A. The number of electrons

B. The number of protons

C. The mass

D. Both A and B

78. **A stable electron arrangement is:**
(Skill 14.2) (Rigorous)

A. An atom with an equal number of electrons and protons

B. An atom that has all of its electrons in the lowest possible energy levels

C. An atom with 8 electrons in its outermost shell

D. An atomic bonding sharing of electrons

79. **Surfaces that touch each other have resistance to motion, this resistance is called:**
(Skill 14.3) (Average Rigor)

A. gravitational pull

B. weight

C. Kinetic energy

D. Friction

80. **When fluid sediments are transformed into sedimentary rocks the process is called?**
(Skill 15.1) (Rigorous)

A. Crystaliization

B. Metamorphisis

C. Lithification

D. Sedimentation

81. **What type of volcano is associated with quiet eruptions?**
(*Skill 15.2) (Average Rigor)*

A. Shield

B. Cinder Cone

C. Composite

D. Upfolded

82. **Any drop of water may circulate through which system?**
(*Skill 15.3) (Rigorous)*

A. Hydrologic

B. Oxygenic

C. Hydro oxide

D. Hydrofussion

83. **Relative Humidity is:**
(*Skill 15.4) (Average Rigor)*

A. The maximum amount of water vapor the air can hold at that temperature,

B. The actual amount of water vapor in a certain volume of air, compared to the potential possible for that temperature.

C. A range which defines the possible amount of water vapor in the air.

D. The air temperature at which water vapor begins to condense.

84. **A "falling star" is actually a:**
(*Skill 15.5) (Rigorous)*

A. Meteor

B. Meteorite

C. Asteroid

D. Meteoroid

85. **Season are influenced by the?**
(*Skill 15.6) (Rigorous)*

A. Obliquity of the ecliptic

B. Equator

C. Wind

D. Gravity

86. **The Articles of Confederation failed because:**
(Skill 16.1) (Average Rigor)

   A. It was not signed by all 13 states.

   B. People did not like the laws it passed.

   C. It did not have the power to tax or enforce law

   D. It gave the government too much power.

87. **Who is credited with having written the Bill of Rights?**
(Skill 16.1)(Easy Rigor)

   A. James Madison

   B. Thomas Jefferson

   C. Ben Franklin

   D. John Adams

88. **Government shall "make all laws which shall be necessary and proper for carrying into execution the foregoing powers, and all other powers vested by this constitution." What is this passage referred to as?**
(Skill 16.1) (Average Rigor)

   A. Constructionist Clause

   B. Powers Clause

   C. Elastic Clause

   D. War Powers Act

89. **The Great Compromise refers to:**
(Skill 16.1) (Average Rigor)

   A. Two houses for state representation, one based on population one that is based on equal representation.

   B. Acceptance of slavery in the South

   C. Uniform currency

   D. Women's right to vote approved.

90. **The Two-thirds Compromise was about?**
(Skill 16.1) (Average Rigor)

   A. Voting rights

   B. Counting the slave population

   C. Counting the Indian population

   D. Legalizing tobacco

91. **The House of Representatives is responsible for:**
(Skill 16.2) (Easy Rigor)

   A. Making laws, commands the military, declaring war

   B. Making laws, impeaching presidents, appointing judges

   C. Making laws, setting taxes, declaring war.

   D. Making laws, appointing ambassadors, enforcing the law.

92. **Which amendment grants you the freedom to own a gun?**
(Skill 16.2) (Rigorous)

A. Fist Amendment

B. Second Amendment

C. Third Amendment

D. Fourth Amendment

93. **McCullough vs. Maryland was a landmark court case because it ?**
(Skill 16.3) (Rigorous)

A. Established the voting age

B. Established judicial review.

C. Established the Miranda Clause

D. Established the right of flexibility of government

94. **A command economy is based on?**
(Skill 16.4) (Average Rigor)

A. Supply and Demand

B. The people deciding what goods and services to produce.

C. The government deciding what goods and services to produce.

D. A cooperative decision based economy.

95. **Capitalism is an economic system that:**
(Skill 16.4) (Easy Rigor)

A. Allows private ownership of business.

B. Allows some private ownership of businesses.

C. Tells companies how much they may sell an item for.

D. Provides welfare for those in need.

96. **Socialism is based on:**
(Skill 16.4) (Rigorous)

A. the belief that the people/the workers should own companies

B. the belief that government should provide most of the peoples needs.

C. The belief that the many should be governed by the few.

D. the belief that the ownership of production, distribution and exchange of wealth is made by private individuals and corporations.

97. **How did September 11, 2001 cause a large economic problem?**
(Skill 16.5) (Average Rigor)

A. Rebuilding the World Trade Center

B. Grounding of airplanes

C. War

D. Freeze on immigration

98. **The war in Iraq is now controversial for many reasons which one below is NOT one of them.**
(Skill 16.5) (Average Rigor)

A. Deaths of young men and women.

B. Financial cost of the war.

C. Questionable reasons we are there.

D. Congress approved the war.

99. **The 10th Amendment declares what department a state controlled department of government?**
(Skill 16.6) (Rigorous)

A. Education

B. Army/National Guard

C. Transportation

B. Criminal Justice

100. **What is the best step to take to be a voice of change in government?**
(Skill 16.6) (Average Rigor)

A. Speeches

B. Political office

C. Meeting and working with your government representative.

D. Civil Disobedience

Answer Key

1.	A	26.	D	51.	B	76.	A
2.	D	27.	D	52.	B	77.	B
3.	A	28.	C	53.	C	78.	B
4.	B	29.	A	54.	C	79.	D
5.	B	30.	B	55.	D	80.	C
6.	D	31.	D	56.	C	81.	A
7.	D	32.	D	57.	B	82.	A
8.	A	33.	B	58.	B	83.	B
9.	D	34.	D	59.	D	84.	A
10.	C	35.	A	60.	B	85.	A
11.	C	36.	C	61.	C	86.	C
12.	D	37.	C	62.	B	87.	A
13.	B	38.	B	63.	C	88.	C
14.	A	39.	C	64.	D	89.	A
15.	A	40.	A	65.	C	90.	A
16.	B	41.	A	66.	A	91.	C
17.	D	42.	D	67.	C	92.	B
18.	A	43.	D	68.	B	93.	B
19.	A	44.	D	69.	B	94.	C
20.	C	45.	A	70.	A	95.	A
21.	C	46.	B	71.	B	96.	A
22.	A	47.	A	72.	C	97.	B
23.	B	48.	D	73.	C	98.	D
24.	A	49.	A	74.	A	99.	A
25.	C	50.	C	75.	A	100.	C

Rigor Table

	Easy 20%	Average Rigor 40%	Rigorous 40%
Question #	2, 9, 11, 12, 16, 22, 24, 25, 27, 34, 35, 36, 49, 54, 55, 61, 67. 74, 85, 87, 91, 95,	3, 4, 5, 7, 8, 13, 14, 21, 28, 32, 37, 39, 40, 41, 42, 43, 45, 46, 48, 56, 57, 58, 59, 62, 63, 64, 69, 71, 76, 79, 81, 83, 86, 88, 89, 90, 94, 97, 98, 100	1, 6, 10, 15, 17, 18, 19, 20, 23, 26, 29, 30, 31, 33, 38, 44, 47, 50, 51, 52, 53, 60, 65, 66, 68, 70, 72, 73, 75, 77, 78, 80, 82, 84, 92, 93, 96, 99

Rationales for Sample Questions

1. **If a student has a poor vocabulary the teacher should recommend that:**
(Skill 1.01) (Rigorous)

   A. the student read newspapers, magazines and books on a regular basis.

   B. the student enroll in a Latin class.

   C. the student writes the words repetitively after looking them up in the dictionary.

   D. the student use a thesaurus to locate synonyms and incorporate them into his/her vocabulary.

A. the student read newspapers, magazines and books on a regular basis.

It is up to the teacher to help the student choose reading material, but the student must be able to choose where s/he will search for the reading pleasure indispensable for enriching vocabulary.

2. **Which of the following is not a technique of prewriting?**
(Skill 1.01) (Easy Rigor)

   A. Clustering

   B. Listing

   C. Brainstorming

   D. Proofreading

D. Proofreading.

Proofreading cannot be a method of prewriting, since it is done on already written texts only.

3.   All of the following are true about phonological awareness EXCEPT:
     (Skill 1.02) (Average Rigor)

     A. It may involve print.

     B. It is a prerequisite for
         spelling and phonics.

     C. Activities can be done by
         the children with their eyes closed.

     D. Starts before letter
         recognition is taught.

A. It may involve print.

The key word here is EXCEPT which will be highlighted in upper case on the test as well. All of the options are correct aspects of phonological awareness except the first one, A, because phonological awareness DOES NOT involve print.

4.   Unlike phonemic awareness, the study of phonics:
     (Skill 1.02) (Average Rigor)

     A. Is solely based on comprehension.

     B. Must be done with the eyes open.

     C. Is the basis of understanding spoken language.

     D. Must be paired with Whole-word Instruction.

B. Must be done with the eyes open.

It is the connection between the sound and the letters on a page. Students would see the "cat." The would sound out each letter until they recognize the word.

5. **Which of the following is a complex sentence?**
   (Skill 1.02) (Average Rigor)

   A. Anna and Margaret read a total of fifty-four books during summer vacation.

   B. The youngest boy on the team had the best earned run average, which mystifies the coaching staff.

   C. Earl decided to attend Princeton; his twin brother Roy, who aced the ASVAB test, will be going to Annapolis.

   D. "Easy come, easy go," Marcia moaned.

B. The youngest boy on the team had the best earned run average which mystifies the coaching staff.

Here, the use of the relative pronoun "which", whose antecedent is "the best run average, introduces a clause that is dependent on the independent clause "The youngest boy on the team had the best run average". The idea expressed in the subordinate clause is subordinate to the one expressed in the independent clause.

6. **The arrangement and relationship of verbal and nonverbal cues in structure best describe:**
   (Skill 1.03) (Rigorous)

   A. style.

   B. discourse.

   C. thesis.

   D. syntax.

D. Syntax.

Syntax is the grammatical structure of sentences. Syntax of communication that is strictly written can be misunderstood because it does not include non-verbal language.

7. **A strategy that can assist in the comprehension of silent reading is:**
(Skill 1.03) (Average Rigor)

    A. Interrupting the class silent reading time and asking detail questions.

    B. Waiting until the students have finished reading a passage to give a definition.

    C. Reading the passage aloud after students have read silently .

    D. Preparing activities related to the printed passage, some may look for specific details, others may look for creative expression.

D. Preparing activities related to the printed passage, some may look for specific details, others may look for creative expression.

Varying activities that question the comprehension of details and a broader sense of comprehension applying the multiple intelligence theory will increase both the students comprehension and your ability to determine the level of comprehension they have of the material.

8. **A major difficulty the English Language Learners have is:**
(Skill 1.04) (Average Rigor)

    A. Some languages having missing phonemes and may have phonemes not present in English.

    B. Word wall organization.

    C. singing.

    D. reading.

A. Some languages having missing phonemes and may have phonemes not present in English.

When a language is missing a phoneme or has an additional one from a person's native tongue comprehension becomes more difficult. Semetic languages such as Hebrew have guttural sounds that do not exist in English and may contribute to difficulty in learning English as a missing phoneme.

9. **The below listed activities all promote phonemic awareness, except?**
    (Skill 2.01) (Easy Rigor)

    A. Using visual cues and movements to help children understand when the speaker goes from one sound to another.

    B. Incorporating oral segmentation activities which focus on easily-distinguished syllables rather than sounds.

    C. Singing familiar songs (e.g., Happy Birthday, Knick Knack Paddy Wack) and replacing key words with words with a different ending or middle sound (oral segmentation).

    D. All of the above.

D. All of the above

All of the methods stated in A, B, and C are stated methods to encourage phonemic awareness.

10. **A structural analysis activity of words would involve:**
    (Skill 2.2) (Rigorous)

    A. Getting together in discussion groups after a reading to discuss a passage.

    B. A group of ELL students discussing the different sounds for a word.

    C. A group selected by a teacher to focus on the relationship between spelling patterns and their consonant sounds.

    D. Encouraging students to compose a list of words they have learned or are interested in learning.

C. A group selected by a teacher to focus on the relationship between spelling patterns and their consonant sounds.

In this activity structural components (i.e., prefixes, suffixes and spelling patterns) of the words are being studied.

11. **One activity that is not encouraged by some in the field of reading is:**
(Skill 2.4) (Easy Rigor)

    A. Checking for understanding

    B. Story mapping

    C. Using the dictionary to look up new words

    D. Story illustration

C. Using the dictionary to look up new words

Cooper is one of the theorists who believe this is not good practice for the students.

12. **Effective teachers encourage the development of vocabulary by:**
(Skill 3.1) (Easy Rigor)

    A. Having student draw pictures of keywords that highlight their meaning

    B. Diagramming words show the prefix, root and suffix

    C. Teacher led discussions about the meaning of a word.

    D. Accepting consistency is good but vocabulary is best developed by using multiple methods.

D. Accepting consistency is good but vocabulary is best developed by using multiple methods

Having a word wall in your room and approaching vocabulary in many different ways applies Gardner's Multiple Intelligence Theory.

13. **Followers of Piaget's learning theory believe that adolescents in the formal operations period:**
    (Skill 3.3) (Average Rigor)

    A. behave properly from fear of punishment rather than from a conscious decision to take a certain action.

    B. see the past more realistically and can relate to people from the past more than preadolescents.

    C. are less self-conscious and thus more willing to project their own identities into those of fictional characters.

    D have not yet developed a symbolic imagination.

B. See the past more realistically and can relate to people from the past more than preadolescents.

Since according to Piaget, adolescents 12-15 years old begin thinking beyond the immediate and obvious, and theorize. Their assessment of events shifts from considering an action as "right" or "wrong" to considering the intent and behavior in which the action was performed. Fairy tale or other kinds of unreal characters have ceased to satisfy them and they are able to recognize the difference between pure history and historical fiction.

14. **Which aspect of language is innate?** *(Skill 3.4)*
    (Average Rigor)

    A. Biological capability to articulate sounds understood by other humans

    B. Cognitive ability to create syntactical structures

    C. Capacity for using semantics to convey meaning in a social environment

    D. Ability to vary inflections and accents

A. Biological capability to articulate sounds understood by other humans

Language ability is innate and the biological capability to produce sounds lets children learn semantics and syntactical structures through trial and error. Linguists agree that language is first a vocal system of word symbols that enable a human to communicate his/her feelings, thoughts, and desires to other human beings.

15. **English Language Learners have difficulty with stories because:** *(Skill 4.1) (Rigorous)*

    A. They can sound out the words to a story but not understand it.

    B. They understand the story only when it is read to them aloud.

    C. Stories must be culturally relevant.

    D. Cognitive ability to process two languages at the same time may be hampered.

A. They can sound out the words to a story but not understand it.

ELL students may understand the sound of letters and how they blend, but that does not mean they understand the words. This makes hearing stories difficult without illustrations being provided.

16. **The following is NOT an example of Inferential Comprehension:** *(Skill 4.3) (Easy Rigor)*

    A. Predicting outcomes

    B. Visually displaying the details of a story.

    C. Looking for the moral of the story.

    D. Inferring cause and effect relationships

B. Visually displaying the details of a story.

Inferences require contemplative thought processing. Noting the details without analysis is not an inferential method.

17. **Which of the following is NOT a benefit of using traditional language to teach reading?** *(Skill 5.1) (Rigorous)*

   A. reader interest stimulated by fanciful/superhuman beings.

   B. repetitive elements.

   C. moral teaching creating predictive literature.

   D. moral message derived at the end of a reading.

D. moral message derived at the end of a reading.

Traditional literature has the moral of a story apparent in its writing making the literature predictable. A fable may not have that moral evident until the very end, and may even require a clarification much like a parable.

18. **The children's literature genre came into its own in the:** *(Skill 5.1) (Rigorous)*

   A. seventeenth century

   B. eighteenth century

   C. nineteenth century

   D. twentieth century

A. seventeenth century

In the seventeenth Century, authors such as Jean de La Fontaine and his *Fables*, Pierre Perreault's *Tales*, Mme d'Aulnoye's Novels based on old folktales and Mme de Beaumont's *Beauty and the Beast* all created a children's literature genre. In England, Perreault was translated and a work allegedly written by Oliver Smith, *The renowned History of Little Goody Two Shoes*, also helped to establish children's literature in England.

19. **Which of the following is NOT a consideration that should be met in order for a teacher to select a "just right" book for a student?**
    (Skill 5.3) (Rigorous)

    A. Analysis of reading behavior

    B. Syllabic readiness

    C. Illustration level

    D. Book length

A. Analysis of reading behavior

Reading behavior can be dependent on a large number of variables. While this is something to look at picking a just right book may actually create an alternative reading behavior. Finding out a child's interests, reading level, and coordinating this with how illustrations assist understanding of literature are far more important. Thus, **A** is the only consideration that may not create an effective choice of a "just right" book.

20. **Which of the following questions most directly evaluates the utility of instructional material?**
    (Skill 5.4) (Rigorous)

    A. Is the cost within budgetary means?

    B. Can the materials withstand handling by students?

    C. Are the materials organized in a useful manner?

    D. Are the needs of the students met by the use of the materials?

C. Are the materials organized in a useful manner?

It is a question of utility or usefulness.

21. **Which is NOT a rule to use when choosing appropriate technology for your classroom?**
    (Skill 5.5) (Average Rigor)

    A. Does it meet the developmental level of your students?

    B. Will the item assist the students learning?

    C. Will your students understand this better than you do?

    D. Is it feasible?

C. Will your students understand this better than you do?

If you ask have to ask yourself this question you either should not use the technology, or you must admit to yourself that students today are more familiar with technology than many adults.

22. **Which of the following indicates that a student is a fluent reader?**
    (Skill 6.2) (Easy Rigor)

    A. reads texts with expression or prosody.

    B. reads word-to-word and haltingly.

    C. must intentionally decode a majority of the words.

    D. in a writing assignment, sentences are poorly-organized structurally.

A. reads texts with expression or prosody.

The teacher should listen to the children read aloud, but there are also clues to reading levels in their writing.

23. **All of the following are examples of ongoing informal assessment techniques used to observe student progress EXCEPT:**
(Skill 6.3) (Rigorous)

   A. analyses of student work product

   B. collection of data from assessment tests

   C. effective questioning

   D. observation of students

B. collection of data from assessment tests

Assessment tests are formal progress-monitoring measures.

24. **Which of the following is a formal reading level assessment?**
(Skill 6.4) (Easy Rigor)

   A. a standardized reading test

   B. a teacher-made reading test

   C. an interview

   D. a reading diary.

A. a standardized reading test

If assessment is standardized, it has to be objective, whereas B, C and D are all subjective assessments.

25. **Which of the following is an essential characteristic of effective assessment?**
    (Skill 6.4) (Easy Rigor)

    A. Students are the ones being tested; they are not involved in the assessment process.

    B. Testing activities are kept separate from the teaching activities.

    C. Assessment should reflect the actual reading the classroom instruction has prepared the student for.

    D. Tests should use entirely different materials than those used in teaching so the result will be reliable.

C. Assessment should reflect the actual reading the classroom instruction has prepared the student for.

The only reliable measure of the success of a unit will be based on the reading the instruction has focused on.

26. **For which of the following uses are individual tests MOST appropriate?**
    (Skill 6.4) (Rigorous)

    A. Screening students to determine possible need for special education services

    B. Evaluation of special education curricula

    C. Tracking of gifted students

    D. Evaluation of a student for eligibility and placement, or individualized program planning, in special education

D. Evaluation of a student for eligibility and placement, or individualized program planning, in special education

See previous question.

27. **Which of the following is an advantage of giving individual rather than group tests?**
     (Skill 6.4) (Easy Rigor)

    A. The test administrator can control the tempo of an individual test, giving breaks when needed.

    B. The test administrator can clarify or rephrase questions.

    C. Individual tests provide for the gathering of both qualitative and quantitative results.

    D. All of the above

D. All of the above

All of the answers listed are advantages of giving individual rather than group tests.

28. **Safeguards against bias and discrimination in the assessment of children include:**
     (Skill 6.4) (Average Rigor)

    A. The testing of a child in Standard English

    B. The requirement for the use of one standardized test

    C. The use of evaluative materials in the child's native language or other mode of communication

    D. All testing performed by a certified, licensed psychologist

C. The use of evaluative materials in the child's native language or other mode of communication

The law requires that the child be evaluated in his native language or mode of communication. The idea that a licensed psychologist evaluates the child does not meet the criteria if it is not done in the child's normal mode of communication.

29. **It is important that teachers should do the following when teaching students how to read from an expository text.**
    (Skill 7.3) (Rigorous)

    A. Model the desired behavior.

    B. Provide a set of guidelines for reading the text.

    C. Show the student the parts of the text (i.e. sub topic headings, illustrations, Table of Contents, index)

    D. All of the above

A. Model the desired behavior.

Teachers can provide guidelines, however for readers in the elementary level this may be of little help. The teacher must demonstrate and model aloud how to read the text pointing out the essentials such as key words and context clues. The teacher also should "think aloud" asking questions about what he/she is reading.

30. **Which of the following is typical of a Middle School student's developmental reading?**
    (Skill 7.5) (Rigorous)

    A. Students begin to comprehend books by using context clues.

    B. Students begin to analyze literature.

    C. Students begin to utilize sight word vocabulary of 500 words

    D. Interpretive literature is read and discussed.

B. Students begin to analyze literature.

New readers learn to use pictures and words as context clues to predict the next word or sentence. Between 3rd and 5th grade students attain a sense of comprehension that allows them to learn from new material. In middle school students begin to expand their reading comprehension by analyzing literature.

31. A good strategy to utilize when teaching literature to young gifted students is:
(Skill 7.6)(Rigorous)

    A. KWL

    B. Reflection/Summarization

    C. Illustration

    D. Literature Circles

D. Literature Circles

Summarization, reflection and illustration are all parts of Literature Circles. Literature Circles also include the position of a leader, and the group now becomes student run with the teacher taking a back seat. Literature Circles utilize Gardner's Multiple Intelligence Theory.

32. You are evaluating Karrie's number sense development. You learn that she has difficulty telling left from right, but she can count from one to ten and pair objects like shoes and gloves with their owners. What number sense is Karrie having difficulty with?
(Skill 8.1) (Average Rigor)

    A. Linear

    B. One-to-one correspondence

    C. Temporal

    D. Spatial relations

D. Spatial relationships

Number sense also includes understanding on, under, next to, beside, as spatial relationships. Left and right are spatial relationships.

33. **A teaching strategy appropriate for developing the cardinality number sense is:**
(Skill 8.1) (Rigorous)

   A. Rearranging the same number of items and having students confirm that the number has not changed.

   B. Providing a bag of marbles and having the students count out the blue ones.

   C. Providing students with two cookies. Removing the cookies and asking how much they have left.

   D. Singing a number song with the class.

B. Providing a bag of marbles and having the students count out the blue ones.

Cardinality answers the question, "how many?" in reference to a group. Counting from a bag of marbles would encourage this as a kinesthetic approach works best in teaching this concept.

34. $\left(\dfrac{^-4}{9}\right) + \left(\dfrac{^-7}{10}\right) =$

   (Skill 8.4) (Easy Rigor)

   A. $\dfrac{23}{90}$

   B. $\dfrac{^-23}{90}$

   C. $\dfrac{103}{90}$

   D. $\dfrac{^-103}{90}$

Find the LCD of $\dfrac{^-4}{9}$ and $\dfrac{^-7}{10}$. The LCD is 90, so you get $\dfrac{^-40}{90} + \dfrac{^-63}{90} = \dfrac{^-103}{90}$, which is answer **D**.

35. $(5.6) \times (^-0.11) =$
    (Skill 8.4) (Easy Rigor)

    A. $^-0.616$

    B. 0.616

    C. $^-6.110$

    D. 6.110

Simple multiplication. The answer will be negative because a positive times a negative is a negative number. $5.6 \times^- 0.11 =^- 0.616$, which is answer **A**.

36. **An item that sells for $375 is put on sale at $120. What is the percent of decrease?**
    (Skill 8.4) (Easy Rigor)

    A. 25%

    B. 28%

    C. 68%

    D. 34%

Use $(1 - x)$ as the discount. $375x = 120$.
$375(1 - x) = 120 \rightarrow 375 - 375x = 120 \rightarrow 375x = 255 \rightarrow x = 0.68 = 68\%$
which is answer **C**.

37. Two mathematics classes have a total of 410 students. The 8:00 am class has 40 more than the 10:00 am class. How many students are in the 10:00 am class?
   (Skill 8.4) (Average Rigor)

   A. 123.3

   B. 370

   C. 185

   D. 330

Let x = # of students in the 8 am class and $x - 40$ = # of student in the 10 am class. $x + (x - 40) = 410 \rightarrow 2x - 40 = 410 \rightarrow 2x = 450 \rightarrow x = 225$. So there are 225 students in the 8 am class, and 225 – 40 = 185 in the 10 am class, which is answer **C**.

38. According to a recipe for 4 people you need 1 2/3 cup of flour but you are expecting 10 people. How much flour do you need? Pick the closest answer.
   (Skill 8.4) (Rigorous)

   A. 3 2/3 cups

   B. 4 1/5 cups

   C. 3 5/3 cups

   D. 4 2/3 cups

B. 4 1/5 cups
If you multiply 2.5 times 1 2/3 cups you get 4.16 which rounds to 4 1/5 cups.

39. If $4x - (3 - x) = 7(x - 3) + 10$, then
    (Skill 8.4) (Average Rigor)

    A. $x = 8$

    B. $x = -8$

    C. $x = 4$

    D. $x = -4$

Solve for x.

$4x - (3 - x) = 7(x - 3) + 10$

$4x - 3 + x = 7x - 21 + 10$

$5x - 3 = 7x - 11$

$5x = 7x - 11 + 3$ The answer is **C**.

$5x - 7x = {}^- 8$

${}^- 2x = {}^- 8$

$x = 4$

40. **A sofa sells for \$520. If the retailer makes a 30% profit, what was the wholesale price?**
    (Skill 8.4) (Average Rigor)

    A. \$400

    B. \$676

    C. \$490

    D. \$364

A. \$400

Let x be the wholesale price, then x + .30x = 520, 1.30x = 520. divide both sides by 1.30.

41. **Given a drawer with 5 black socks, 3 blue socks, and 2 red socks, what is the probability that you will draw two black socks in two draws in a dark room?**
(Skill 8.4) (Average Rigor)

   A. 2/9

   B. 1/4

   C. 17/18

   D. 1/18

A. 2/9

In this example of conditional probability, the probability of drawing a black sock on the first draw is 5/10. It is implied in the problem that there is no replacement, therefore the probability of obtaining a black sock in the second draw is 4/9. Multiply the two probabilities and reduce to lowest terms.

42. **303 is what percent of 600?**
(Skill 8.4) (Average Rigor)

   A. 0.505%

   B. 5.05%

   C. 505%

   D. 50.5%

Use x for the percent. $600x = 303$. $\dfrac{600x}{600} = \dfrac{303}{600} \rightarrow x = 0.505 = 50.5\%$, which is answer **D.**

43. **Given the formula $d = rt$, (where d = distance, r =rate, and t =time), calculate the time required for a vehicle to travel 585 miles at a rate of 65 miles per hour.**
   (Skill 9.2) (Average Rigor)

   A. 8.5 hours

   B. 6.5 hours

   C. 9.5 hours

   D. 9 hours

D. 9 hours

We are given d = 585 miles and r = 65 miles per hour and $d = rt$. Solve for t. $585 = 65t \rightarrow t = 9$ **hours, which is answer** D.

44. **Solve for x:** $\quad |2x + 3| > 4$
   (Skill 9.2) (Rigorous)

   A. $-\frac{7}{2} > x > \frac{1}{2}$

   B. $-\frac{1}{2} > x > \frac{7}{2}$

   C. $x < \frac{7}{2}$ or $x < -\frac{1}{2}$

   D. $x < -\frac{7}{2}$ or $x > \frac{1}{2}$

D. $x < -\frac{7}{2}$ or $x > \frac{1}{2}$

The quantity within the absolute value symbols must be either > 4 or < -4. Solve he two inequalities $2x + 3 > 4$ or $2x + 3 < -4$.

45. **Graph the solution:**
    $|x| + 7 < 13$
    (Skill 9.2) (Average Rigor)

    A.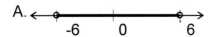

    B.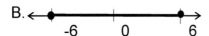

    C.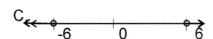

    D.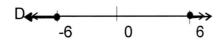

A.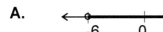

Solve by adding -7 to each side of the inequality. Since the absolute value of x is less than 6, x must be between -6 and 6. The end points are not included so the circles on the graph are hollow.

46. **Given segment AC with B as its midpoint find the coordinates of C if A = (5,7) and B = (3, 6.5).**
    (Skill 9.2) (Average Rigor)

    A. (4, 6.5)

    B. (1, 6)

    C. (2, 0.5)

    D. (16, 1)

B. (1, 6)

47. **In similar polygons, if the perimeters are in a ratio of x:y, the sides are in a ratio of**
    (Skill 9.2) (Rigorous)

    A. x : y

    B. $x^2 : y^2$

    C. 2x : y

    D. 1/2 x : y

A. x | y   The sides are in the same ratio.

48. **Find the midpoint of (2,5) and (7,-4).**
    (Skill 9.2) (Average Rigor)

    A. (9,-1)

    B. (5,9)

    C. (9/2 , -1/2)

    D. (9/2, 1/2)

D. (9/2, 1/2) Using the midpoint formula

$$x = (2 + 7)/2 \qquad y = (5 + -4)/2$$

49. **Which of the following is an acute triangle?**
    (Skill 9.3) (Easy Rigor)

    A.

    B.

    C.

A.

An **acute** triangle has exactly three *acute* angles.

50. **The measure of the interior angles of a polygon can be found by using what formula?**
(Skill 9.3) (Rigorous)

A. Measure of $\angle$ = 180 (n-2)

C. Measure of $\angle = \dfrac{180(n-2)}{4}$

C. Measure of $\angle = \dfrac{180(n-2)}{n}$

D. Measure of $\angle = \dfrac{360(n-2)}{n-4}$

C. Measure of $\angle = \dfrac{180(n-2)}{n}$

Find the measure of the interior and exterior angles of a regular pentagon.

Since a pentagon has five sides, each exterior angle measures:

$$\frac{360}{5} = 72^{o}$$

Since each exterior angle is supplementary to its interior angle, the interior angle measures 180 - 72 or 108°.

51. **You want to get a new rug for your bedroom which is a combined shape of a square and a trapezoid, the only measurements you have are below. How much do you need to order?**
   (Skill 9.4) (Rigorous)

   A. 16.5 square feet

   B. 20.5 square feet

   C. 18 square feet

   D. 21.5 square feet

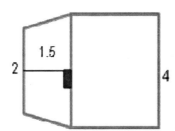

B.   20.5 square feet

Two Shapes—square---trapezoid
$A_{trapezoid} = \frac{1}{2}h(b_1 + b_2)$
$ASquare = bH$
$(BH) + (\frac{1}{2}h(b_1 + b_2))$
$(16) + (.75(2 + 4)) = 20.5$ square feet

52. **Find the area of this trapezoid.**
   (Skill 9.4) (Rigorous)

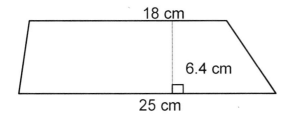

   A. 100 cm^2

   B. 105.6 cm^2

   C. 131.8 cm^2

   D. 211.2 cm^2

B. 105.6 cm^2

The area of a trapezoid equals one-half the sum of the bases times the altitude.

$$A_{trapezoid} = \frac{1}{2}h(b_1 + b_2)$$
$$= 0.5 (6.4) (18 + 25) = 105.6 \text{ cm}^2$$

53. **What measure could be used to report the distance traveled in walking around a track?**
   (Skill 10.1) (Rigorous)

   A. degrees

   B. square meters

   C. kilometers

   D. cubic feet

Degrees measures angles, square meters measures area, cubic feet measure volume, and kilometers measures length. Kilometers is the only reasonable answer, which is **C.**

54. **What is the closes equivalent to 1 gram?**
   (Skill 10.1) (Easy Rigor)

   A. 1 pint

   B. 1 Quart

   C. 1 ounce

   D. 1 millimeter

C. 1 ounce

One gram is approximately equivalent to one ounce.

55. **3 km is equivalent to:**
   (Skill 10.2) (Easy Rigor)

   A. 300 cm

   B. 300 m

   C. 3000 cm

   D. 3000 m

D. 3000 m

To change kilometers to meters, move the decimal 3 places to the right.

56. **The mass of a cookie is closest to:** *(Skill 10.2)(Average Rigor)*

    A. 0.5 kg

    B. 0.5 grams

    C. 15 grams

    D. 1.5 grams

C. 15 grams a cookie is measured in grams.

57. **A car gets 25.36 miles per gallon. The car has been driven 83,310 miles. What is a reasonable estimate for the number of gallons of gas used?**
    (Skill 10.2) (Average Rigor)

    A. 2,087 gallons

    B. 3,000 gallons

    C. 1,800 gallons

    D. 164 gallons

Divide the number of miles by the miles per gallon to determine the approximate number of gallons of gas used.

$$\frac{83310 \text{ miles}}{25.36 \text{ miles per gallon}} = 3285 \text{ gallons.}$$ This is approximately 3000 gallons, which is answer **B**.

58. **What is the probability of drawing 2 consecutive aces from a standard deck of cards?** *(Skill 10.3) (Average Rigor)*

   A. $\dfrac{3}{51}$

   B. $\dfrac{1}{221}$

   C. $\dfrac{2}{104}$

   D. $\dfrac{2}{52}$

There are 4 aces in the 52 card deck.

P(first ace) = $\dfrac{4}{52}$. P(second ace) = $\dfrac{3}{51}$.

P(first ace and second ace) = P(one ace)xP(second ace|first ace)

= $\dfrac{4}{52} \times \dfrac{3}{51} = \dfrac{1}{221}$. This is answer **B.**

59. **What is the median of the following?** *(Skill 10.3) (Average Rigor)*

   83, 75, 12, 65, 69, 90, 12, 73, 77, 80

   A. 73

   B. 70

   C. 12

   D. 74

D. 74

The median is the middle number of a range. When an even number of items is given the two middle number must be averaged.

60. Corporate salaries are listed for several employees. Which would be the best measure of central tendency?
(Skill 10.3) (Rigorous)

$24,000 $24,000 $26,000 $28,000 $30,000 $120,000

A. Mean

B. median

C. mode

D. no difference

B. median

The median provides the best measure of central tendency in this case where the mode is the lowest number and the mean would be disproportionately skewed by the outlier $120,000.

61. Which statement is true about George's budget?
(Skill 10.4) (Easy Rigor)

A. George spends the greatest portion of his income on food.

B. George spends twice as much on utilities as he does on his mortgage.

C. George spends twice as much on utilities as he does on food.

D. George spends the same amount on food and utilities as he does on mortgage.

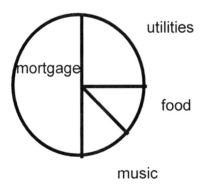

C. George spends twice as much on utilities as he does on food

George spends twice as much on utilities as on food.

62.   **A person whose test score falls in the 60th percentile has:**
      (Skill 10.5) (Average Rigor)

      A. scored a 60 on the test.

      B. Has outperformed 60% of those who took the test.

      C. Has out performed 40% of those who took the test

      D. Has failed the test

B. Has outperformed 60% of those who took the test.

Percentile rankings determine how well you performed compared to others.

63.   **A good reason to use manipulatives when teaching math concepts is because:**
      (Skill 11.2)(Average Rigor)

      A. Alternate presentation of math problems

      B. Concrete model

      C. Both A and B

      D. Abstract presentation of math concepts

C. Both A and B

Manipulatives benefit students because they can become a model, a form of alternative representation of a math problem.

64. **Which of the following is NOT considered a necessary skill for problem solving?**
    (Skill11.3) (Average Rigor)

    A. Identify the main idea

    B. Identify the important facts

    C. Ability to perform the computation.

    D. Understanding of substitution

D. Understanding of substitution

All others stated in problem are essential to problem solving. The main idea asks the question, "What are they looking for?"

65. **Individualizing instruction for a student within an inclusive math environment should require the teacher to:**
    (Skill 12.3) (Rigorous)

    A. Assess the current strengths and weaknesses of the student

    B. Shorten the assignment

    C. Observe student needs of all students

    D. To understand the current goals on the IEP.

C. Observe student needs of all students

The unfortunate truth of the inclusive classroom is that you must deliver as close to "normal" all curriculum, without calling attention to the student. In order to individualize the material you need to understand the all the student levels, the classroom, their deficiencies and strengths, in comparison to the students assigned to you.

66. **What cell organelle contains the cell's stored food?**
(Skill 13.1) (Rigorous)

   A. Vacuoles

   B. Golgi Apparatus

   C. Ribosomes

   D. Lysosomes

A. Vacuoles

In a cell, the sub-parts are called organelles. Of these, the vacuoles hold stored food (and water and pigments). The Golgi Apparatus sorts molecules from other parts of the cell; the ribosomes are sites of protein synthesis; the lysosomes contain digestive enzymes. This is consistent only with answer (A).

67. **Identify the correct sequence of organization of living things from lower to higher order:**
(Skill 13.2) (Easy Rigor)

   A. Cell, Organelle, Organ, Tissue, System, Organism.

   B. Cell, Tissue, Organ, Organelle, System, Organism.

   C. Organelle, Cell, Tissue, Organ, System, Organism.

   D. Organelle, Tissue, Cell, Organ, System, Organism.

C. Organelle, Cell, Tissue, Organ, System, Organism

Organelles are parts of the cell; cells make up tissue, which makes up organs. Organs work together in systems (e.g. the respiratory system), and the organism is the living thing as a whole. Therefore, the answer must be (C).

68. **Autotrophs are:**
    (Skill 13.3) (Rigorous)

    A. Tertiary Consumers

    B. Producers

    C. Primary Consumers

    D. Decomposers

B. Producers

Autotrophs are the primary producers of the ecosystem. Producers mainly consist of plants. Primary consumers are the next trophic level. The primary consumers are the herbivores that eat plants or algae. Secondary consumers are the carnivores that eat the primary consumers. Tertiary consumers eat the secondary consumer. These trophic levels may go higher depending on the ecosystem. Decomposers are consumers that feed off animal waste and dead organisms. This pathway of food transfer is known as the food chain.

69. **A good definition of a "parasite is:**
    (Skill 13.4) (Average Rigor)

    A. A host that has a being
       eating of its sustenance.

    B. A predator living on a host causing negative effects to the host.

    C. A predator that lives on a host leaving positive effects to the host.

    D. A species that competes for sustenance against the direct community

B. A predator living on a host causing negative effects to the host.

Parasites feed of the host often stealing needed sustenance and at times taking an inordinate amount of space as it grows within the host.

70. **A possible detrimental effect of disturbing a bat's niche is:**
   (Skill 13.4) (Rigorous)

   A. An increase in population of insects

   B. The negative effects of Bat guano

   C. Necessary relocation of a bat lair.

   D. The density-dependency factor created on small animals.

A. An increase in population of insects

The term "Niche" describes the relational position of a species or population in an ecosystem. Niche includes how a population responds to the abundance of its resources and enemies.

71. **Which of the following is a correct description of 'evolution' theory? (Skill 13.5) (Average Rigor)**

   A. Giraffes need to reach higher for leaves to eat, so their necks stretch. The giraffe babies are then born with longer necks. Eventually, there are more long-necked giraffes in the population.

   B. Giraffes with longer necks are able to reach more leaves, so they eat more and have more babies than other giraffes. Eventually, there are more long-necked giraffes in the population.

   C. Giraffes want to reach higher for leaves to eat, so they release enzymes into their bloodstream, which in turn causes fetal development of longer-necked giraffes. Eventually, there are more long-necked giraffes in the population.

   D. Giraffes with long necks are more attractive to other giraffes, so they get the best mating partners and have more babies. Eventually, there are more long-necked giraffes in the population.

B. Giraffes with longer necks are able to reach more leaves, so they eat more and have more babies than other giraffes. Eventually, there are more long-necked giraffes in the population.

Although evolution is often misunderstood, it occurs via natural selection. Organisms with a life/reproductive advantage will produce more offspring. Over many generations, this changes the proportions of the population. In any case, it is impossible for a stretched neck (A) or a fervent desire (C) to result in biologically mutated baby. Although there are traits that are naturally selected because of mate attractiveness and fitness (D), this is not the primary situation here, so answer (B) is the best choice.

72. Accepted procedures for preparing solutions should be made with
    _____ .
    (Skill 13.6) (Rigorous)

    A. alcohol.

    B. hydrochloric acid.

    C. distilled water.

    D. tap water.

C. Distilled water.

Alcohol and hydrochloric acid should never be used to make solutions unless instructed to do so. All solutions should be made with distilled water as tap water contains dissolved particles which may affect the results of an experiment. The correct **answer is (C).**

73. **Chemicals should be stored:**
    (Skill 13.6) (Rigorous)

    A. in the principal's office.

    B. in a dark room.

    C. according to their reactivity with other substances.

    D. in a double locked room

C. According to their reactivity with other substances.

Chemicals should be stored with other chemicals of similar properties (e.g. acids with other acids), to reduce the potential for either hazardous reactions in the storeroom, or mistakes in reagent use. Certainly, chemicals should not be stored in anyone's office, and the light intensity of the room is not very important because light-sensitive chemicals are usually stored in dark containers. In fact, good lighting is desirable in a storeroom, so that labels can be read easily. Chemicals may be stored off-site, but that makes their use inconvenient. Therefore, the best answer is (C).

74. **Computer simulations are most appropriate for:**
    (Skill 13.6) (Easy Rigor)

    A. replicating dangerous experiments.

    B. mastering basic facts.

    C. emphasizing competition and entertainment.

    D. providing motivational feedback.

A. Replicating a dangerous experiment

A computer simulation is a computer program that attempts to simulate an abstract model of a particular system.

75. **Density is determined by:**
    (Skill 14.1) (Rigorous).

    A. dividing mass by volume

    B. dividing volume by mass

    C. using a scale

    D. Determining water displacement

A. dividing mass by volume

Density is stated in grams per cubic centimeter (g/cm^3), where the gram is the standard unit of mass. To find an object's density, you must measure its mass and its volume. Then divide the mass by the volume ($D = m/V$).

76. **Plasma is considered a:**
    (Skill 14.1) (Average Rigor)

    A. Gas

    B. Solid

    C. Liquid

    D. Form of energy

A. Gas

Plasma is an ionized gas with unique properties.

77. **The Atomic number of an element represents:**
    (Skill 14.2) (Rigorous)

    A. The number of electrons

    B. The number of protons

    C. The mass

    D. Both A and B

B. The number of protons

The Atomic number is the total number of protons in an atom.

78. **A stable electron arrangement is:**
    (Skill 14.2) (Rigorous)

    A. An atom with an equal number of electrons and protons

    B. An atom that has all of its electrons in the lowest possible energy levels

    C. An atom with 8 electrons in its outermost shell

    D. An atomic bonding sharing of electrons

B. A stable electron arrangement is an atom that has all of its electrons in the lowest possible energy levels.

79. **Surfaces that touch each other have resistance to motion, this resistance is called:**
    (Skill 14.3) (Average Rigor)

    A. gravitational pull

    B. weight

    C. Kinetic energy

    D. Friction

D. Friction

Surfaces that touch each other have a certain resistance to motion. This resistance is **friction**.

80. **When fluid sediments are transformed into sedimentary rocks the process is called?**
    (Skill 15.1) (Rigorous)

    A. Crystaliization

    B. Metamorphisis

    C. Lithification

    D. Sedimentation

C. Lithification

When fluid sediments are transformed into solid sedimentary rocks, the process is known as lithification.

81. **What type of volcano is associated with quiet eruptions?**
   (Skill 15.2) (Average Rigor)

   A. Shield

   B. Cinder Cone

   C. Composite

   D. Upfolded

A. Shield

Shield volcanoes are associated with quiet eruptions, Cinder cone volcanoes are noted for the explosiveness. Composite volcanoes are built by lava flows. Mt. St Helens is one, and her explosion in the 1980s was explosive.

82. **Any drop of water may circulate through which system?**
   (Skill 15.3) (Rigorous)

   A. Hydrologic

   B. Oxygenic

   C. Hydro oxide

   D. Hydrofussion

A. Hydrologic

Hydrologic Cycle is a technical term for the Water Cycle.

83.   Relative Humidity is:
        (Skill 15.4) (Average Rigor)

        A. The maximum amount of water vapor the air can hold at that
            temperature,

        B. The actual amount of water vapor in a certain volume of air, compared
            to the potential possible for that temperature.

        C. A range which defines the possible amount of water vapor in the air.

        D. The air temperature at which water vapor begins to condense.

**B. The actual amount of water vapor in a certain volume of air, compared
to the potential possible for that temperature.**

The word relative requires a comparison/allowance for potential.

84.   A "falling star" is actually a:
        (Skill 15.5) (Rigorous)

        A. Meteor

        B. Meteorite

        C. Asteroid

        D. Meteoroid

A. Meteor

The burning meteoroid falling through the Earth's atmosphere is called a **meteor**
(also known as a "shooting star").

85.   **Season are influenced by the?** *(Skill 15.6) (Rigorous)*

   A. Obliquity of the ecliptic

   B. Equator

   C. Wind

   D. gravity

A. Obliquity of the ecliptic

Because the earth is tilted 23.45° from the perpendicular. The tilt of the Earth's axis is known as the obliquity of the ecliptic and is mainly responsible for the four seasons of the year by influencing the intensity of solar rays received by the Northern and Southern Hemispheres.

86. **The Articles of Confederation
      failed because:
      *(Skill 16.1) (Average Rigor)***

   A. It was not signed by all 13 states.

   B. People did not like the laws it passed.

   C. It did not have the power to tax or enforce law

   D. It gave the government too much power.

C. It did not have the power to tax or enforce law

The Articles of Confederation failed because it was dependent on the states for both power and money. They could make law but they had no ability to enforce it. Also, there were two many forms of currency. The government also could not regulate interstate trade.

87. **Who is credited with having written the Bill of Rights?**
    (Skill 16.1)(Easy Rigor)

    A. James Madison

    B. Thomas Jefferson

    C. Ben Franklin

    D. John Adams

A. James Madison

Many people make the mistake of crediting Jefferson. He was in France at the time.

88. **Government shall "make all laws which shall be necessary and proper for carrying into execution the foregoing powers, and all other powers vested by this constitution." What is this passage referred to as?**
    (Skill 16.1) (Average Rigor)

    A. Constructionist Clause

    B. Powers Clause

    C. Elastic Clause

    D. War Powers Act

C. Elastic Clause

These few words made the Constitution a living form of government that could adapt to the needs of the present time.

89. **The Great Compromise refers to:**
(Skill 16.1) (Average Rigor)

   A. Two houses for state representation, one based on population one that is based on equal representation.

   B. Acceptance of slavery in the South

   C. Uniform currency

   D. Women's right to vote approved.

A. Two houses for state representation, one based on population one that is based on equal representation.

Big states argued that they had a larger population and should be represented by population. Smaller states felt that they would have no power and wanted equal representation.

90. **The Two-thirds Compromise was about?**
(Skill 16.1) (Average Rigor)

   A. Voting rights

   B. Counting the slave population

   C. Counting the Indian population

   D. Legalizing tobacco

A. Counting the slave population

Northern states were concerned that if the Southern slave states would have an unfair advantage in the House of Representatives if slaves were counted. The compromise decided that a slave should be counted as two-thirds of a person.

91.   The legislative branch of government is responsible for:
        (Skill 16.2) (Easy Rigor)

  A. Making laws, commands the military, declaring war

  B. Making laws, impeaching presidents, appointing judges

  C. Making laws, setting taxes, declaring war.

  D. Making laws, appointing ambassadors, enforcing the law.

C. Making laws, setting taxes, declaring war.

Congress not the president makes laws. Congress not the president sets the tax rates for the people. The president also cannot declare war. He can go before Congress and ask them to vote on declaration of war, but he has no power in this area.

92.   **Which amendment grants you the freedom to own a gun?**
        (Skill 16.2) (Rigorous)

  A. Fist Amendment

  B. Second Amendment

  C. Third Amendment

  D. Fourth Amendment

B. Second Amendment

The Second Amendment states: "A well regulated Militia, being necessary to the security of a free State, the right of the people to keep and bear Arms, shall not be infringed."

93.   **McCullough vs. Maryland was a landmark court case because it ?**
       (Skill 16.3) (Rigorous)

   A. Established the voting age

   B. Established judicial review.

   C. Established the Miranda Clause

   D. Established the right of flexibility of government

B. Established judicial review.

This case as the first case to establish judicial ability to review laws and rule on the constitutionality of them.

94.   **A command economy is based on?**
       (Skill 16.4) (Average Rigor)

   A. Supply and Demand

   B. The people deciding what goods and services to produce.

   C. The government deciding what goods and services to produce.

   D. A cooperative decision based economy.

C. The government deciding what goods and services to produce.

This the command of the government it cannot be ignored.

95.   **A planned economy conflicts with:**
        (Skill 16.4) (Rigorous)

        A. Supply and demand.

        B. Public facility ownership.

        C. Private ownership of business.

        D. Welfare for those in need.

A. Supply and demand.

A "Planned Economy" places bureaucratic controls on economic principles. This lessens the impact of supply and demand..

96.   **Socialism is based on:**
        (Skill 16.4) (Rigorous)

        A. the belief that the people/the workers should own companies

        B. the belief that government should provide most of the peoples needs.

        C. The belief that the many should be governed by the few.

        D. the belief that the ownership of production, distribution and exchange of wealth is made by private individuals and corporations.

A. the belief that the people/the workers should own companies

Karl Marx believed that the people would one day rise up against the owners of businesses and take over giving ownership to the workers.

97. **How did September 11, 2001 cause a large economic problem?**
    (Skill 16.5) (Average Rigor)

    A. Rebuilding the World Trade Center

    B. Grounding of airplanes

    C. War

    D. Freeze on immigration

B. Grounding of airplanes

When planes were grounded on 9-11 businesses were kept from interacting. The lack of confidence in the airlines industry contributed to a huge decline in the economy which shortly thereafter recovered.

98. **The war in Iraq is now controversial for many reasons which one below is NOT one of them.**
    (Skill 16.5) (Average Rigor)

    A. Deaths of young men and women.

    B. Financial cost of the war.

    C. Questionable reasons we are there.

    D. Congress approved the war.

D. Congress approved the war.

The one answer that has not become controversial is the Congressional declaration of War on Iraq.

99. The 10th Amendment declares what department a state controlled department of government?
(Skill 16.6) (Rigorous)

 A. Education

 B. Army/National Guard

 C. Transportation

 D. Criminal Justice

A. Education

The responsibility of educating children was left to the states. It is not claimed as a federal responsibility in the Constitution nor in any of the Amendments. Therefore the 10th amendment declares this as a state controlled department.

100. What is the best step to take to be a voice of change in government?
(Skill 16.6) (Average Rigor)

 A. Speeches

 B. Political office

 C. Meeting and working with your government representative.

 D. Civil Disobedience

C. Meeting and working with your government representative.

Your elected representative is your voice in the government. The best way to begin seeking any change in government is through your representative. Any US citizen has this ability.

XAMonline, INC. 21 Orient Ave. Melrose, MA 02176

Toll Free number 800-509-4128

TO ORDER Fax 781-662-9268 OR www.XAMonline.com

ILLINOIS TEACHER CERTIFICATION SYSTEM - ICTS - 2008

PO#   Store/School:

Address 1:

Address 2 (Ship to other):

City, State Zip

Credit card number_____-_____-_____-_____   expiration_____

EMAIL _____

PHONE   **FAX**

ISBN	TITLE	Qty	Retail	Total
978-1-58197-975-6	ICTS Special Education Learning Behavior Specialist I 155			
978-1-58197-576-5	ICTS Special Education General Curriculum Test 163			
978-1-58197-694-6	ICTS Basic Skills 096			
978-1-58197-293-1	ICTS Assessment of Professional Teaching Tests 101-104			
978-1-58197-978-7	ICTS Science- Biology 105			
978-1-58197-979-4	ICTS Science- Chemistry 106			
978-1-58197-673-1	ICTS Science- Earth and Space Science 108			
978-1-58197-594-9	ICTS Elementary-Middle Grades 110			
978-1-58197-599-4	ICTS Early Childhood Education 107			
978-1-58197-981-7	ICTS English Language Arts 111			
978-1-58197-982-4	ICTS Social Science- History 114			
978-1-58197-643-4	ICTS Mathematics 115			
978-1-58197-999-2	ICTS Science: Physics 116			
978-1-58197-985-5	ICTS Social Science- Political Science 117			
978-1-58197-987-9	ICTS Foreign Language- French Sample Test 127			
978-1-58197-988-6	ICTS Foreign Language- Spanish 135			
978-1-58197-989-3	ICTS Physical Education 144			
978-1-58197-990-9	ICTS Visual Arts Sample Test 145			
978-1-58197-992-3	ICTS Library Information Specialist 175			
978-1-58197-993-0	ICTS Reading Teacher 177			
978-1-58197-994-7	ICTS School Counselor 181			
978-1-58197-995-4	ICTS Principal 186			
			SUBTOTAL	
			Ship	$8.70
			TOTAL	